"With the busy schedule I maintain, I look forward to relaxing for a few minutes each evening with a good novel. I especially enjoy contemporary fiction, since I can relate to the struggles and issues the characters face, and I appreciate Christian fiction because I can take in God's truths through its pages. *The Invitation* has everything I like and it is wonderfully crafted. I was immediately drawn into the story. I look forward to the next title in the series."

MARITA LITTAUER

PRESIDENT, CLASSERVICES INC.; SPEAKER AND AUTHOR

"*The Invitation* is a fascinating tale of four different people who are called together for a mysterious purpose. Through their intriguing story and the suspenseful ending, Nancy Moser sends her own invitation to the reader, asking us to consider how God can use us and all ordinary people in the most extraordinary ways."

FLORENCE LITTAUER

FORMER PRESIDENT, CLASS SPEAKERS, INC.; INTERNATIONAL SPEAKER; AUTHOR OF OVER 25 BOOKS, INCLUDING *PERSONALITY PLUS*, *SILVER BOXES*, AND *GETTING ALONG WITH ALMOST ANYBODY*

"*The Invitation,* Nancy Moser's first novel in The Mustard Seed series, is an experience in God's power. Whenever sin, lack of faith, and doubt linger, God's love can move in to change and to heal. The strangers who gather in Haven, Nebraska find in the power of God a newness of life and a strength in hope. Few novels in the marketplace are quite as inspirational, nor offer as a background real-life relationships, danger, and intrigue. *The Invitation* is fiction, but its message of hope is real for us all."

JOY FISHER

MANAGING EDITOR FOR *PARENTLIFE* AND *LIVING WITH TEENAGERS*

the Invitation

NANCY MOSER

ALABASTER

BOOKS

This is a work of fiction. The characters, incidents, and dialogues are products of the author's imagination and are not to be construed as real. Any resemblance to actual events or persons, living or dead, is entirely coincidental.

THE INVITATION
Published by Alabaster Books
A division of Multnomah Publishers, Inc.

© 1998 by Nancy Moser
International Standard Book Number: 1-57673-115-4

Cover design by Brenda McGee

All Scripture quotations, unless otherwise indicated, are taken from *The Holy Bible,* New International Version © 1973, 1978, 1984 by International Bible Society. Used by permission of Zondervan Publishing House. All rights reserved.

Library of Congress Cataloging-in-Publication Data:
Moser, Nancy.
  The invitation/by Nancy Moser.   p. cm.
  ISBN 1-57673-115-4 (alk. paper)   I. Title.
PS3563.08841715   1998   98-5569
813'.54–dc21   CIP

98 99 00 01 02 03 04 05 — 11 10 9 8 7 6 5 4 3 2

To my sister, Crystie

Together our mustard seeds grew and mountains moved.

Thanks for accepting the invitation—on faith.

⁓

"Your love has given me great joy and encouragement,
because you, brother, have refreshed the hearts of the saints."

PHILEMON 1:7

Prologue

Come and see.

"Are the invitations ready?"
"They are being delivered."

One

Give thanks to the LORD, for he is good; his love endures forever.
Let the redeemed of the LORD say this—those he redeemed
from the hand of the foe, those he gathered from the lands,
from east and west, from north and south.

PSALM 107:1–3

JULIA CARSON STARED out the window of the bus. She smiled at the children waiting for her.

What a relief from politicians.

"Stop here, Murray," she told the driver of the Book Bus.

Murray stopped the vehicle in front of the Minneapolis Magnet summer school. Two dozen children ages six through sixteen waved at their ex-governor.

"Is it always like this?" Murray asked. He was new on the job.

"Word is definitely getting around." Julia waved at the children through the window. "Some of these kids have never owned a book, so getting a free one every time I come makes it feel like Christmas—for all of us."

"Ho, ho, ho," Murray said.

Julia put a hand on his shoulder. "Hey, I'll take one happy kid over a dozen grumpy politicians any day."

Murray opened the door, and Julia stepped out amid cheers and hugs. She found the open adulation satisfying but also embarrassing. All this gratitude for a few books. For something that was a basic need in every child's development. She vowed as long as she and Edward had money to fund the Book Bus, it would continue.

"Mrs. Carson, Mrs. Carson, I read my last book two times already," said a little boy whose oversized T-shirt skimmed his knees.

She put a hand on top of his head. "I'm proud of you, David. Are you ready for another one?" He nodded, looking up at her with dark eyes. She leaned close and whispered. "Do you want to go first?"

He smiled like he'd won the lottery.

"Me, too!" said ten-year-old Telisha. "I finished *Little House in the Big Woods* all by myself."

Julia tugged her hair affectionately. "Then you shall be second."

David and Telisha's good fortune spurred the other children to talk at once as they vied for Julia's approval. She was relieved when the director of the summer school clapped her hands, quieting them.

"Get in line, kids. You know the rules. Six at a time. No dawdling when it's your turn. Mrs. Carson will help if you have questions."

The children got in line with a minimum of commotion. There was another cheer as Murray exited the bus carrying a cooler, Dixie cups, and a box of cookies.

Julia eased her way past the children and entered the bus. She stood in the door. "David, Telisha, come on in. And then you, Sarah? Is that your name, hon? You and Gaylord and Grant, and we'll end the first group with the handsome young man with the gorgeous smile...yes, that's you, honey. Come, children."

The children scrambled in, shoulders bumping shoulders as they jockeyed for position near their favorite bookshelf. Julia loved this part. She delighted in helping each child pick out a special book he or she could take home forever. Books had been such an important part of her childhood. One of her most precious memories was her family's evening ritual: after the dinner dishes were cleared, her father had read to them around the walnut dining table with the tatted lace tablecloth. It was there that Julia was introduced to Charles Darnay, D'Artagnan, and Anna Karenina.

If only she could do the same for all the children who searched the limited shelves of the Book Bus. With a hot meal warming their stomachs, she'd gather them close and safe and read aloud to them. She'd marvel as their faces glowed to ageless stories.

Julia's attention was brought back to the crowded bus by the sound of a book falling to the floor. "Don't grab, Sarah. There are plenty of books for all of you." She retrieved the book. "*Christy,*" Julia said, reading the title as she handed it to the girl. "A very good choice." Sarah beamed and held the book to her chest as she headed for the door.

Julia watched the little girl step out of the way so a middle-aged woman could enter the bus. *Probably someone's mother or grandmother,* she thought. The woman's clothes were rumpled, and a wisp of black hair pointed left when it should have pointed right. Her eyes studied the titles of young-adult books. She seemed to be looking for something.

"May I help you, ma'am?" Julia asked.

When the woman turned to look at her, Julia felt an odd jolt pass through her. She had the kindest eyes…they were the eyes of an old friend, yet Julia was certain they'd never met.

"Do you know anything about Haven?"

The woman's question pulled Julia out of her thoughts. "Haven? I don't think I've heard of it. I'm afraid we don't have adult books." She looked around at the children, trying to match one of them with the woman. Then she thought of something, "Haven? Perhaps you mean *The Raven?* The poem by Edgar Allan Poe?"

The woman smiled. "No, Julia. I mean Haven." She held out a white envelope.

Julia took it, then looked at the woman. "What's this?"

"You've been chosen, Julia. You have things to do." With that she moved toward the door.

Julia frowned, confused. "Things to do? What are you talking about?"

As the woman stepped down onto the pavement, she turned back and pointed to the envelope, then gave Julia a wink.

"Mrs. Carson? Mrs. Carson?" A child tugged at Julia's skirt. "David took *The Dawn Treader* and I wanted that one. Do you have another copy?"

Julia watched the woman walk away from the Book Bus.

"Mrs. Carson? Do you?"

Julia let her attention return to the immediate needs of the little girl. "I'll bring a copy for you next time, Telisha. I'll even put your name on it. Why don't you pick another book for today."

Telisha nodded and wove her way down the aisle to find another book.

Julia looked down at the envelope in her hand. Her name was written in an elegant cursive across the front. She slid a finger under the flap, breaking the seal. She pulled out a white card. On the front was a botanical drawing of a broad-leafed plant bearing a cluster of small flowers.

"Mrs. Carson, can you help me find a book about spaceships?"

Julia held up a hand, her eyes scanning the contents of the card. "Just a minute, honey, I'll be right with…" She trailed off.

> *Julia Eugenia Carson is invited to Haven, Nebraska.*
> *Please arrive August 1.*
> *"If you have faith as small as a mustard seed,*
> *you can say to this mountain,*
> *'Move from here to there' and it will move.*
> *Nothing will be impossible for you."*

"Haven?" Julia mumbled.

"What'd you say, Mrs. Carson?" asked the boy.

Julia shook her head, trying to clear it. She walked to the door of the bus and called to Murray and the school director. "Do either of you know who that woman was? The grandmotherly type who came in the bus?"

They looked at each other over the heads of the last few children in line. "I don't remember seeing anyone, Julia."

"Me, neither," Murray said. "But we *were* busy with the juice."

"Mrs. Carson, the spaceships?" asked the boy again.

Julia shrugged. She didn't have time to worry about the odd woman. Or the invitation. She stuffed the card into the pocket of her skirt and turned to help the boy.

~~~

Walter Prescott was dying. At least, that was the worst-case scenario.

Walter stared out the third-story window of his office at KZTV, St. Louis. He barely noticed the traffic merging and converging below. His mind was still going over the call he'd just received from his doctor scheduling a biopsy. He had a shadow on his lung. "Suspicious" was the doctor's word.

Walter took a drag from his cigarette, swallowed the smoke into his lungs, and held it there. He coughed. With a muffled oath, he snuffed the cigarette into the ashtray on the windowsill. Stupid cigarette. Stupid lungs. Stupid shadow.

A car pulling in front of the building drew his eyes. He gave a silent whistle of appreciation. This wasn't just any car. It was a champagne-colored Mercedes that oozed sophistication. Walter watched, fascinated. Anyone who owned such a car most likely wore thousand-dollar suits, carried a car phone to be in constant contact with his broker, and lived in a cozy five-bedroom mansion on a tree-lined street. He'd be successful. He'd have his life together.

He wouldn't have a shadow on his lung.

The man who climbed out of the car didn't fit Walter's fantasy. He was sixtyish and balding. Far from a thousand-dollar suit, his nondescript cardigan vest covered a short-sleeved shirt. Walter frowned. The man looked as if he'd be more comfortable in a beater car like his own—a Chevy van held together by rust and dust.

Of course, Walter could afford to trade in his van (though certainly not for a Mercedes), but he'd held on to it. He was good at that—holding on to his past, no matter how rusty and dusty it was. When the network headquarters of WBS had offered him a producer's job in New York City, he'd declined. Striking out into new horizons was not Walter's style. He was comfortable in his life. He had a tolerable job, a more than tolerable girlfriend, Bette…and a totally intolerable shadow on his lung.

"Excuse me, Mr. Prescott," his secretary's voice came through the intercom. "I know you asked not to be disturbed, but there's a Gabe Thompson to see you. He doesn't have an appointment but…"

Her voice trailed off, and Walter stared at the intercom. *Gabe Thompson?* Walter hadn't seen Gabe in five—or was it six years? He strode across his office and yanked open the door. He scanned the reception area, searching for the skinny, scarecrow face of Gabe Thompson.

"Right here, Mr. Prescott," his secretary said. She indicated a small man with stooped shoulders, wire rim glasses, and a balding head that he made no attempt to disguise with those absurd wisps some men combed across their pates. He wore a sweater vest over a short-sleeved shirt. The gentleman took a step forward and held out his hand. "Gabe Thompson, Mr. Prescott. Thank you for taking the time to see me."

Walter blinked a few times, trying to adjust his anticipation of seeing an old working buddy to seeing this stranger with his working buddy's name…this stranger he'd just seen emerge from a champagne-colored Mercedes.…Belatedly, he shook Mr. Thompson's hand.

"May I come in?" the man asked.

"Actually, I'm rather busy—"

"Please."

Walter felt the heat in the old man's eyes. There was a passion there. There was *com*passion there.

"I suppose I can spare a minute," Walter said. He led the man into his office and offered him a chair. The older man got comfortable. Then he smiled at Walter, absently fingering the buttons of his cardigan.

Walter jerked a thumb toward the window. "Is that your car down there?"

"I'm using it. Do you like it?"

"What's not to like?" Walter shifted in his chair, shoving his back against the comfort of the leather. He removed a number two pencil from above his ear and tapped it on the arm of the chair. "I apologize if I seemed disappointed when I first met you, Mr. Thompson, but I expected someone else. I have a friend named Gabe Thompson, and when my secretary said that name, I assumed..."

"I feel honored to share a name with so good a friend," said this other Gabe.

Walter looked at his desk. "Actually, I haven't seen or talked to Gabe in years. I'm not good at that—keeping up with old friends."

"He is well."

"He—" Walter sat forward. "You know him?"

"I know of him."

"Now that's amazing," Walter said. "Gabe Thompson knows Gabe Thompson. Is he still in Kansas City? What's he doing?"

"All I can tell you is he is well."

Walter froze. His instincts snapped to attention. What kind of answer was that? For that matter, who *was* this guy? He probably wasn't even named Gabe Thompson.

He probably used the name to get into my office, flashing those puppy eyes of his, making me think he was harmless. He's probably some sicko out to sell me a time-share in Timbuktu....

Walter's face hardened. "What do you want, Mr. Thompson? I really don't have time—"

The man reached under his vest into his shirt pocket. "I'm here to deliver this." He held out an envelope.

15

Walter reached out and took it, then tossed it on his desk. "There. You've done it. Now, I think you'd better leave."

"As you wish." The man walked to the door, then paused and turned back to Walter. "Open your mind, Walter Prescott, and *you'll* be well. Just open your mind and your heart."

He walked out, sidestepping Walter's boss, Dave Hanlin.

"Who was that?" Dave asked as he came into Walter's office.

Walter leaned back in his chair, shaken. *He said I'd be well. Well from this cancer? I know it's cancer. It would serve me right if it was cancer.*

"Walter?"

Walter cleared his throat and his thoughts. "You know Gabe Thompson, don't you, Dave? He worked here in programming the first year you came."

"I knew him," Dave said. "Too bad."

"Too bad?" Walter said. "He's a great guy."

"Was, Walter. Was. Didn't you hear he died of cancer a few months back? I only found out last week when I was in Kansas City visiting the station where Gabe went to work."

Walter stared at his boss. "Dead? Gabe?"

"Sorry, Walter."

Gabe was my age. He's dead? He shook his head. "I can't believe he's gone. He was a great—hey!"

He bolted from his chair and rushed to the window, pointing down at the Mercedes. "That guy said Gabe was well. That's what he said, 'He is well.'" Walter reached for the white envelope. "And he gave me this."

"What is it?"

Walter ripped open the envelope. An ink drawing of a mustard plant decorated the front of a white folded card. He opened it.

Walter Ralph Prescott is invited to Haven, Nebraska.
Please arrive August 1.
"If you have faith as small as a mustard seed,

16

you can say to this mountain,
'Move from here to there' and it will move.
Nothing will be impossible for you."

"Haven?" Walter turned the card over. Surely there had to be more information.

"Haven what?" Dave asked. "What is it? Some kind of invitation?"

Walter moved back to the window. The Mercedes was still there. "I don't know, but I'm going to find out." He ran to the door. "Talk to you later, Dave."

Walter hurried past his secretary and punched the button for the elevators. When he saw they were floors away, he detoured toward the stairs. He slammed through the door, the echo following him down the three flights to street level. He shouldered his way past the people in the lobby and burst onto the sidewalk. The Mercedes was still parked across the street.

"Gotcha!" Walter said, gasping for breath. He scanned the faces, looking for the bogus Gabe Thompson. *How dare he use my friend's name to get into my office to give me some bizarre invitation to Haven, Nebraska...wherever that is.*

A man in a navy suit walked toward the Mercedes, balancing his briefcase while he fumbled for the key. He pushed a button and the locks clicked open for him.

"Hey!" Walter said, dodging cars as he crossed the street. "That's not your car!"

The businessman looked up. His expression changed from surprise to indignation. "What do you mean this isn't my car?"

"You stole the keys! Where's Gabe Thompson?"

The businessman slid onto the leather driver's seat and shut the door.

Walter slammed his hands against the window. "Where's Gabe?"

The doors locked.

The engine started and the car lurched forward. Walter ran after it, thumping his hands on its trunk as it pulled into traffic. When he saw what was on the license plate of the Mercedes, he froze in the middle of the street.

A car honked. "Hey, bud! Move it!"

Mechanically, Walter shuffled to the sidewalk. He kept moving until his shoulder met the cool stone of a building. He leaned against it, hoping it was strong enough to hold him.

The license plate had said HAVEN.

～⌒

Natalie Pasternak sat on a boulder. The steepest section of the trail lay ahead. Natalie bit the end of her pencil and stared at the pad of paper in her lap.

Her eyes lit up. She smiled and nodded to herself. She scribbled on the paper, her hand struggling to keep up with her thoughts.

Natalie often escaped into the mountains surrounding Estes Park, Colorado. Escaped from the never-ending work of her family's resort to the solitude of the perfect wilderness. Her family thought her writing frivolous. Although they'd come to the mountains twenty years ago to "do their own thing": sing folk songs and get high on life (or whatever else was handy), now they cared about such trivialities as money and food rather than the payment of satisfaction and the nourishment of creative thought. Hypocrites.

Natalie heard the crunch of boots on the path below. A woman appeared, dressed in the brown uniform of a forest ranger. Her flame-colored hair was remarkable. She seemed to burst from the confines of the dull uniform both physically and emotionally.

"Hideeho!" the woman said. "Nice to see a fellow nature lover."

Natalie scribbled a final few words on the paper before they were lost forever, then smiled at the ranger. "Something up?"

she asked. "I don't see rangers hiking the trails unless they're on a mission."

The ranger considered this, then nodded. "You're absolutely right."

"So?"

The ranger ignored the question and shrugged off her pack, arching her back muscles. She took a deep breath of the thin air. "Ahh. Inspiration and nature go together, don't they?"

"*I've* always thought so."

"You a writer?"

"I try to be."

"Reached many people yet?"

"Reached...?" Natalie hesitated. "I don't know about that, but—"

"Isn't that why you write? To reach people? To move them?"

Natalie shrugged. "I write because I can."

"You write because you have to. It's a gift. Use it." The ranger rummaged through her pack. "Gotten anything published yet?"

"I've sent stuff out. But nothing's happened."

"Maybe you're sending to the wrong people."

Natalie squinted at her. "You know the right ones?"

"Maybe." The ranger found what she was looking for and pulled out a white envelope. She held it toward Natalie. "This is for you."

Natalie took it. "What is it?"

The ranger walked past her to the steep part of the trail. She didn't answer. Natalie turned the envelope over and saw her name written on the front.

"Hey!" Natalie called after her. "This has my name on it. How did you know my name?"

The ranger stopped on the incline and turned back to Natalie, her eyes twinkling. "He knows, Natalie."

Natalie frowned. "What do you mean *he* knows? Who knows?"

19

The ranger smiled and continued up the trail.

Natalie sat there, totally confused. She turned the envelope over in her hand. *Maybe it's a list of agents or publishers. I don't know how that ranger knew I was here, but—*

She tore open the flap and pulled out a white card with a plant drawn on the front. *What's a plant have to do with the publishing business?* She opened the card.

Natalie Jasmine Pasternak is invited to Haven, Nebraska.
Please arrive August 1.
"If you have faith as small as a mustard seed,
you can say to this mountain,
'Move from here to there' and it will move.
Nothing will be impossible for you."

"What is this?"

Natalie looked up quickly, but the ranger was gone. She slid off the rock and ran up the trail after the woman. The steep grade slowed her, working her legs and lungs.

"Hey! Where are you?" she called after the ranger. "Come back here and explain this!"

There was no response. The trail was empty. Natalie tried to glimpse a patch of brown uniform against the green of the forest. Or a flash of red hair. Nothing. Only a mountain goat could have scrambled up the rocky terrain so quickly.

Out of air, Natalie stopped climbing. Drawing in breaths, she took another look at the invitation in her hand.

"Where's Haven, Nebraska?" she asked aloud. "And who's asking me there?"

For once in Natalie's life, the woods did not supply an answer.

⟨⁀⟩

Kathy Kraus pulled the box of Lucky Charms from Lisa's grip. "You can't open the box in the store, sweetcakes. We have to pay for it first."

She handed the box to four-year-old Ryan, who pushed his

own kid-sized cart. He could be trusted to guard it from his two-year-old sister, who Kathy was sure had the biggest sweet tooth in existence. Ryan wasn't into sugar. He was a cornflakes fan. Any generic brand would do. Kathy's grocery budget appreciated Ryan's simple tastes—and cringed at Lisa's.

Lisa squirmed in the seat of the cart, her rubber-toed sneakers kicking close to Kathy's stomach. Kathy diverted her with a box of macaroni, and the little girl shook it, enjoying the clatter of its music. After topping off the cart with a gallon of milk, Kathy headed toward the checkout. All the lanes were busy. Had *everyone* decided to stop at the store after work? Oh, well, it was her own fault. She'd spent the afternoon painting a picture of a child in a swing and hadn't wanted to break the spell of her inspiration to buy something as mundane as toilet paper and soup. Especially not when the kids were napping. Nap times were a gift from heaven.

"I'll help you over here, ma'am."

Kathy looked up to see a cashier opening a lane and detoured her cart. Lisa raised her arms, wanting out, and Kathy lifted her to the floor.

"How are you today?" asked the cashier. Her blue eyes were as pale as her lashes. Her blond hair was drawn into a tight bun in the style of a ballerina.

"I'm fine," Kathy said, excavating through the wet wipes, emergency lollipops, and coupons of her purse to find her checkbook. "Are you new here?"

The cashier nodded cheerfully. "Today's my first day. My name's Anne."

"You'll like it here," Kathy said. "The employees are great. I come to Arkansas Grocery all the time because of them."

The procession of groceries ended, and the cashier looked under the cart where Lisa had crawled. "Well, here's a special treasure," she said. "We're saving the best for last?"

Lisa climbed off the rack and found the security of her mother's leg.

21

"That will be $28.63, Mrs. Kraus."

Kathy paused with her writing. How had the woman known her name?

"Is it all right if I give them a peppermint?" Anne asked, looking at Kathy's children with a smile.

Kathy nodded and finished writing her check. *I must have introduced myself.* She lifted Lisa into the cart full of sacks and watched as the cashier handed Ryan the receipt.

"You take care, Mrs. Kraus. And God bless."

Kathy nodded, trying to remember the last time she'd heard that wonderful phrase.

Ryan ran ahead and activated the automatic door, then took his place holding the front of the cart as they crossed the parking lot. Kathy strapped them in the backseat, unloaded the groceries, and put the cart in the cart corral.

"This is for you, Mommy," Ryan said as she got into the car. He held a white envelope over the seat.

"You hold on to the receipt, cookie. I don't need it right—"

"No, Mommy," Ryan said. "This card. The cashier lady gave this to me while you were putting Lisa in the cart. She said it's for you."

Kathy took the envelope and turned it over in her hands. *Kathy Kraus* was written in script on the front.

"What's it say, Mommy?" Ryan asked.

"Say, Mama?" repeated Lisa.

"Maybe I'm invited to a special sale," Kathy said.

"Will it be like free sample day?" Ryan asked. "I like when we get ice cream samples and cottage cheese on crackers."

"Cackers," Lisa echoed.

Kathy slid her finger under the flap and pulled out a card. On the front was a drawing of a plant. There were no words. Inside it said:

> *Kathleen Mary Kraus is invited to Haven, Nebraska.*
> *Please arrive August 1.*

"If you have faith as small as a mustard seed,
you can say to this mountain,
'Move from here to there' and it will move.
Nothing will be impossible for you."

Kathy turned the invitation over to see if she'd missed something. *Who's it from?*

"Anything wrong, Mrs. Kraus?"

Kathy looked up to see one of the sackers standing at her window. A caravan of shopping carts stood near the back of her car, ready to be pushed back to the store.

"I'm fine, Billy...I..." Kathy closed the invitation and ran her fingers across the drawing of the plant. "Maybe you can answer a question for me."

"Sure thing, Mrs. Kraus."

"Is that new cashier a practical joker?"

Billy glanced toward the building. "Who are you talking about?"

"That new cashier, Anne. She handed Ryan this invitation and it—"

"We don't have a new cashier named Anne."

"Maybe I misunderstood her name," Kathy said. "I'm talking about the new woman. The one with the blond hair that's drawn tight in a bun. The one with the pretty blue eyes."

Billy stared at her as if her own hair were drawn back too tightly. "We don't have *any* new cashiers, Mrs. Kraus. Just the same old bunch who've been here for years."

"But—"

A car honked, blocked by Billy's row of carts. "Got to go, Mrs. Kraus. Have a nice day."

Kathy watched him leave, her mind racing.

"Are you okay, Mommy?" Ryan asked.

She flinched at his voice. When she realized she had the invitation clutched against her chest, she set it on the passenger seat, shoving it toward the door. As far away as possible.

She turned in her seat, facing the children. "Ryan, did you hear the cashier's name?"

"It was Anne," Ryan said. "Just like you told Billy."

"And she had blond hair and blue eyes?"

"And a pretty necklace."

"I didn't see a neck—"

"A cross one," Ryan said, marking a cross on his chest. "Gold."

"Pitty," Lisa said.

"And she *was* there?" Kathy asked.

Ryan got a wrinkle between his eyes. "Sure she was, Mommy. Do you want to go inside and see her?"

Kathy shivered. "No," she said with more force than she'd intended. "I want to go home."

*My heart is not proud, O LORD, my eyes are not haughty; I do not
concern myself with great matters or things too wonderful for me.
But I have stilled and quieted my soul; like a weaned child with its
mother, like a weaned child is my soul within me.*

PSALM 131:1–2

"WHAT'S THIS ABOUT an invitation?" Kathy's husband, Lenny,
flipped through the mail on the kitchen table. "Ryan said you
got some fancy invitation at the grocery store today?"

Kathy gave Ryan a dirty look as the little boy slinked past,
just out of her reach. He grabbed a cookie from the counter
before scrambling out of the kitchen. Gutsy kid. She'd asked
him not to tell Daddy about the invitation, though she wasn't
quite sure why.

Of course, that didn't matter now. Lenny knew.

"It's nothing," Kathy said, stirring the ground beef browning
on the stove. "A promotion at the grocery, that's all." She turned
her back on him, her shame at lying making her blush.

Lenny shrugged and grabbed the newspaper to read before
dinner. He headed toward the living room, and Kathy relaxed
when she heard the evening news come on. Her secret was
safe.

Some secret. It's a secret from me, too.

She added some sloppy joe spices to the simmering meat
and opened the cupboard that held her grandmother's china.
She lifted the top plate and pulled the invitation out of its hiding place. She held it lovingly, then opened it with as much
reverence as if it were an invitation to Cinderella's ball.

"You're mine," she whispered, "but who are you from?"

She read the quote again, feeling a mixture of comfort and
excitement at the flowing words: "If you have faith as small as a

mustard seed, you can say to this mountain, 'Move from here to there' and it will move. Nothing will be impossible for you."

She'd heard those words somewhere before. Images drifted into her mind...dangling legs and patent leather Mary Janes...a quarter held tightly in a fist, waiting for the offering plate to go—

Church. The Bible.

Kathy hurried to the bookshelf in the living room. She pulled out the black-leather Bible.

"Dinner ready yet?" Lenny asked, not looking up. "I've got things to do."

"Almost." Kathy pressed the Bible to her chest so Lenny wouldn't see it as she went back to the kitchen. How absurd, hiding the Bible from him. He'd seen her read it before. Although he never got into religion much, he never begrudged Kathy her beliefs—as long as she didn't push them off onto him. Which she wasn't likely to do by hiding the Bible from him. Hiding the Bible *and* the strange invitation with the verse. She flipped to the concordance.

"Mustard seed...mustard seed..." She moved her index finger down the columns of references. "Here it is." There were five verses listed from Matthew, Mark, and Luke. Might as well start with the first one: Matthew 13:31. She turned the pages hungrily, needing the words on the invitation to match the words in the Bible. She fumbled for the invitation, comparing the verse word for word, like a teacher checking a test.

It didn't match. Fighting disappointment, she went to the second verse: Matthew 17:20.

She read it, then read it again. A shiver started in her midsection, spread to her head and toes, and then traveled back again.

"It matches," she whispered. The sizzle of the meat caught her attention. Hurriedly, she stuck the invitation in the Bible, marking the place. "But what does it mean?"

"What does what mean, Mommy?" Ryan asked from the doorway to the kitchen.

Kathy leaned toward him and whispered, "You told Daddy. That wasn't nice."

"Sorry. I forgot."

She flicked the end of his nose, and his grin said he knew he was forgiven.

Kathy set further thoughts of the invitation aside as the reality of feeding her family intruded. The next twenty minutes were spent passing, chewing, and wiping up spills. An ordinary meal.

At least it was until Lenny said, "I've got to leave in a couple days to go up into Missouri. Boss says I've neglected the northern part of my territory. There's a carpet promotion he wants us to push."

"Where in Missouri?" Kathy asked, helping Lisa with a spoonful of fruit cocktail.

"Springfield, Marionville, and Haven."

The spoon clattered to the table. *"Haven?"*

Lenny glanced at her. "Haven? I didn't say Haven. I said Branson."

"You said Haven," she said. "The first time, you said Haven."

"Why would I say that?"

"I don't know," Kathy said. "But I heard—"

"You heard wrong."

"You said…I heard…" Kathy pushed her plate aside, feeling dizzy.

Lenny looked at her, then Ryan. The two males exchanged a bewildered shrug. "What's wrong, Kath?" Lenny asked. "What's Haven? Where's Haven?"

"Nowhere," Kathy said, getting up to clear the table. "Nowhere at all."

Kathy couldn't sleep. The rhythm of Lenny's snores grated against her nerves. The ticking of the Garfield clock in the kids' bedroom across the hall were like the clicks in a torturer's wheel as he tightened the rack, wrenching her muscles tighter and tighter.

Finally, she grabbed her robe and escaped into the hall, shutting the bedroom door behind her. Out of habit, she checked on the children before closing their door against her jumbled thoughts.

She turned on the light in the kitchen and got a glass of water, careful to barely run the tap so as not to wake her family. She needed to be alone.

As she set the glass on the counter, her thoughts fell into line as if she had triggered some magic stimulus. "A map," she whispered.

She carefully turned the knob on the kitchen door leading to the garage and went into Lenny's car to retrieve the road atlas. Only two small clicks and the wisp of the nightgown against her legs cut into the night's silence. Tiptoeing, she took the Bible and set it with the atlas on the kitchen table. She flipped to the map of Nebraska.

She had no idea where Haven was. North, south, east—
Her finger pegged it.

"It's real." She lifted her finger as if the entire town of Haven would be revealed beneath it. "It's a real place. It's not a joke."

She found herself mapping a route from Haven to their home in Eureka Springs, Arkansas. Interstate 80 east to 29. South through Kansas City to 71—

She slapped the map shut, cringing at the sound.

What am I doing? I'm not really going there. Besides, August first is in four days.

So Haven, Nebraska was real. So the verse in the invitation matched a verse in the Bible. So what? There were too many questions unanswered.

Who was the invitation from? What was happening in Haven? And most of all, why was she invited?

Nothing important ever happened to Kathy. She'd been born in Eureka Springs, grown up there, gotten pregnant there, and married there. Although her "cart before the horse" (her mother's words) was not the proper way to start her adult life, everything had worked out. She and Lenny had married. Ryan was born six months later, and Lisa twenty months after that. Yes, they had struggled—were still struggling—but they were happy. Most of the time. But those good times took turns with the other times when Kathy felt like a prisoner, stuck in a life she had not planned, held by chains of responsibility. Her deepest emotions were buried beneath necessity, swept under the neutral plane she lived on while she kept her family satisfied and the house clean.

In high school she'd had a counselor, Mrs. Robb, who'd seen her potential. She'd commented on Kathy's painting and her willingness to lend a listening ear to her friends. Mrs. Robb had teased that if she wasn't careful, Kathy would take her job.

Where was her potential now? Her painting was relegated to a dank basement; her listening ear wasted on the whiny pleas of her children. She was a slave, locked away from her dreams....

Lenny's job as a carpet salesman meant he was on the road a lot, covering northern Arkansas, southeastern Kansas, and southern Missouri. From what Kathy could tell, he was pretty good at it. They'd rented this two-bedroom home a few months earlier. There was a backyard for the kids to play in (as long as the neighbor's dog wasn't outside yipping at them) and even a washer and dryer in the unfinished basement.

The basement held Kathy's "studio." It had horrible light, a cold concrete floor with dead crickets in the corners, and the sound of plumbing churgling in the exposed pipes. But it was hers. And every chance she got, she went there to paint. Her subjects were children. Children she'd seen. Children she imagined. Children playing, crying, sleeping, jumping, shouting. She captured their innocence in the sweeping strokes of her brush.

Mrs. Robb had told her many times that she was good. But

was she? She didn't know. In fact, when it came right down to it, she didn't know a lot of things. She didn't know why she'd gotten pregnant in high school, she didn't know why she was lucky enough to have two great kids.

And she didn't know why Lenny was cheating on her.

She hadn't confronted him, though she had played out a few scenarios as to how she'd do it. If she'd do it. A part of her wanted the situation to go away. She'd simply forgive him and they'd go on with their life, such as it was. She was into forgiveness, having needed a passel of it herself over the years. But the hardest part was the imagining. Imagining him on the road, eating dinner at a restaurant alone, but then not alone. Laughter. Lingering conversation. A touched hand. Questions asked and answered with passionate looks. And then the motel…

She shook her head, forcing the thoughts away. She looked at the Bible, then at the invitation. Maybe this was her way out. She could run away to Haven—an appropriate name, now that she thought about it. She could take the kids and go to Nebraska to…to what?

She jerked her head erect, suddenly alert.

"Ma-maaaa…"

Although Lisa's cry was muffled through the closed bedroom door, Kathy heard her. She glanced around the kitchen, an oasis of light in the dark night, with the smell of sloppy joes lingering in the air.

"Ma-maaa…"

She sighed at her ridiculous impulses, scooped up the evidence of her folly, turned off the kitchen light, and went to comfort her child.

The phone call from Lenny was unexpected. "Get a sitter, Kath. Since I have to leave tomorrow, I'm taking you out to dinner tonight. A new place on the highway to Springfield where that awful greasy spoon used to be. I'll be home to pick you up at 6:30."

Kathy called the neighbor girl to baby-sit and hopped in the shower. She tried not to question why Lenny was taking her out. Was he feeling guilty about something? She didn't want to know.

Lenny hadn't said what kind of restaurant it was, but since it had taken over where Dolly's Diner used to be (home of fly droppings on the windowsills and chipped coffee cups) she didn't expect it to be fancy. That didn't matter. It was *out*.

She put on a red skirt and a striped blouse. Sandals. A pair of earrings. A spray of Sweet Honesty perfume. And without thinking about the whys of it, Kathy stuck the invitation into her purse. Having it with her gave her a kind of comfort—a reminder of what could have been.

"You look great," Lenny said when he walked in the door. He put a hand behind her waist and pulled her close. "I'm sorry if I neglect you sometimes, Kath. I do love you, you know."

Kathy knew exactly how much he loved her. Yet she laid her head on his shoulder, finding the place where she could listen to the beating of his heart. Maybe these few moments were enough.

He kissed the top of her head and broke away. "Let's go. I'm starved."

They said good-bye to the kids, who were playing Chutes and Ladders with the baby-sitter, and headed out. Lenny held the passenger's door of his car open, and Kathy cringed at a sudden memory. Lenny's car was where she'd first suspected...

One Saturday they'd taken it to go to the lumberyard to get supplies for a shelf they were building in the garage. That's when she'd smelled it. Perfume. A woman's scent. Not her own. Even Lisa had noticed and in her child's way had mentioned it.

"Don't you like my new cologne, honey?" Lenny had said, but Kathy thought his laughter was brittle.

Lenny had been especially nice that day while they built the

31

shelf. Making up for past wrongs?

Luckily, the scent had faded, along with Kathy's suspicions. Until she received the phone call from a motel manager saying that she—Mrs. Kraus—had left behind a blue sweater and did she want him to mail it to her....

She didn't own a blue sweater. And she hadn't traveled with Lenny in a long time.

As they drove, Lenny was in a good mood. Talking loud. Joking. Kathy tried not to read anything into it, but he *was* going out of town tomorrow. He'd be on his own, gone at least a week....

"I hope you like this place, Kath," he said, as they crossed the state line into Missouri. "I ate here a week ago when I took the owner of Kaleidoscope Karpets to lunch. It was his idea. They have the best chicken fried steak and mashed pota—" He stopped his monologue when Kathy grabbed his forearm. "Kath? What's wrong?"

She couldn't speak. She could only point to the new, freshly painted restaurant sign at the side of the road.

Highway Haven.

"You're acting stupid," Lenny said, as they pulled into McDonald's parking lot. "I still don't understand why we couldn't eat at the other place just because of its name."

Kathy rode in silence, her hands limp in her lap. She felt as though she'd run a twenty-mile race. Uphill. Her shoulders slumped with the weight of this Haven that kept intruding into her life. First the invitation, then Lenny's list of towns, now this. Out of all the restaurants in the area, Lenny had chosen the one with *that word* in its name.

Lenny shut off the car and turned toward her in his seat. "You've got some explaining to do."

Kathy didn't think her mind could hold a thought for more than a passing second, much less put words together in a coherent sentence. With great effort, she managed a shrug.

"That's it?" Lenny said. "You act strange at dinner last night, you ruin our dinner tonight when I'm really trying to be nice, and you blame it on a word? What aren't you telling me?"

Kathy gave up. She couldn't keep it a secret any longer. Taking the invitation out of her purse she handed it to her husband.

Lenny opened and read it. "This is the invitation Ryan was talking about?"

Kathy nodded, avoiding his eyes.

"You lied to me."

Kathy opened her mouth for the perfect comeback: *"You lied to me!"* But she shut the words away. Now that the secret was loose, she wanted Lenny's opinion. She took a deep breath and tried to force energy through her veins.

"I'm sorry about lying," she said. "But it's so odd. It's a Bible verse. I looked it up. But I still don't understand what it means. Maybe I should pray about it."

Lenny flipped the card in the air. Kathy made a move to save it from being wrinkled or bent. He pulled it out of her reach. "You're acting like this is a gift from God or something."

Kathy froze at his words. Maybe it was.

She held out her hand and waited. She didn't want him to know how important the invitation was to her. If he knew he might crumple it up or toss it out the window. After a moment, Lenny laid the invitation in her hand. She slipped it safely into her purse.

"So," Lenny said, "what wacko do you think sent it to you?"

"I don't think it's a wacko."

"You should. There's no name, no explanation, nothing but a weird quote about a mustard seed."

"It's a Bible quote. Matthew 17:20."

"So some religious cult wants you to join them?"

Kathy shook her head adamantly. "I'm sure that's not it."

"But the mention of faith moving mountains. That's holy-holy stuff. They probably want you to give them all your worldly goods and they'll promise to move a mountain—though why anyone would want a mountain moved—"

"They aren't asking for anything."

"Except for you to go to Haven, Nebraska with no idea of what's there or what people will—"

"They want me to go there on faith," Kathy said, mostly to herself.

"What?"

She raised her head, feeling a sudden surge of energy. "I've been invited to go to Haven, Nebraska on *faith*. The verse talks about faith as small as a mustard seed and implies if I have faith amazing things will happen."

"What kind of amazing things?"

Kathy's gaze flitted around the car. "I don't know, but I have to go. I *have* to go."

Lenny raised a hand. "No, you don't. You don't have to go nowhere."

"But I've been invited—"

"No wife of mine is traveling hundreds of miles, by herself, to some nowhere of a place I've never even heard of before."

Kathy felt her prison chains tighten. "But I have to—"

"I don't like the words *have to*, Kath. You don't *have* to do nothing except be my wife and a mother to our kids. Isn't that right?"

"Yes, but—"

"Besides," he said. "Who knows if this Haven even exists?"

"But it does!" Kathy popped open the glove compartment and pulled out the road atlas. She found the map of Nebraska and placed a finger on the dot that was Haven, south of the Platte River.

Lenny pulled the map from her and stared at it. He flipped to the index of towns. "It's not listed in the index."

"Maybe it's too small."

Lenny scanned the page and shook his head. "There are towns listed that only have a population of 150."

34

"Maybe it's smaller than that."

He raised an eyebrow. "What would a tiny town be doing sending an invitation to a woman two states away?"

Kathy sank back against the seat, her enthusiasm gone. "I don't know, Lenny. I don't know anything anymore."

He put a hand at the nape of her neck. "Forget about it. It can't be anything important. Nothing important ever happens to ordinary people like us. Put it out of your mind. You've got a family to take care of. A house. And your painting, if anyone ever buys any of it. You don't need that stupid invitation messing up your life."

Kathy didn't answer.

"Do you?"

She managed to shake her head. "No, I suppose not."

But even as she said it, she knew she was lying. Again.

Kathy sat at the kitchen table, nursing her second cup of coffee. She'd seen Lenny off on his trip and she felt empty. The sense of excitement that had been created by the invitation was now null and void. Breakfast, lunch, dinner. Dishes, laundry, dusting. Over and over. Finished in time to start again.

Stuck.

Ryan clomped into the room, wearing his Daffy Duck pj's and Lenny's shoes.

"What do you want, sweetie?" she asked.

"We want to play shopping. Lisa's the mommy, and I'm the daddy. We're going to the store. Lisa wants your purse."

The patter of tiny bare feet on the floor foretold Lisa's arrival. She burst into the kitchen wearing two of Kathy's necklaces, a scarf, three bracelets, and a month's supply of lipstick covering the general area of her mouth. She dragged her Bunny Bob by one ear.

"Me Mama!"

Kathy took her purse from the back of the chair and handed it to Lisa. "I sincerely hope Mama looks a little better than that."

Lisa frowned.

Kathy amended her words. "You look gorgeous, sweet-cakes."

Lisa beamed and sat on the floor where she promptly emptied Kathy's purse. Ryan grabbed the billfold and keys.

"I get these," he said.

Lisa lunged for the billfold. "Mine!"

Kathy reached between them and rescued her billfold, checkbook, a nail file, lipstick...and the invitation. "Now, you can play," she said.

Lisa picked a pen and a cherry DumDum off the floor. She put them in the purse and ran into the living room, leaving the crumpled coupons, used Kleenex, and a compact of wet wipes on the floor.

"That's one way to clean out a purse," Kathy said to herself.

She got up to freshen her coffee and returned to the table where the invitation sat waiting for her. She slapped open the front page of the newspaper, veiling her view of it. She read an entire news story on the economy before she realized the words had drifted through her brain, unnoticed.

"This is ridiculous." She lowered the newspaper into a crumpled mess and peered over it. The invitation called to her. She tossed the newspaper aside and grabbed the envelope. "Is this what you want?" she asked it. "You want my full attention?"

"Who you talking to, Mommy?" Ryan asked as he attempted to get a drink of water from the sink.

Kathy got out of her chair and helped him.

"Who *am* I talking to?" she asked herself. She laughed as she realized she'd asked the question out loud. Using Ryan's glass, she got a drink for herself. "I'm going bonkers, completely bonkers."

Ryan moved to the table and rummaged through her billfold. "Can we have money, Mommy? We won't spend it. Not really."

Kathy opened the coin purse and got out seventy-some

cents in change. Ryan clomped away, grinning happily.

Without thinking about it, Kathy found herself looking through her checkbook, checking its balance. *Would there be enough money for gas to get us all the way to Nebraska?*

"It doesn't matter," she said, tossing the checkbook aside. "The car would never make it that far. Not with those tires. And what about Lenny? Although maybe...maybe we could be home before he gets back."

She looked at the phone book Ryan sat on during meals. She grabbed it, flipped to the yellow pages under Buses, then carried it to the phone and dialed the 800-number.

As the phone rang, Kathy had to use all her willpower not to hang up. She didn't understand what was driving her, leading her in this direction, but she felt she had to let it run its course. For a little while. It was as if she could hear the footsteps of the jailer getting closer, closer, the clinking of his keys teasing her as he came to unlock the chains and set her—

"Hello?"

The word startled Kathy, and she quickly asked for a price quote.

"From what city and state will you be departing?"

"Eureka Springs, Arkansas."

"And where is your destination?"

Kathy swallowed hard. "Haven, Nebraska."

"Departing what date?"

Kathy glanced at the calendar hanging by the refrigerator. Today was July 30. The invitation said to arrive August 1.

"Tomorrow," she said, not believing she was actually considering it.

"I'm sorry, we do not serve Eureka Springs and we do not show a Haven, Nebraska on our route—"

Kathy closed her eyes. It was over. There was no way she could get there even if she had the money—

"But we do have a bus leaving Springfield, Missouri, going to Grand Island, Nebraska. Would that work?"

Not really, but…

"When does it leave?"

"We have a departure at 5:30 P.M. on July 31 arriving in Grand Island at 8:20 A.M. on August 1 with two transfers in Kansas City, Missouri and Omaha, Nebraska."

Kathy's heartbeat quickened. *It would work. We could get to Haven—or close to Haven.*

"How much for one adult and two children, ages four and two? Round trip."

"For the adult and older child it would be $154 each. The younger child would be $77."

Kathy mumbled a good-bye and hung up. $385. The sound of the jailer faded. He'd given up and put the keys away.

"None of it matters. I don't have a way to get to Springfield, or from Grand Island to Haven." Kathy closed her eyes and was surprised to find herself praying, "Lord, if I'm supposed to go to Haven, let there be a way."

The ringing of the phone set Kathy's heart racing. She answered it, breathless.

"Hello?"

"Kathy, Kathy, Kathy. Do I have good news for you!"

"Sandra? What's up?" Sandra Perkins was the owner of one of the shops that sold Kathy's paintings on consignment.

"You must have a guardian angel looking after you," Sandra said. "Just this morning—a few minutes ago, in fact—a couple came into the store from New York City. They were captivated by your paintings and bought all four! Did you hear me, Kathy? They bought all four!"

Kathy put a hand to her mouth, stifling a gasp. "How much do I get?" she managed.

"Well, with the 40 percent I get for commission—we did agree on that amount—I'll be writing you a check for $385. Shoot, I'm feeling generous, I'll make it an even $400. Not bad, huh?"

Kathy slumped in her chair, her knees suddenly too weak to hold her up.

"Kathy?"

"When can I pick up the check?"

"Anytime, kiddo. And bring me more of your paintings ASAP. You're hot, young lady. You are sizzling."

"Can I pick it up today?"

"Sure thing. In fact, that'd be perfect because I'm planning to drive to Springfield tomorrow afternoon so I won't be in—"

"You're going to Springfield?" Kathy broke in, stunned. "Tomorrow?"

"They're having a craft fair up there. I want to check out some of the local artists. You won't mind a little competition, will you, Kathy?"

"No, I don't mind…can the kids and I ride along?"

"To Springfield? Sure thing. The more the merrier."

After making the arrangements, Kathy said her thanks and hung up. Then she hit the redial button and made bus reservations, the sound of keys and falling chains ringing in her ears.

The door of her life had swung open. She was free.

She was going to Haven.

Three

He stilled the storm to a whisper; the waves of the sea were hushed.
They were glad when it grew calm,
and he guided them to their desired haven.

PSALM 107:29–30

"YES, BENJAMIN, I know," Julia said into the phone. She rolled her eyes for her husband, Edward's, benefit. "But I don't *want* to run for Congress. I'm out of politics. Done. *Fini.*"

While Julia listened to her old campaign manager ramble on, she pointed at the suitcase near the floor and the sacks of groceries on the counter. She waved her hand toward the door, indicating Edward could take them out to the car.

"Talk to me in a couple days, Benjamin. Edward and I are heading out the door on the way to the cabin." She opened the refrigerator door, took out the milk, and chugged the last few swallows. "Two days, Benjamin. The political system will not come to an end in two days. If only it would." She rinsed the plastic jug and set it on the floor, then stomped on it.

"What was that?" she said into the phone. "That's my patience exploding, Benjamin. Got to go." She hung up and tossed the jug into the recycling bin.

Edward leaned against the doorjamb, grinning.

"What?" she asked.

"Such tact. Such grace. It's a wonder anyone voted for you."

She snatched her purse off the counter and strode out the door, giving him a shove as she passed. "If the public can't take the truth, they don't want me."

"I want you." He grabbed her hand and pulled her close, lowering his head to kiss her. She wrapped her arms around his neck, dangled her purse down his back, and gave him her full attention.

She pulled away first, though her arms held him captive. "You're perfect," she told him.

"I know."

"And conceited."

"Most definitely."

She put her hands on her hips. "And exasperating."

"Just for you, darling."

She pointed a finger at him. "And late."

"You're the one who was on the phone."

"Duty called."

"Tell it to call back."

"I did."

"Then what are we waiting for?"

She smiled. "Your arm, sir."

Edward extended his arm and she took it. They walked together to the car.

Julia and Edward's lake cabin was their sanity. While she was governor, it had been a place of escape. With no phone, no television, and only an ancient transistor radio, it was perfect. Her staff had urged her to add a phone, but she had declined saying the only beings she wanted to talk to when she was at the cabin were fish and Edward, in that order. Besides, if there was a dire emergency (Julia had emphasized the word *dire),* they could call Maniken's Market up the road and Manny would get a message to her.

Julia hit the scan button on the car radio as the last station faded out. Seconds later the radio homed in on a clear signal. Julia tapped her hand against the steering wheel in time to the tune.

"Just as I am, without one plea, but that thy blood was shed for me. And that thou bidd'st me come to thee, O Lamb of God, I come, I come!"

"Neat song," Julia said.

"I'll give it an eighty-five," Edward said. "It's got a good beat and it's easy to dance to."

"Your age is showing, Mr. Carson."

"Don't gloat. You're right behind me."

The song ended and the announcer came on. "The verse for today comes from Psalm 107, verse—"

"This must be a Christian station," Julia remarked. "I've always meant to give them a listen but I've never—"

"Shh," Edward hushed her.

"'He stilled the storm to a whisper; the waves of the sea were hushed. They were glad when it grew calm, and he guided them to their desired haven.'"

"Haven?" Julia echoed, startled. *Do you know Haven?* the woman on the Book Bus had asked her.

"What a comforting—Julia! Watch the road!"

She jerked the car back into their lane.

"What are you doing?" Edward yelled, his eyes darting between her and the highway. "Forget haven! You're going to send us both to heaven if you don't watch the road."

"Sorry," she said. "It just hit me—"

"No, that truck nearly hit you." He drew a deep breath. Then, apparently confident car and driver were doing all right, he lowered his voice. "What's with the word *haven*? Why did hearing that word send you into a panic?"

"It's the woman," Julia said. "This morning. A woman came into the Book Bus and asked if I knew anything about haven."

"Haven what?"

"I have no idea. I asked if she meant *The Raven*. After all, it was a Book Bus and I—"

"And she didn't want *The Raven*."

Julia shook her head, glanced at her skirt, and reached her hand in her pocket. "Here," she said. "The woman gave me this. I forgot all about it, what with Benjamin's phone call and getting ready to go to the lake."

Edward read the invitation. "So Haven's a place."

"Apparently."

"Maybe they want you to speak there. Talk about your views

on education, that sort of thing."

"They would have called or sent a letter with more details than this." She pointed at the invitation. "It doesn't even say who it's from."

"The people of Haven, Nebraska."

"An entire town?"

"Maybe it's a small town."

"It still doesn't say why I'm invited. There's no phone number. No address. And that verse. I think it's from the Bible."

"It is," Edward said, tapping the invitation against his knee. "Did the woman who gave you the invitation have any explanation?"

"She left as soon as she gave it to me. Then the kids wanted my attention and I forgot all about her." Julia turned the car onto the dirt road leading to their cabin. "But she did say one thing before she left. She said I'd been chosen. She said, 'You have things to do.' Then she left the bus…and winked at me."

"Winked?" Edward smiled. "You have an admirer."

"Or a psycho."

Edward slipped the invitation into her purse. "Don't worry about it, Julia. We're at the cabin. Worry is not allowed here."

"But what does it mean?"

He reached over and put a finger to her lips. "If they really want you to come to Haven, they'll get a hold of you. As I heard you tell Ben, the political system will not come to an end in two days. The same holds true for speaking engagements."

The sight of the water lapping on the dock and the gentle swaying of the hammock under the maple trees helped Julia push her worries aside.

"We're here," she said.

"Amen to that."

"Julia, are you sure you want to go fishing?" Edward asked. "It looks mean out there."

The lake reflected the gray of the sky. The western horizon, which often treated them to magnificent sunsets, now showed only the dimmest glow as the sun sank behind layers of clouds.

Julia pulled her wrinkled, faded, totally ugly fishing hat down around her ears. "Fish like rain, and so do I."

Edward handed her the tackle box. "Are you sure you don't want me to go with you?"

She gave him one of her looks. "You'd only talk. You know you would. A good fisherman is a *quiet* fisherman."

"I'd whisper."

"Bye, Edward." She stepped into the boat and sat on the seat next to the small motor. She pulled the strip and the motor hummed into action. Edward tossed the tie-off rope into the boat. Julia blew him a kiss as she left him on the dock.

She turned the boat north and lifted her face to the breeze, smiling at her own contentment.

Two miles up the lake was a cove where a group of dead trees stuck their leafless limbs through the water, looking like struggling victims reaching for air. The bass and crappie congregated there in the early evening, darting in and out amongst the maze of submerged branches. She steered around the point and set her anchor at the edge of the grove. She tied on a feather-jig and cast the line.

Julia popped open a can of Sprite and settled in, resting her arms on her knees. It was time to wait. Julia wasn't good at waiting. She wanted results. Now. That's why she fished. Self-therapy. It forced her to slow down, mentally and physically. Catching the fish was secondary. The lesson came from the process.

She closed her eyes and let her mind drift with the boat. It was so nice to do nothing, to have no deadlines, no meetings, no phone calls…Benjamin wanted her to run for Congress. He wanted her to fish for votes, be a fisher of men…who'd said that phrase before? Wasn't it biblical? That was it. Jesus told his disciples to be fishers of men.

The Bible. She'd thought about the Bible three times in one

day. First the invitation, then the verse in the car, and now her "fishers of men." Julia *was* a believer, but her faith was private. She'd tried to go public with it when she was running for governor because so many of the things she stood for had their basis in the Bible—virtues like common sense and basic values. But her consultants had stopped her, telling her religion and politics did not mix.

"Why not?" Julia had asked. "'One nation under God' is the basis of our country's birth."

"Believe what you want," they said. "But don't say it out loud. You might tread on somebody's toes."

"Whose toes?"

They hemmed and hawed at that one. "People."

"What people?"

"People who don't believe in God."

"That's a small minority," Julia said.

"People don't like hearing God stuff from their politicians."

"Are you sure?"

"Trust us. Don't do it."

That was one of the reasons Julia hadn't sought a second term. The sidestepping necessary to please everyone made her dizzy. No one spoke the truth. No one stood up and said what they meant, truly meant, deep inside. All the breakthroughs she'd tried to get through the legislature were dissected and molded and remolded until they were a sanitized version of her original intent.

Julia did not mind raising a ruckus—especially in politics. It was when her blatant, truth-talking ways were muzzled that she didn't recognize herself. Being a common citizen was much more liberating. At least her thoughts were her own and no political handler could squeeze them into his or her idea of politically corr—

Plop!

Julia opened her eyes toward the sound. Her empty Sprite can had blown off the seat into the water. She tried to reach for it, but the wind blew it away, making it skim across the top of the water.

That's when Julia noticed the storm clouds directly overhead and the water slapping against the sides of the boat. The twilight had surrendered to the dark; the moon shone timidly between the clouds, reflecting off the whitecaps scattered across the once-gentle lake.

"Now you've done it," Julia told herself, reeling in her line.

A sudden sheet of rain swept across the bow, catching her by surprise. Torrents of rain followed, drenching her.

Julia pulled the starter cord on the engine. Nothing happened. She yanked it again. Nothing.

"No!" Julia yelled. Over and over she tried, knowing she was flooding the carburetor, but not caring. She needed to get home.

She looked around, fighting panic. Over her right shoulder, she caught a glimpse of something in the darkness. Looming. She turned in time to duck under a limb as the boat was pushed into the sunken grove of trees.

She put out her arms, fending off the attacking branches. The sounds of wood scraping against the bottom of the boat were like fingernails across a blackboard. In the dark she couldn't see her antagonists, but they were there, threatening her. Julia grabbed one of the oars and held it over the water like a knight's jousting stick. As the boat drifted deeper into the maze, the oar was jostled as if the branches were fighting back.

"Stop it!"

The rain stung her eyes; the clouds conquered the moon. Thunder rumbled, and lightning ripped the sky as though cackling at her.

I'm in a metal boat. In the dark. In a lightning storm. Without a working motor. I'm in big trouble.

"Please, God. Please, God. Help me get home!"

Julia felt something bump into her foot. She reached down and found a flashlight floating at her feet.

Floating?

She switched on the light, thankful to be drawn out of the darkness, and shone it across the bottom of the boat. Two inches of rainwater covered the bottom with the storm adding more every minute. The light flashed on something orange near the bow. Julia carefully crawled forward and grabbed the life vest. She strapped it on.

At least I won't sink.

With the life vest removed from the bow of the boat, an old tin cup that had been sitting beneath it caught Julia's attention by clanking against the side.

"Thank you, Edward," she said aloud. He'd been the one to tie the cup onto the boat. "You never know when you might need it for bailing," he'd said.

She needed it now. She yanked it hard, breaking its string. She dipped it into the water at her feet and bailed. And bailed.

The boat bumped into a tree with a thud. Julia reached out and touched a huge, barkless trunk. It felt solid compared to the constant bobbing of the boat.

Abandoning her bailing, she tied the boat to the tree, pulling as close as possible. Stationary, she was safe. Safer, anyway. Drifting, she was vulnerable to unseen branches that could poke a hole in the hull. She thought of trying the motor again but realized even if it did work, the rotors would become fouled in the woody water. And no way could she row. The muscles of her upper body were no match for the strength of the wind and waves.

Julia shone the flashlight across the water. She was surrounded by the black fingers of the trees. The thunder and the rain pounding against the water were like a scene from a nightmare. She looked toward shore but knew it was useless. There were no cabins around this cove. The submerged trees were a colossal deterrent for landowners who wanted a beach and a boat dock. There was a road not too far away, but no one in a passing car with its windows closed tight against the storm would be able to hear her screams for help.

"I'll have to wait it out." She felt water lapping around her ankles and resumed bailing. She found a rhythm: dip-pour, dip-pour. Her mind fell into a corresponding chant of *Please-God, please-God*—

The crack of a lightning bolt split the sky, zapping a tree on shore. The explosion sent a shock wave through Julia, making her skin tingle. Bark and branches shot from the tree as the electricity sped to its roots.

"No-o-o-o-o..." Julia stopped bailing and wrapped her arms around herself, seeking comfort. She ducked her head against the pelting rain, drawing herself in. Deeper. Deeper in. "No, no, no, no, no—"

"Julia!"

She raised her head, squinting against the rain and dark.

"Julia? Are you there, Julia?"

Edward!

Quickly, she switched on the flashlight and directed it toward shore. There, directly in line with the lightning-struck tree was a figure waving a flashlight back at her.

Relief swept over her. "I'm here, Edward!"

He waved the flashlight up and down, up and down to tell her he'd heard. "Are...all right?" His words broke between the wind and rain.

"Yes, but get me out of here!"

He nodded with the light again. "I'll...help!"

Although she hated to see him go, she knew he'd be back. He'd drive to the nearest cabin, use their phone, and call the marina. Someone would be out to rescue her soon. She knew it.

As his headlights disappeared down the winding road, Julia resumed her bailing. "Do your part, Julia," she muttered. "Help will be here soon."

She paused in her bailing as realization dawned. Help had been there already.

"Thank you, God," she said. She repeated it over and over just to make sure he heard.

Julia sensed the bedroom door opening and could feel Edward's presence in the room. Although she was content in her cozy cocoon, she forced her eyes open to acknowledge him.

"Hi," she said as she saw him lay a book on the bedside table.

He sat on the bed and took her hand. "Hi, yourself. You feeling okay this morning?"

"I feel safe."

He kissed her forehead. "You are safe."

"Thanks." She snuggled deeper in the covers.

"Don't thank me."

"Why not? You're the one who found me. You're the one who brought help, even though the storm did pass right after you left."

Edward glanced at the book he'd brought into the room. Julia frowned. "What's up, Edward?"

He stroked a stray hair away from her eyebrow. "I'm not the one who found you, Julia."

"But I saw you on the shore. Right under the tree that was struck by lightning. Now, if that wasn't a scary—"

"That's the key, Julia," he cut her off. "When the storm started I headed out to find you. You hadn't said where you were going, but I assumed you'd be one of three places, the cove, the point, or by the dam. But which one? They're spread out, so if I chose wrong, it could cost you your life."

She squeezed his hand. "But you chose right."

Edward shook his head. "I had no idea where to look. I was sitting in the car at the end of our driveway trying to figure out which direction to go when I prayed. I said, 'Help me find her, Lord. Show me where she is.'"

"And...are you telling me he did?"

"He did."

"How?"

Edward swallowed with difficulty. "The lightning. I saw the lightning off to the north. It wasn't the ambiguous flashes I'd seen earlier, it was one distinct bolt ripping through the sky. I could tell it hit something. And I knew. It was God's finger, pointing the way to you."

A shiver flowed from Julia's arms, traveling up and down her body. "That's where I first saw you," she whispered. "Right at the foot of that tree."

Edward nodded. "I could tell the lightning struck toward the cove. I drove there, saw the tree, called your name...and there you were."

"There I was." Julia grabbed his hand and held it to her chest.

He glanced at the book again.

"So, what's with the book, Edward?"

He pulled his hand away and took it from the nightstand. Keeping the pages open, he lifted it toward himself so she could see the cover.

"The Bible?"

He nodded. "Remember the verse we heard on the radio yesterday, the one that upset you?"

"The one with the word *haven* in it?"

"You just lived that verse, Julia."

"I don't—"

He held up a hand. "Listen." He began to read: "'He stilled the storm to a whisper; the waves of the sea were hushed. They were glad when it grew calm, and he guided them to their desired haven.'"

Chills washed over her again, and she stared at him. "Are you telling me this is some sort of sign?"

His gaze didn't waver. "Think about it. The woman asking you about haven, the invitation, the verse, your experience on the water."

"Coincidence."

"Some people don't believe in coincidence."

"Are you some people?"

He hesitated. "Maybe."

She sat up in bed. He adjusted the pillows behind her. "Let's say you're right," she said. "Let's say everything that happened yesterday happened for a purpose. A divine purpose, you're telling me?"

"Perhaps."

"I'm afraid you're giving me too much importance, Edward. I can't see why God would do all this for me."

"Neither can I."

She crossed her arms in mock indignation. "Well, thanks for your vote of confidence, Mr. Carson. I thought you were the one who thought God was involved in this?"

"I am, I am," he said, rubbing the space between his eyes. "Just because I believe it doesn't mean I understand it."

"Oh, *that's* reassuring."

He shrugged. "All I know, Julia, is that you are a good woman who has given a lot—"

"You betcha."

"But who has a lot more to give."

She fixed him with a look. "If you're wanting me to enter politics again, I don't think—"

Edward extended a calming hand. "All I want you to do is open your mind. Somebody's trying to tell you something."

"That somebody being God?"

He shrugged again.

"Are you telling me you want me to go to Haven, Nebraska?"

"Yes."

"Even though we have no idea who sent the invitation or what it's about?"

He nodded.

She put a hand to his forehead. "Did you take a gullible pill this morning, Edward?"

He stood and placed the Bible in her lap, then pointed to the 107th chapter of Psalms. "Think about it."

With that, he left her alone with her thoughts.

Julia found him in the kitchen making soup. He shooed her away.

"Back to bed, missy. You're going to stay warm and relax the entire day. I am your humble and obedient servant."

She got back in bed, and he adjusted the covers around her. "You really are a nudzh," she said.

"But a loving nudzh."

"Do I smell vegetable soup?"

"You do," he said. "And toast with peanut butter."

"You'll spoil me."

"For one day."

He started to leave the room. "Will you bring me the newspaper, too?" she asked. "Pretty please?"

"Give her an inch…"

"I know, I know, and she thinks she's a ruler." She smiled coaxingly. "Please?"

He left, only to return a few minutes later with a bed tray set with soup, toast, milk, and a vase of daisies plucked from the garden.

"I could get used to this," she said, spreading a napkin over her chest.

"It's my turn next."

"You planning to get caught in a storm?"

"The next one we have." He left again and came back with his own bowl of soup in hand and the paper tucked under one arm. They ate in silence, sharing the newspaper.

As Edward cleared away the dishes he asked, "Have you thought more about going to Haven?"

"Not now, Edward," she said, opening the paper to the comics. "Today is my day of rest. Remember?"

He nodded and took the dishes to the kitchen. Julia took a

pen out of the drawer in the nightstand and folded the newspaper so she could tackle the crossword puzzle. Confident in
her extensive vocabulary, she worked in ink. As she whipped
through the down clues, alternating with those that went
across, she heard Edward clanging around the kitchen, washing the dishes.

Twenty-one down: To blister. Ten letters.

"Vesiculate," Julia said aloud. She smiled with satisfaction as
she filled in the boxes.

Fifteen across: A place for growth of the spirit. Five letters,
the middle letter v—

Haven.

Julia's hand shook. She stared at the newspaper.

Edward's voice echoed in her mind: *"Some people don't
believe in coincidence."*

"Edward..." she called, her voice weak.

The dishes were clattering. He didn't hear.

"Edward!" she called again, desperate.

He came running. "What's wrong?"

She handed him the newspaper and fell back onto the pillows. "Fifteen across. Read it."

His eyes scanned the paper, finding it. "A place for growth
of the spirit."

"Five letters. Middle letter a v," she said.

He looked up, meeting her eyes. "Haven."

She nodded.

"You're going."

She nodded again.

Four

Two are better than one, because they have a good return for their
work: If one falls down, his friend can help him up.
ECCLESIASTES 4:9–10

SWEAT RAN DOWN Natalie's face even though the afternoon had
turned cool. A gentle rain fell outside the windows of the
Osage cabin. She'd propped the door open, letting in the
breeze—and Sam Erickson.

"Knock, knock."

"Hey, Sammy," Natalie said, tossing a rotted floorboard onto
the growing pile. "Want to help?"

"Not in this lifetime," he said. He came inside and straddled
a kitchen chair. "You're making a mess, you know."

"Gee. What would I do without you?"

He gave her a deep sigh. "Merely exist."

"Hand me the saw, will you?"

"Where were you this afternoon?"

Natalie took the saw and looked at him, gauging her
answer. *Should I tell him?*

Sam was her best friend, her only real friend in the entire
world. They'd met in grade school and had suffered through
bouts of hate, love, and annoyance ever since. Their relationship was as rocky as the mountains themselves. And just as
majestic. And treacherous.

She decided to take a chance. "Look in the pocket of my
jacket." She pointed across the room to the couch where she'd
tossed her jacket after being assigned work duty. He pulled out
the white envelope.

"Open it."

He read it, then looked in the envelope to see if he'd missed
something. "Who's it from?"

"I dunno."

"Who gave it to you?"

"A ranger while I was on a hike up by Loch Vale."

He blinked. "While you're on a hike, a ranger finds you and hands you an invitation to Nebraska?"

Natalie climbed out of the hole in the floor. "That's it."

"Did you ask him about it?"

"Her. She was a woman ranger. By the time I'd read it, she'd hiked up that really steep part of the trail. I started to go after her but she'd disappeared."

"As in *poof,* disappeared?"

"You make it sound as if there were a puff of pink smoke like in that genie show."

"So are you going?"

Natalie stared at him. "Just like that? You think I should go?"

"Why not? Someone went to a lot of trouble to make sure the invitation was hand delivered."

"I suppose they could have mailed it."

"But they didn't. They searched you out on a wilderness trail. Doesn't that make you curious?"

"Of course…"

"Then go see what it's about."

"But it might be some sicko person selling swampland or something. Or a band of perverts wanting beautiful young girls to be their slaves."

Sam rolled his eyes. "You're the sicko. A conceited sicko."

"Just thinking out loud."

He read the invitation again. "I like this verse about moving mountains. It makes you think anything's possible."

"I wish."

He rose from the chair, came to kiss her cheek, then headed for the door. "Get done with your work, and we'll get pizza."

He left her. The cabin felt empty without him.

"Gin!" Natalie yelled, slapping her cards on the table.

Sam tossed his down, beaten. "You are the luckiest—"

"Most talented and skilled—"

"Pain in the behind I have ever—"

"Loved." She rubbed her hands together, adding up the points against him. "A few more hands and I can add Italy to my itinerary."

"When are you going to Europe?" Natalie's sister asked from across the room.

Natalie shuffled and dealt another hand. "Someday."

"You're strange," Beth said. "Who'd want to go to a weird place like Europe? I want to go to Hollywood."

"The capital of weird," Natalie said.

Beth turned her attention back to the Scrabble game she was playing with their mother. "I'm going to be a movie star."

"Double weird," Natalie mumbled, rearranging her cards.

"I'm going to be famous before you are," Beth said.

"Uh-huh."

"I am!"

"Good thing you don't need talent to be famous."

The letter *U* flew across the room and hit Natalie on the forehead.

"Hey!" she yelled.

"Beth!" their father said over his newspaper. "You want to throw something, little girl, I'll throw *you*."

Natalie picked up the Scrabble letter and displayed it. "No need, Dad. Beth already threw *U*."

"Very funny."

She tossed Beth the letter, and they resumed their games.

"Your turn, Mom," Beth said. "You're taking forever."

"I'm thinking."

"Just because it's a triple-word score—"

"I've got it!"

Natalie's mother laid the letters across the board, spelling out loud: "H-a-v-e-n. Haven. Now that's a great score!"

Natalie dropped her cards. "What did you say, Ma?"

"I got a triple-word score with the word *haven*. That puts me in the lead!"

Natalie rushed to her mother's side, looking at the board.

"Hey, Nat, get away," Beth said, putting a protective arm around the board. "This is our game."

Natalie stared at the word. She felt Sam squeeze her arm. She looked to her mother. "What made you think of that word?"

Her mother shrugged, clearly puzzled at the hubbub one word was causing. "I was trying to use my *V* and, I don't know…I guess I was looking around the house, trying to see some object that had a *v* in it…oh, now I remember!" She pointed to the newspaper. "I saw your father's paper. See the headline? It says, 'Hikers Find Haven from Storm'. I saw the word in the headline and I used it." She looked at Beth triumphantly. "And I took the lead. Nah, nah, nah, nah, nah."

Natalie grabbed Sam's hand and pulled him toward the door.

"Where are you going?" her father asked. "It's getting late and you've got to get up early to caulk the windows in the Pawnee cabin."

"We won't go far," Natalie said. "We're going for a walk."

Sam jogged to keep up with Natalie's stride. "Slow down!" he said. "You said walk, not run."

Natalie jerked to a stop, causing Sam to run into her back.

"I didn't say *stop*, I said slow down."

She turned to face him, grabbing his upper arms. "What's going on, Sam? Why is this happening to me?"

Sam looked at her. "You're scared, aren't you?"

Natalie stormed away, shoving her hands in her pockets. Sam came after her. "It's just an invitation," he pointed out.

She stopped again, but this time he was ready for her. "It's *just* an invitation with my name on it. My full name that nobody but family and close friends know. It's *just* the name Haven that's magically come up three times in one day."

"Three times?"

Natalie counted on her fingers. "First on the invitation itself. Later, Ma uses the word *haven* in a Scrabble game, and finally the word's written across the front page of the newspaper. Three."

"Coincidence."

"I don't believe in coincidence."

"What *do* you believe in?"

Natalie walked to the side of the dirt road and climbed onto a car-sized boulder. She raised her face to the black of the sky. A thousand stars stared back. "I believe in something more than you and me."

She held out her hand and pulled him up.

"You mean God?" Sam asked.

"Yeah, I guess I do."

There was a moment of silence. Then Sam said, "I believe in him, too."

"Then why haven't you said anything? Why haven't *we* ever said anything?"

Sam shrugged. "We talk around it enough, talking about how gorgeous things are around here, how perfect. We both know the mountains didn't happen by accident. But we've never said the *G* word."

"He's out there, isn't he, Sam?"

"I think so. I hope so."

She turned to face him on the boulder. "What if God sent me the invitation?"

He raised his hand, blocking the words. "Whoa there, Natty. You got the invitation from a ranger, a flesh-and-blood ranger. Don't you think if God were sending you an invitation it'd come blazing down from heaven...or at least be printed in gold leaf." He laughed. "Or maybe it would glow in the dark."

He lay on the boulder and swiped his hand across the sky. "Or maybe there'd be a sky banner that only you could see. 'Hey you! Natalie Jasmine Pasternak! Come on down to Haven!'"

Natalie turned her back to him. "Don't laugh at me, Sam. Not you."

He sat up and moved behind her, scooting forward until they fit together like two riders on a toboggan. "Not me," he said, wrapping his arms around her. "Never me."

Natalie leaned her head against his cheek and closed her eyes. She knew so little about God. She'd never been to church. Not once. She'd asked her mom about it when she was six or seven but had been told there was no need to go to a building to find God. God was inside her. That had been the end of it.

Natalie didn't accept the idea of God being inside her. She was too flawed. Any God who wanted to take up residence in *her* body was obviously none too particular. Definitely not a perfectionist.

And Natalie wanted God to be a perfectionist. That's why she saw him in nature. People were flawed, but nature wasn't. Nature was pure. Sometimes, she would go on hikes early in the morning before the trails were full of people. She'd climb until she reached the furthermost lake nestled in the niche of two mountains. There she'd see the lake as glass, each rock, fish, and twig visible until the sun hit the snow on the mountain and the trickle of snowmelt ran into the lake. The intrusive ripples would spread, dissolving the mirror until sunset when the absence of sunlight and the cool of night would make the mirror reappear in time to reflect the moon.

She could sit for hours looking at such a scene, painting it in her mind. There was no way to improve on it. That fact alone proved to her there was a God.

But if nature was so perfect, why was mankind so flawed? Why was her dad so stern and her mother so dull? Why was Beth so selfish? Why was she so confused and Sam so...Sam so...

She opened her eyes and saw that the moonlight had cut a swath across their legs. She noticed how they'd synchronized their breathing, as if two bodies took a single breath, shared it, and let it out. Soul mates…

She lunged forward, startling him.

"What are you—"

She dropped to the road, pulling him after her. "We're going!"

"But I don't want to go home so soon."

"Not home! We're going to Haven!"

"Whoa, Natty. I wasn't invited. Whatever is happening in Haven…it's for you, not me."

"It doesn't matter." She walked in circles.

"Who says?"

Natalie waved her arms in the air. "I say. The trees say. God says."

"You're hearing voices?"

"Just my own."

"You *are* getting kind of loud—"

She grabbed his hands. "Not that voice, Sam. This voice." She pulled his hands to her heart. "My inner voice says we're supposed to go."

"Well, *my* inner voice wants to tell *your* inner voice…" he hesitated, looking into her eyes. "You're serious about this, aren't you?"

"As serious as I can be without being crazy."

He pulled away and walked to the other side of the road. "Let's say we're supposed to go. Have you thought about the hows of it? How we're going to get to Nebraska by August 1? That's four days away. You're working for your parents. I've got a job at a souvenir shop. Do you really think anyone will let us leave? And whose car are we going to take? Do you have money for gas and food…and where are we going to sleep?"

Each question made Natalie beam. She strutted across the road and linked an arm through his, turning them toward

60

home. "Have no fear, Nat is here. It will all work out. I know it will."

Sam shook his head. "Why did I feel safer when you were scared?"

Natalie finished caulking the living-room window of the Pawnee cabin. She moved to the window over the kitchen sink and spotted Sam walking toward the cabin. He was wearing his work uniform: khaki shorts and an Estes Park T-shirt. She met him at the door.

He came in without a word and sank into a chair. He draped a leg over the arm.

"What's wrong?" Natalie asked. "You having second thoughts?"

Sam made a face. "A part of me wants things to stay exactly as they are—good, bad, and boring. But another part of me wants to head out on the open road with my girlfriend and find adventure." His face clouded. "Leave our troubles behind. Conquer new worlds."

"Haven, Nebraska?"

He shrugged. "I looked it up on a map. It's south of the Platte River, two-thirds of the way across the state. Four hundred miles."

"Can my slug bug make it?"

"If the chipmunks running the engine don't give out."

"We'll bring along lots of nuts to feed them."

"And us. Corn Nuts. We love our Corn Nuts. And root beer. Lotsa root beer." Sam stretched out on the couch. "What are you going to tell your parents?"

"I thought I'd make it seem like a Barzeenian terrorist—a drop-dead gorgeous Barzeenian terrorist—kidnapped me, flinging me over his shoulder as he carried me to their secret hideout in the mountains. We'll hate each other at first, but then my quick wit and innocent beauty will win him over, and he'll propose and take me back to Barzeenia where I'll be queen—"

61

"I do hope that's not the plot of one of your stories," Sam said dryly.

"Maybe I should be a princess instead—"

"Oh, that's much more believable."

She threw her hands in the air. "Where's your imagination, Sam? Don't sentence me to write about ordinary people, people like Ned at the store. Ned who thinks 'yup' is a complete sentence and who puts his French fries in a neat row before eating them."

"He does that?"

"Tallest to shortest."

"That is so—" Sam shook the subject away. "You got off on a tangent, Natty."

"I should have been a math major."

"Natty!"

"Fine!" She flung herself in the chair. "I'll tell my parents I'm going camping with Cindy or something. I don't know. I'll handle it."

"You're not going to tell them the truth?"

"No way. I avoid confrontation. Especially with adults of the parental persuasion."

"Maybe you shouldn't tell them anything."

"Just leave? They'll think you kidnapped me."

"Oh, please."

"They will. Or they'll think we eloped." Natalie leaned close. "We could get married."

It wasn't the first time the subject had come up. "I love you, Natty, but we're only eighteen."

"My parents were eighteen when they got married."

"That was the seventies. They were hippies."

"This is the nineties, and we're friends."

"Best friends."

"That sounds like the basis of a great marriage."

He shook his head. "It's good as it is. I don't want to risk ruining it."

"We love each other, Sam. That can't be ruined, can it?"

"Things are fine the way they are."

"Things change."

"They don't have to," he said.

Natalie picked at a fingernail. "But sometimes they change even when we don't want them to." With a sigh, Natalie went back to her caulking. "Do you think we're doing the right thing?"

Sam looked out the window. "I think we're doing what we have to do. Can you live your entire life never knowing what's in Haven? Or who's in Haven?"

Natalie took a deep breath and studied him. After a moment, she shook her head. "No, I can't. That's why I'm going. *We're* going. Together."

Five

Listen to advice and accept instruction,
and in the end you will be wise.
PROVERBS 19:20

WALTER STORMED PAST his secretary's desk.

"Mr. Prescott?" The voice wasn't right.

He turned and tried to focus. "Who are you?" he barked.

The secretary blinked. "I'm Mary Ellen. I'm the swing-secretary. Belinda had a doctor's appointment so I'm taking her place this afternoon." She held a pile of pink message slips. "These are for you."

He took them with as much emotion as a computer accepting data.

"Is there anything special you'd like me to do for you, Mr. Prescott?"

His eyes came back to life and he moved to his office. He paused in the doorway. "Leave me alone." He slammed the door.

Regret. Remorse. Shame. Too many emotions, too fast. Yet he didn't have the energy to make amends. Not now.

Walter tossed the messages on his desk and sank into his chair, turning toward the window. He took the pencil out of his hair and chewed on it vigorously, ignoring the taste of paint and wood. It was either chew a pencil or smoke. He'd already had three cigarettes this morning. That was three more than he should have had.

He looked through the windows at the office building across the street and watched a presentation being made in a conference room. A woman holding a pointer stood before six people, who sat around a table looking bored. A typical day in the business world.

Except this day hadn't been boring at all. Not for Walter. Finding out you're going to die was hardly boring. Being visited by a stranger who'd stolen a dead man's name was hardly boring. Receiving a bizarre invitation from this cryptic man, who said Walter would be well, was hardly boring.

Walter swiveled his chair just enough to see the white card sitting on his desk.

"You're the cause of all this," he said, pointing his pencil at the invitation. "You and that phony Gabe."

Walter watched the card, expecting it to move…or talk back…or better yet, disappear. Predictably, it sat there, inanimate and mute. Then suddenly, the top flap of the card began to stir. Just slightly. Up, down. Up, down. Waving at him. Mocking him.

Walter grabbed the arms of his chair, tensing himself for an attack. He felt a trickle of sweat run down the back of his neck.

The entire desk seemed to be alive. The corners of the pink messages joined in, fluttering, accompanying the mocking invitation in its impossible dance.

I'm going crazy. Papers can't come to life!

Walter wiped his face with his handkerchief. He loosened his tie, tilting his face toward the cool breeze of the air-conditioner. His eyes focused on the ceiling. The air-conditioning vent was positioned directly above his desk. He looked from it to the desk, following the airflow, feeling it blow on his face, watching how it hit the papers and made them flutter….

Walter's shoulders relaxed. He closed his eyes. "You are going crazy, Prescott. One hundred percent."

He extended his arms and tensed his muscles until his upper body shook, as if the movement would put everything—every thought—back where it had been at the beginning of the day. He sat forward in his chair and lay his hands on his desk.

"I am in control here. I am in…" He paused, staring at his desk, then reached out to lift the invitation by its corner as if it were a defiled object. "You have caused enough trouble for one day." His hand hovered above the wastebasket, but at the last moment it detoured and dropped the invitation in his open briefcase. He promptly closed the lid and secured it.

"There. Take that you…you…" He let the sentence die.

Walter flipped through a pile of messages, repeatedly transferring the top message to the bottom of the stack. Occasionally, he would draw the message close to his face, trying to decipher the swing-secretary's atrocious handwriting. The fourth message halted his rhythm.

The name and number were illegible, but the message blazed like neon. *Re: HAVEN*.

Walter stormed out of his office, the door ricocheting off the wall.

"What is this?" He held the pink note under Mary Ellen's nose.

The secretary's initial flash of fear changed to agitation. "There's no need for shouting, Mr. Prescott." She plucked the message away from him and held it at arm's length. She opened her mouth to read it out loud, then closed it as her own handwriting eluded her.

"I can't seem to make out the name…or the number…" She held the note to her forehead like Johnny Carson doing his swami act. She shook her head, resigned. "I'm sorry, Mr. Prescott. Sometimes when I'm in a hurry, my writing gets a bit messy—"

He grabbed the note away from her and pointed to the message. "You managed to get the message down clear enough: Haven."

The secretary sat back in her chair. "Oh, yeah. I remember that one. A nice man. Very polite, wanted you to call him. But the other lines were ringing and I had to write fast. I got the message so clear because he spelled it out and I wrote it slow. H-a-v-e-n. He said you'd know what it meant."

"But I don't!"

She shrugged. "He said you would."

As Walter stuffed the message into his pants pocket and huffed into his office, he heard her mumble, "If *he* doesn't know what haven means, how am I supposed to know?"

Walter walked calmly to his door and glared at her. "Obviously, you're not *supposed* to know," he said. Raising his voice he added. "Besides, *you're* not invited!"

He slammed the door a second time, then stood there, staring at the floor. No doubt about it. The office grapevine would be ripe tonight.

Walter pulled the door of his apartment open at the same moment Bette rang the doorbell.

"I need you," he said. He pulled her inside, nearly spilling the sack of groceries she'd brought with her. He set the groceries aside and hugged her. Enveloped her.

"Such a welcome," she said. "Who's dying? Me or you?"

He pushed her to arm's length. "That's not funny." He picked up the sack and took it to the kitchen.

"Oh, Walter. I'm just kidding. Everything will be all right. I know it will."

He stopped and turned toward her. "They scheduled the biopsy for August 6."

She hurried after him. "But that's good. The sooner you know, the better you'll feel."

"I'm sure when they tell me it's cancer I'll feel loads better."

"God will take care of you."

"Not when I'm the one who did the smoking."

She ran a hand across his forehead, her fingers skimming his hairline. "Is that why you wanted to eat in tonight? You're worried?"

"I feel the need to be home, and it has nothing to do with my health. I don't want to go where *they* can find me."

"Are we talking about boogie men, doctors, or aliens?"

He took a bunch of celery from the sack and pointed it at

her. "This is not the time for jokes."

She made a locking motion over her lips.

"Let's eat first and talk later," he said.

"Are you implying your news can't be handled on an empty stomach?"

"Yes…no…I'm implying I'm starved."

After four months of dating—and a lot of joint ventures in the kitchen—Bette and Walter worked together as a finely tuned cooking machine. Chow mein and hot tea were served over small talk, and then the dishes were cleared. Bette took a seat on the couch, while Walter chose a CD of Bach's Brandenburg Concertos.

"That's nice," Bette said, leaning her head against the cushions and closing her eyes.

"Calming," Walter said.

She opened one eye. "We're going to need calming?"

He raised an eyebrow and shrugged.

Sighing, she sat upright and faced him on the couch. "So tell me about your day. What's up? What's the scoop? Somebody has to talk and I choose you."

Walter grimaced. "Not a good choice of words."

"Which words?"

"The choosing part."

"You got chosen for something today?"

"Sort of."

"Is it a good choosing or a bad choosing?"

"I don't know."

"This isn't going to be twenty questions, is it?" she asked, shaking her head. "I hate twenty questions."

Walter squeezed her knee. "So do I." He got up and lit a cigarette, ignoring her frown. Then he retrieved the invitation from his briefcase.

"Ooh, pretty," Bette said, looking at the ink drawing.

"Read the inside."

She opened it, read it, and—in what Walter was beginning

to think was the universal reaction—turned it over, looking for more. She looked at him. "Who's it from?"

"I don't know."

"What's in Haven, Nebraska?"

"I don't know."

"Why is this Bible verse quoted?"

Walter grabbed the invitation away from her and read it again. "This is a Bible verse?"

"Sure," Bette said. "From Matthew or Mark, one of the two. It's a well-known verse."

"Not by me."

She leaned forward and kissed his forehead. "Give yourself time, Walter. You've only been going to church with me six weeks."

"So what do you think the invitation means?"

She shook her head and took it back. "Because of the verse, I assume this is a picture of a mustard plant."

"Sounds logical."

"The fact they included your full name is interesting." She looked up at him. "Ralph?"

"My paternal grandfather."

"But there's so much they don't tell you....Why Haven? What time on August 1? Who's giving the party...or whatever it is?"

"And why the Bible verse?" Walter said. "It's not chic to go around spouting the Bible, much less put it in an invitation."

"Somehow, I don't think this has anything to do with being chic."

"But it's well done," he said. "Simple, but elegant."

"Maybe it's a retreat for the station? They're gathering the executives hoping you'll find yourselves."

Walter shook his head. "A TV station isn't going to quote the Bible. They wouldn't be caught dead acknowledging God."

"You need to do something about that, Walter," Bette said. "You know how it bothers me and a lot of other people that the news is so negative, that programming is so suggestive, that the good of the world is overlooked as not newsworthy."

He held up a hand. "I know, I know. And I agree with you—to a point. But I can't cut a swath through the entire system screaming that it has to be changed. I have to do it a little at a time."

She crossed her arms. "So when are you going to start?"

"You've changed the subject," he said, pointing to the invitation.

"That's my prerogative."

"Bette…"

Her arms flew in the air. "Fine. I'll drop it. For now."

"Praise the Lord," he said, mockingly.

She glared at him. "Did anyone else at the station get an invitation?"

"Not that I know of. It was hand delivered to me by a nondescript little man, who used the name of an old friend to gain access to my office."

"He could have been going through the building handing them out."

"I don't think so. When he pulled out the envelope from his inner pocket, it seemed to be the only one. As soon as I read it, I went after him to ask about it. That's when the fun really started."

Walter told her about the man's car. The Haven license plate. The dancing invitation. And the telephone message. He pulled the pink sheet out of his pocket as proof.

"I can't make out the name or number," Bette said.

"But you can read the message, can't you?"

"Haven."

"Exactly."

She sat a moment, looking at him. Then she took his hand. "God works in mysterious ways, Walter. Maybe all that happened to you today is meant to reinforce the invitation. He wants you to go, and he wants you to know he's serious about it. He wants you to have faith."

Walter stood, pacing in front of the couch. "And I'm supposed to believe that a man like me is being chosen by God to do...to do *anything*."

Bette's voice softened. "He's forgiven you, Walter. You need to forgive yourself."

Walter stopped pacing. "How can I? I lived with a woman for two years, but I wouldn't commit. I was in this life to work hard and have fun. Taking, taking, taking. Never giving back. When I was through using Donna, I dumped her. I did more than dump her, I crushed her like a bug under my heel. I took great joy in bringing her down. And when she took the pills..."

"She lived, Walter."

"Luck. Pure luck."

"Providence."

Walter shrugged. "See? I can't even give God credit for saving Donna. No God, no man, nowhere, has a use for someone with as little faith as that."

Bette slipped her arms around his waist and leaned her head against his chest. He resisted her comfort, keeping his hands at his sides.

"I forgive you, Walter. And God forgives you. Christ took care of it for you. It's over. You're sorry. God's sorry with you. Now you go on."

His resolve melted. He put his arms around her and held her close. Then he suddenly pushed away. "But I can't. I don't deserve it—whatever it is. Besides, there's the biopsy. Maybe that's my punishment. *That* I deserve."

He snatched the invitation off the couch and took it to the wastebasket in the kitchen. He tossed it among the celery leaves and wet tea bags. He carried the wastebasket to the front door and outside. Bette followed behind him.

"Walter? What are you doing?"

He walked down the stairs and out the front door of the apartment complex. He marched around the side of the building where he emptied the wastebasket into a trash can. He replaced the lid with a clatter.

"I'm going on with my life the best I can. I don't need any mumbo jumbo messing it up. I have enough problems."

"But Walter—"

"Case closed."

Bette went home early. Walter couldn't blame her. He'd effectively squashed the mood of the evening with his adamant rejection of the invitation.

Had he made the right decision?

He didn't know. All he knew for sure was that he was tired. He checked the front door, lit a cigarette, and turned out the lights. Heading toward the bedroom, he unbuttoned his shirt. He wadded it into a tight ball and drilled it into the laundry basket. He emptied his pants pockets into the bowl on the dresser. Keys, change, a breath mint, his handkerchief. And a wrinkled pink phone message from work.

"I should have thrown you away, too," he told it. He held his cigarette beneath the paper, threatening it with a death by fire. "All it would take would be a few seconds and you'd be—"

Walter cocked his head. Something was different about the note.

He held it close. The name was still illegible and the message was still bold. But the space where the phone number had been scrawled was different. Gone was the scribbled row of numbers. In its place was a list of three phone numbers—including area codes—written in perfect penmanship.

He crumpled the message, tossed it on the dresser, and backed away. He shook his head, denying his eyes.

Turning, he went to the bathroom and washed his face—scrubbed it—hoping the splash of hot water and the vigorous rubbing would force common sense into his brain.

He came out of the bathroom and approached the pink note cautiously. Standing near the bed, he closed his eyes, willing the phone numbers to be gone so he could throw the thing away and be done with it. With all of it.

God, if you're up there, listen to me. I don't know what's going on, but it's scaring me. I'm not good at games. I'm a facts man. If there's something I'm supposed to do, you need to tell me plain.

He took a deep breath and opened his eyes, moving toward the dresser. The note was waiting for him. His eyes widened. No longer a crumpled ball, it lay flat and unwrinkled. "Do you press shirts, too?" he asked the air.

He picked up the note. He made himself look at it.

The three phone numbers were there, waiting for him.

"I take it I'm supposed to call these?"

The room answered with silence.

"Fine," he said, bolting to the head of the bed. "I'm calling. It's only three phone calls. I can hang up anytime. What can it hurt?"

What can it help?

He dialed the first number before the logical part of his brain talked him out of it. A 501 area code. He had no idea where that was.

As the phone rang for the third time he had a rush of panic. *What am I going to say?*

Before he could slam the phone into the cradle he heard a woman's voice. "Hello?"

Walter's thoughts fell in a jumble. "Hello…I mean hi…I mean my name is Walter Prescott and I'm calling from St. Louis. I got your number today from a man who came into my office and—"

"I'm not interested in buying anything, thank—"

"No!" yelled Walter. "Don't hang up! I'm not selling anything. Please listen, just one minute."

"I'm really busy," the woman said. "I'm going out of town tomorrow with my two kids and I have a lot of stuff to get ready.…"

Walter's stomach clenched. "May I ask where you're going?"

73

There was a pause on the line. "I don't think that's any of your business, Mr. Preston—"

"Prescott. And I understand," he said. "But will you tell me I'm right if I guess your destination?"

"Is this some kind of contest?"

"No, no," he said, trying to make his voice sound normal. "Please, just…are you going to Haven, Nebraska?"

Her intake of breath was answer enough. She whispered into the phone. "How did you know?"

"I got an invitation, too."

"Oh-h-h," she moaned. "I've got to sit down."

There was the rattle of chair legs against a floor.

"Miss? Miss? Are you all right?"

"I'm fine," she said, her voice stronger. "How did you get my number?"

"Long story," Walter said. "In fact I've got two other numbers to call. They must be Haven people too."

"Haven people," she repeated. "What do you suppose it means?"

"I have no idea. In fact I threw my invitation away just this—"

"You threw it away?"

"It didn't make any sense," Walter said. "It didn't say who it was from or why we were invited."

"But it's from God."

Walter snickered. "Have you been talking to Bette?"

"Who?"

"Never mind." He ran a hand across his eyes. "As far as it being from God, I don't think—"

"What else can it be?"

"What else…?" Walter stifled a laugh. "Anything else. Anyone else. You and Bette are hurdling all common sense and zeroing in on the least likely explanation."

"Why is it the least likely?" the woman snapped. "Because it's not splashed across the evening news? Because it's not the

74

topic of every talk show? Because it's happening to us?"

Walter decided not to tell her his business *was* the news.

"These things don't happen," he said.

"Why not?"

"Because they're...spiritual. They're not of this world. They're...odd."

"Don't you think the miracle of conception is spiritual? Don't you think the feel of a child's head against your cheek is out of this world? Don't you think the fact a human being can learn to talk or walk or trust at all is odd?"

"I don't have any children—"

"Then think of your own life, Mr. Prescott. Haven't you ever come frighteningly close to being in a car wreck and been saved? Haven't you felt a shiver run through your soul when you hear a choir sing a hymn, like the words and music are a direct link with God himself? Haven't you ever been blessed with an idea when your mind was blank only moments before?"

"I suppose."

"You may have chalked those things up to luck or inspiration or your own smarts, but you're wrong. God's around us all the time, working with us, working through us, working *in spite* of us." She took a deep breath and laughed self-consciously. "I have no idea why I'm talking to you this way. You're a stranger and I'm not usually one to express my opinion like this. But I have a strong feeling—"

"I'm not a religious man, Miss...Miss..."

"Mrs. Kathy Kraus. Of Eureka Springs, Arkansas."

"Nice to meet you. And call me Walter."

"Walter," she repeated. "I'm not particularly religious, either. I go to church—sometimes—but I have a husband who's out of town a lot, and when he is home he wants to spend his Sunday mornings relax—" She hesitated. "No. It's not Lenny's fault I don't go to church. I use him as an excuse. Funny how I've never realized that before. So you see, I'm not talking above you, Walter. I'm far from perfect."

"Amen to that."

She laughed. "We're a flawed pair."

"Why does that make me feel better?"

"Because it means we're allowed to fail. There are no great expectations for us to do this completely right."

"Then how do we do it?"

"We follow our instincts. We pray for guidance."

"My instincts are tuned into things men do, not things God does."

"Maybe that's his point."

Walter lay back on his bed. The pillows threatened to envelop him, take him captive into sleep.

"Are you still there, Walter?"

He sat up, forcing himself to think. "I'm here. I'm just overwhelmed."

"Be overwhelmed later. We have to make a plan."

"A plan? Why?"

"You said you've got more phone numbers to call?"

Walter looked down at the pink note. "Two more."

"For some reason we're all supposed to meet. Be a team of some sort."

"Could be."

"How are you getting to Haven?" she asked.

I'm not going. I threw away my invitation. "I—"

"You live in St. Louis?" she went on.

"Right."

"Do you have a car?"

"Such as it is."

"We're taking a bus."

"We?"

"My kids and I. I have to take them with me. Lenny's gone on a business trip."

"What's he think of all this?"

"He told me to forget about it."

76

"Then maybe you should—"

"I'm going." Her voice was strong. "Everything has fallen into place so I can go. But the bus only goes as far as Grand Island, Nebraska. Would you pick us up there? It'd be on your way."

"Sure," he said, though he was far from sure.

"The bus gets in at 8:20 A.M."

"On the first?"

"Can you be there?"

I wasn't going. I wasn't going. I wasn't—

"I'll be there."

"I thought you threw your invitation away?"

"I made a mistake."

"Only a wise man will admit that."

"Then I must be the wisest of them all."

She laughed, then her voice softened. "It will be okay, Walter. I know it will."

"I hope so."

"Now, call the others," she said. "Arrange for us to meet somewhere so we can discover Haven together."

"Anything else?"

She laughed again. "I'm usually not so bossy. In fact, one of my many faults is I'm too submissive and quiet. You probably hate me."

"Not at all. I like you." And he did.

"Really? It's been a long time since anyone's said—" She cleared her throat. "Good luck, Walter."

He hung up and stared at the phone. "We're going to need it."

There was a pause on the line.

"Did you hear me?" Walter asked. "I asked if you got an invitation to Haven, Nebraska."

Walter heard a muffled, "It's for me, Ma." Then, "Yeah, I got one. Who are you?"

77

"Walter Prescott. I'm calling from St. Louis. Who are you?"

"Hey, mister, you're the one who called me," the girl said.

"I got your number, but it didn't have a name next to...long story."

"You're not some pervert, are you?"

"Listen, girlie girl," Walter said, rubbing the space between his eyes. "I don't need to take this kind of—" he broke off, calming himself. "If you don't want to talk about this, I'll hang up right—"

"No! Don't hang up." The girl's voice quieted as though someone else were in the room. "It's just weird, you know?"

"I know."

"I'm Natalie Pasternak. I live in Estes Park, Colorado."

"Estes Park. I've been there," Walter said. "Pretty place."

"I know."

"You sound young. How old are you?"

"You sound old," Natalie said. "How old are *you?*"

"Touché."

"Eighteen. And that's not so young."

"Forty-six. And that's very, very old."

They laughed. Then Natalie asked, "Are you going to...you know?"

"I'm thinking about it. Are you going to...you know?"

"Me and my best friend are leaving tomorrow."

"You're bringing someone?"

"Is that okay?"

"I don't know. I suppose it is."

"I've never driven nine hours by myself. Besides, if the wind blows the wrong direction my car will stop running. What if it broke down, and I was alone in western Nebraska somewhere? Not that me or my friend know much about cars but—"

"It's scary, isn't it?" Walter said.

"What?"

"Going to a place you know nothing about. It's scary."

"Weird."

"Scary."

"Creepy."

"Scary."

"All right," Natalie said. "It's scary."

"At least we agree."

"What do you think it means?" she asked. "The invitation, the verse, the whole thing."

"You first."

"Uh-uh. I asked you."

Walter hesitated, annoyed because it was so hard for him to say the words. "It might be, it could be...I don't know, maybe it's from God."

"You think so?" Natalie asked.

"That's what you thought, too?"

"Well...yeah. But it sounded so dumb. I mean, I'm a nobody. I've never even been to church. Why would God pay attention to me?"

"Exactly."

"Thanks."

"I mean, I feel the same way," Walter said.

"Exactly."

"There's another woman in Arkansas. I've already called her."

"Wow. Arkansas. Is she going?"

"She is. She's taking a bus as near as it will go. I'm going to pick her up in Grand Island."

"I envy you," Natalie said. "Meeting ahead of time. Not having to go in alone."

"We could do that," Walter said. "All of us. Maybe that's why I got the phone numbers of the three of you so we could meet before we got to Haven."

"Three? Me, the Arkansas lady, and who else?"

"I don't know," Walter said, looking at the last phone number on the pink note. "I haven't called them yet."

"Well, whoever they are, I want to meet," Natalie said. "But where?"

"Just a minute." Walter set down the phone and got an atlas from the bookshelf. *Odd how I haven't even looked up this place until now.* He spotted the city of Grand Island along Interstate 80, which spanned Nebraska from east to west. Haven had to be close…there it was. Maybe an hour further west, just a few miles south of the interstate.

"There's an interchange off 80 heading to Haven," Walter explained. "Why don't we meet there. There should be a gas station or something."

"What if there isn't?" Natalie asked.

"Then pull off the side of the road and wait."

"What time?"

"Kathy's bus gets in at 8:20—Kathy's the name of the lady from Arkansas—so let's say 9:30, the morning of the first. I drive a green Chevy van."

"I've got a blue Volkswagen Beetle."

"When I call this next person, I'll tell him or her, too."

"Where does that person live?" Natalie asked.

"I have no idea. The area code's 612."

"That's Minnesota."

"Really," Walter said. "They've got us coming from north, south, east, and west, haven't they?"

"Whoever *they* are."

"Exactly."

Natalie was right. Area code 612 was Minnesota.

"Carson residence," came the man's voice on the phone. He was out of breath.

Walter was tongue-tied again. What was he supposed to say?

"Hel-lo-o," said the voice. "Anybody there?"

"Yes, I'm here," Walter stammered. "I'm calling regarding Haven. Haven, Nebraska."

Walter heard a hand move over the receiver, then a garbled, "Julia! It's about Haven!"

A woman came on the line. "This is Julia Carson. What about Haven?"

Minnesota....Julia Carson...

"*Governor* Julia Carson?" Walter asked.

"Ex-governor. Who's calling please?"

Walter introduced himself and explained the reason for his call. He told Julia about Kathy Kraus and Natalie Pasternak.

"There are four of us?" she finally asked.

"That's all that appeared on *my* note."

"Define *appeared.*"

Walter explained about the note.

"You're lucky you got hold of me at all," Julia said. "My husband, Edward, and I were planning to be at our cabin for a few days, but there was a storm and I got caught out on the lake...anyway, we came home early so I could get ready to go to Haven."

"So you *are* going."

"What choice do I have?" Julia asked.

"I think you have plenty of choices. No one's forcing you to—"

"No, you don't understand," she said. "The finger of God sent lightning, marking the place where I was in the storm. That's how Edward found me."

"Finger of God?" He was skeptical.

"Hey, you be caught in the middle of a grove of submerged trees with your boat filling up with water and a motor that won't work. Thunder, lightning, darkness. It was the finger of God, I tell you."

"Fine, fine," Walter said. "After today I'd believe anything."

"You'd better."

Walter remembered news stories about the feisty governor of Minnesota. She was a plain-talking, alarmingly honest woman who made waves just by entering a room. This was going to be interesting.

"We're going to meet ahead of time so we can go into

Haven together," Walter explained. "Would you like to join us?"

"You betcha."

Walter stood at the counter, watching the mug of water heat in the microwave. He readied a tea bag. The microwave buzzed, and he took out the mug and dipped the bag into the steaming water. The amber color spread, darkening the water.

"I'm really going. I, Walter Prescott, am actually going to drive to Haven, Nebraska. The biopsy will have to wait." He lifted the tea bag and squeezed it between his fingers. He reached toward the wastebasket to throw it away. The empty wastebasket.

He jerked his head toward the front door. The invitation! He'd thrown it away!

Walter raced through the front door, leaving it open. He ran down the stairs, nearly crashing into a man as he rounded the corner at the back of the building. He tore off the lid of the trash can and was relieved to see the familiar celery debris of his trash. He sifted through it, expecting to find the invitation near the top.

It wasn't there.

He dug deeper into someone else's garbage, pushing aside a Trix box, bread wrappers, and an old *Time* magazine.

"Where is it?" he yelled.

"Lose something, mister?" asked the man Walter had nearly collided with.

Walter looked up hopefully, but after one look went back to work. The man wasn't a fellow apartment dweller, but a bum with a scraggly ponytail, dirty T-shirt, and torn pants. "I'm fine. I'll find it," Walter mumbled.

"Turn the can upside down," the man suggested.

"But it should be on top. I just put it here."

"What should be on top?"

Walter hesitated, then shook his head. This ragtag man was

82

no threat to his invitation from God. "I'm looking for an invitation. A card with the drawing of a plant on the front. I threw it away…and I shouldn't have."

The man moved closer, shifting his plastic grocery sack behind his back.

"Is it an invitation to a party?"

"No, not exactly…actually, I don't know for sure. But it's very, very important to me." Walter took a second look at the man. His expression seemed too smug, his eyes too interested in following Walter's search through the trash. "You didn't see it, did you?"

The man put a hand to his chest in mock indignation. "Me? What would I want with an invitation?"

Walter eyed him a moment, then nodded. "I suppose you're right." He gathered the trash he'd strewn on the ground and dumped it back in the can. "And I suppose I can go without the invitation. I'm sure he wouldn't mind."

"Who's *he?*"

"The host."

"What's his name?"

Walter hesitated, then hurriedly put the lid on the can and walked toward the front of the building. "Nice talking to you."

The man tipped his baseball cap. "Have a good time at your party."

Walter walked faster, nearly running. "Thanks," he called back as he raced around the corner of the building.

⁓

Antonio Delatondo—known to everyone as Del—took a seat in the bus shelter three blocks from Walter Prescott's apartment building. He took out his haul for the night: a half-eaten Mars bar, the end piece from a loaf of bread, two soggy tea bags, a celery stick, six pennies, and a small, white invitation.

He wrapped the food in his handkerchief and set it on the bench beside him. Using the bottom of his T-shirt, he wiped the tea stain off the front of the invitation. *His* invitation.

He passed over Walter's name and mentally filled in his own.

Antonio Michael Delatondo is invited to Haven, Nebraska.
Please arrive August 1.
"If you have faith as small as a mustard seed,
you can say to this mountain,
'Move from here to there' and it will move.
Nothing will be impossible for you."

"Thank you very much, I'd be glad to come," he said.

The bus pulled to the curb and Del gathered up his things and got on, pooling his change for a ride to the shelter where he could get a shower, a meal, and a good night's sleep. He had to be back at the apartment building early.

They had a long trip ahead of them.

Six

Do two walk together unless they have agreed to do so?
AMOS 3:3

THE SUN WAS STILL LOW in the sky when Del strolled through the parking lot of Walter Prescott's apartment building. He'd taken the 5:20 A.M. bus in order to get back before Walter went to work. Somehow he had to stow away in Walter's vehicle. Trouble was, which car was Walter's?

Del walked beside the cars, trying to match the vehicles with the Walter Prescott he'd met the night before. A red pickup? Walter didn't seem the truck type. A compact? Walter would have had to be a pretzel to fit inside. And his appearance had been way too haphazard to belong with the immaculate black sedan.

Then Del spotted it. A sickroom green Chevy van held together by rust. A shoe box on wheels. Somehow, it seemed to fit.

He made a beeline toward the van. Peeking in the window, he saw some partially opened mail that had been tossed on the dash. Del craned his neck to read the envelopes through the windshield. Mr. Walter Prescott.

"Bingo!"

Del patted the vehicle, making friends. He looked around the parking lot. It was empty. Now all he needed was…he spotted a piece of wire among some trash blown against bushes. He bent the wire, deftly molding it into the tool he needed. At least Walter's van was an old one, with the kind of locks you could get hold of with a hanger if you angled it just right….

Pop.

He was in. Del tossed the wire aside and climbed in. There

were bucket seats for the driver and front passenger, then two bench seats. The middle seat would accommodate two riders and was covered with sacks of crushed pop cans. The backseat, which could hold three, was full of crumpled fast-food sacks and a stack of old newspapers. There was a plaid stadium blanket tossed on the floor and a rumpled raincoat on the seat.

"Clean your van much, Walter?" Del took off the suit jacket he'd gotten from the shelter and folded it carefully. It would be his pillow. He moved the blanket, newspapers, and trash off the backseat and climbed in. The sacks of cans threatened to fall, but Del caught them in time. He lay down on the backseat and hid himself with the blanket and raincoat.

It was 6:45 A.M.

By seven o'clock, Del had shed the blanket and coat. The humid heat of the day was starting early. At seven-fifteen, when he heard someone humming, he peeked out and saw Walter Prescott walking toward the van, a camera on his shoulder and a suitcase in one hand. He fumbled for his keys.

Del scrambled to cover himself. He froze when the back cargo doors opened. Walter tossed his suitcase and camera behind the seat Del was lying on, slammed the door shut, and walked around to the driver's side.

Don't let him see me, Lord. Please, don't let him see me.

Walter got in the van, making it wobble as he got comfortable. He draped his suit coat over the passenger's seat, then started the engine and turned the air conditioner on high. Del sighed with relief and pushed aside the blanket so he could breathe the blessed air. Walter turned on the news, making snide comments to the newscaster. Del smelled cigarette smoke and stifled a groan. *Why couldn't I have stowed away in a nonsmoking van?* The air conditioning pushed the foul air toward Del. He smothered a cough. Walter sang along with a jingle for a local health spa, the effort sending him into his own fit of coughing.

"Serves you right, Walter Prescott," Walter told himself.

Del agreed completely.

The ride to Walter's office took a half hour. The seat was more comfortable than the thin mattress at the shelter. This wouldn't be half bad. Del dozed until the van started up the incline of a parking garage.

Suddenly the van pulled to a stop, and Del heard Walter get out and lock the door. Del stuck his head up and watched Walter go through a door, probably toward an elevator. As soon as the door swung shut, Del threw off the blanket and coat and sat up, stretching his muscles. He had no idea how long Walter would be gone. Was he working the entire day? Was he merely stopping in at the office on his way out of town?

Del pulled the invitation from the pocket of his suit coat. It was for August 1. Today was July 31.

"You've got to be leaving today," Del said to the absent Walter. "But when?"

He spent the next four hours reading the newspapers Walter was recycling. Around twelve he realized he had to go to the bathroom. Should he risk it? As twelve turned to one, he had no choice.

Del scouted the garage and waited in pain while a woman with a stroller got her child into a car seat, the stroller packed away, and her car started. While he was waiting for her to arrange her paraphernalia, his growling stomach added to his misery. If only he had some money…he climbed into the driver's seat and reached his hand into the storage pocket in the door. Just as he'd hoped. Change. Del grabbed handfuls of coins and dropped them into his pocket.

Finally the coast was clear. Del exited the van via the driver's door. He held his body confidently and checked his watch as if he were late for an appointment. In a way he was. If Walter came back to the van while he was gone, he'd miss a big appointment—in Haven, Nebraska. Somehow Del felt that particular appointment had the potential to be very important.

Del took the stairs to the ground floor. No rest room. He hurried out to the street and walked next door into the KZTV building. Although he had on a clean T-shirt and a newer pair of pants, he wished he'd worn his suit coat. It would've helped him blend with the other suits moving through the building.

Putting on his best smile, Del asked the receptionist by the elevators where the rest rooms were located. She smiled warily and told him down the hall to the left.

He used the facilities and gave her a wave when he walked past her on his way out. Feeling lucky—and rich with the change in his pockets—he stepped into a hole-in-the-wall snack bar and bought an apple, a Milky Way, a Coke, and a Butterfinger. At the last minute he added a roll of breath mints. He wanted to smell nice when he got to the party in Haven.

As Del was pushing open the door to leave the snack bar, he saw Walter walking by, heading toward the parking garage. Del sprinted out the door and hurried up the street, hugging the wall of the building, keeping his head down.

"Hey, Walter!" a man called, coming toward them on the street. "Hold up a minute."

Walter stopped to talk to the man, and Del rushed past them to the garage. Again he chose the stairs, taking them two at a time. Two floors. Three. Del burst through the door onto the parking floor and ran to the van. He tried the sliding door. *It was locked!* A few seconds were lost as he remembered he hadn't gone out that way. He dashed around to the driver's door. Yanking it open, he climbed inside, scrambled between the two front seats, sidestepped the smaller bench seat, and dove into his hiding place. He stuffed his sack of food on the floor and grabbed the coat and blanket, pulling them into place.

"Quit moving! You're shaking the entire van," he mumbled to himself. He forced his movements to be deliberate, controlling the final adjustments of his covers.

He heard a jingling of keys.

I didn't lock the door!

Walter turned the key in the lock, tried the door, found it

locked, tried it again, and opened the door.

He didn't notice. I can't believe he didn't notice.

Walter got in the car, humming the theme to *Rocky*.

How appropriate, Del thought with a silent chuckle, *after what I've just been through.*

As Walter snaked the van out of the garage and onto the street, Del had a chance to calm his breathing. He'd made it. They were on their way.

To Haven.

To their destiny.

The smell of French fries filled the van. Del's stomach churned. Was there any smell in the world that could pique a person's taste buds like that of hot, salty fries?

Del adjusted his suit-coat pillow. He'd heard Walter order a number one from McDonald's. Super-sized. It wasn't fair. It was after five o'clock and Del hadn't had the guts to risk opening his sack to eat one of his candy bars for lunch, much less dinner. And now to be assailed with the smell of heaven itself...if only he'd had time to pop open his Coke before they'd left St. Louis. As it was, there was no way Del could get a drink until Walter left the van. *If* he ever left the van. Walter had used the drive-through to order dinner.

Doesn't this guy ever stop?

Del heard a squeak as a straw was pushed through the opening in the super-sized Coke.

Torture. Pure torture.

Besides the hunger, there was the stale smoke—and the annoying music Walter listened to. At first it had been a classical piece—Rachmaninoff, Eighteenth Variation from Rhapsody on a Theme of Paganini, if Del wasn't mistaken. That had been nice. But then Walter had put on a tape of Barry Manilow. Rachmaninoff was acceptable, even enjoyable—but Del drew the line at "Copacabana." And when Walter started to sing along...

The volume rose to an obnoxious level. Del's only consolation was the racket covered the noise of two candy bars being unwrapped. Del waited for the chorus to pop the top of his Coke.

Ah.

After a while, Del dozed, only to be awakened by his bladder. His muscles ached. He desperately needed to lie on his back and straighten his legs. He needed a bathroom, he needed fresh air. He needed silence.

He was given a brief moment of peace when Walter ejected the Manilow tape. But Del's relief was short lived. The opening notes of "We've Only Just Begun" filled the air.

Del groaned silently. The only thing worse than Barry was the Carpenters. Haven or no Haven, there was only so much a man could—

He sat upright. The raincoat and blanket fell away. The rush of air felt as refreshing as a cold shower. Taking a few deep breaths, Del waited for the chorus before adding his lusty baritone to Walter's creaky tenor.

The van skidded side to side as Walter slammed on the brakes. His eyes in the rearview mirror were huge as they stared back at Del.

"Keep your eyes on the road, Mr. Prescott. I don't feel like dying today." Del turned sideways and leaned against the window, arching his back. He straightened his legs on the bench. "Though with your taste in music and the capacity of your bladder, I might consider death a blessing."

The van shuddered as Walter pulled onto the shoulder and turned off the engine, fumbling with his door, escaping outside. Only then did he turn to Del and scream, "What are you—?" He coughed. "You're that bum. What are—?"

Del climbed out the side door, stemming the flow of words. *"Bum* is such a harsh word, Walter. I am merely a man challenged by life, challenged by the—"

Walter coughed again violently.

"Choking on your pride?"

Once Walter finished the spasm of coughing, he asked, "What are you doing in my van?"

Del raised a hand indicating he needed a moment. He walked toward the back of the van and took two steps into the grassy ditch. "Give me a minute, Walter. I need to do my duty and then I'll answer your questions."

While Walter looked on dumbstruck, Del took care of business, then walked toward Walter, his hand outstretched. Walter put his own hands behind his back.

Del nodded. "So be it. I can understand your hesitance in being neighborly since my presence in your van was a surprise, but I want you to know that I am absolutely, positively, no threat to you. The name is Antonio Delatondo—Del to my friends and all relatives except my mother. And friend or not, you can call me Del since you've been kind enough to give me a ride."

"*Give* you a ride?" Walter asked. "I don't recall you asking, or me saying yes."

"An unfortunate oversight, I assure you," Del said, bowing. "But you see, I desperately needed a ride, and since we are both headed to the same destination, I decided to tag along."

"The same destination?"

Del nodded. "Glad to see you've calmed down a bit."

"You're going to Haven?"

"Yes, sir, I am."

"But why?"

Del straightened. "I've been invited."

Walter hesitated, then pointed at him. "You stole my invitation from the trash."

"I believe the simple definition of trash is worthless material that has been discarded," Del said. "Thrown away. Disposed of."

"But I went back to get it. You saw me."

"By then the invitation technically wasn't yours anymore,

91

was it, Walter? It was my possession. And *I'm* not about to throw it away."

"You don't even know what it's for. Or who sent it."

Del pondered this for a moment. "Do you?"

Walter stared at him, clearly flustered. "That doesn't matter! It was given to *me*. Not you."

"You obviously didn't hold it in high regard."

"I was mistaken."

"Your confession is commendable," Del said. "A wise man admits his—"

Walter kicked the fender of the van. "If one more person tells me that, I'll…I'll…"

"I forgive you," Del said.

Walter stared at him again, his mouth hanging open. "*Forgive* me? For what?"

"For being rude. And ungrateful."

"Me?" Walter paced in front of his van, his arms waving. "You steal from me, then you stow away in the back of my van, scaring me half to death by popping—"

"If you'd stopped for a potty break in a reasonable amount of time you never would have known I was there," Del said. "Of course, there is the fact that the EPA should issue air-quality warnings for your van. And then there's your questionable taste in music.…These were the factors which finally drove me over the edge."

"My taste—"

"The Rachmaninoff was quite enjoyable, but the rest. Really, Walter, Barry and the Carpenter siblings?"

"You have no right—"

"That is true. I don't have any right. But I do have a need, and since you're a God-fearing man, I was hoping you could help meet that need."

"What do you know about me? How do you know I'm a God-fea—"

"The verse in the invitation. It's from the Bible."

"How do you know that?"

"Just because I'm without residence or sustenance doesn't mean I wasn't brought up right. Don't be such an elitist, Walter. I was raised a good Catholic. I was an altar boy." Del made the sign of the cross and chanted, "Christ has died. Christ is risen. Christ will come again."

"You sound well educated."

Del almost laughed at Walter's look of confusion. "Bachelor of philosophy from Illinois."

Walter's eyes widened, then he studied Del, even more confused. "Then...how...why?"

Del moved to the van and leaned against it. "I suppose you deserve something of an explanation since I have forced myself on you."

"I'd appreciate it."

Del filled his lungs with the country air. "I had a bit of trouble. I considered myself invincible. Better than the rest. I was an arrogant, selfish, egotistical—"

"Hey, I'm not Dear Abby. This is not the time for true confessions."

Del smiled. "Would you care for a false one?"

Walter crossed his arms. "All I wanted to know was how you came to be a...how you ended up in my van."

"You want the *Reader's Digest* condensed version?"

"Fifty words or less."

Del sighed. "Because of me a woman is dead."

⁓

Walter stood there, staring at his stowaway, stunned. What in the world had he meant, "Because of me a woman is dead"? What kind of man was he dealing with?

He remained silent, waiting for more. When Del didn't continue, he prompted, "And?"

Del shrugged. "That's it."

Walter snorted. "That's not the condensed version, that's downright lean."

"I don't like to talk about it."

Yeah? Well, I don't like people stowing away in my van…scaring me half to death. "How'd she die?"

"Beaten to death."

Walter swallowed around a suddenly constricted throat. "Not…certainly not by you?"

Del shook his head, looking to the ground. "Not by me, no, but certainly because of me."

The man's grief was almost tangible. Walter felt a wave of compassion. "Was she your wife?"

"She was a prostitute."

The word slapped Walter in the face. And he'd been feeling bad. "Well, then…" he let his voice trail off, giving a careless shrug.

Del took a step toward him, his shoulders suddenly tense. "'Well then,' what?" he asked. "Since she was a hooker it doesn't matter that she's dead, is that what you're implying?"

Walter edged around the van toward the driver's door. "Hey, I didn't mean anything—"

"You think you're better than she was?"

"No," Walter said, opening the driver's door. *God, just get me out of this alive, okay? Let me get away from this crazy man.* "Just forget it," he said, trying to soothe Del. "Forget the whole thing."

He slid into the van, but Del grabbed the door, preventing him from closing it. He fixed Walter with a glare. "I was just like you, Walter. I looked down on her, judged her—"

"Hey, I am *nothing* like you," Walter said, pulling at the door. His mind calculated the chances of starting the van and pulling away without running over this lunatic. Even *with* running over this lunatic…

Without warning, Del released the door, letting Walter pull it shut. The man stood immobile, his body gone limp, his eyes glazed over. Walter had the impression Del was seeing other times. "I can't forgive myself. Don't you see? I can't forgive myself."

Walter put the key in the ignition but didn't turn it. There was something about this man. Something so basic, so common, so innocent…He rolled down his window. "Look, I'm not good at talking about stuff like this. My girlfriend is but I'm…you're not the only one who needs…Bette keeps telling me God forgives, if you ask him."

Del smiled smugly. "I know. That's why I don't ask."

"You don't want to be forgiven?"

Del's jaw tightened and his eyebrows twitched as he fought for control. "Not yet. Maybe someday, but not yet."

A car drove by and honked, bringing Walter back to reality. He stared at the steering wheel, fingering the keys in the ignition. After a few moments, he nodded and looked at Del. "We'd better get going."

Del's eyes narrowed. "Am I right to note the choice of pronoun?"

"You're the one who said I was a God-fearing man. I'm not going to leave you out in the middle of nowhere."

Del opened the side door to get back in the van.

"Hey," Walter said. "No need to sit in the back. You can sit in the front with me if you want."

Del smiled through the opened door. "Only if I get to pick the music."

"I suppose you like that country babble—"

Del slid the door shut and got in the passenger door. "I appreciate many kinds of music. Garth, Twila, Barbra, Elvis—"

"Elvis?" Walter said. "You complain about Barry and you like *Elvis?*"

"Elvis lives forever."

Walter pulled onto the highway, fighting a grin. He gave Del a sideways glance. "You're not him, are you? I mean under that ponytail and your questionable taste in clothes, you're not Elvis in disguise?"

Del closed his eyes, took a deep breath, and sang "Hound Dog" at the top of his lungs.

Seven

I lift up my eyes to the hills—where does my help come from?
My help comes from the LORD, the Maker of heaven and earth.
PSALM 121:1–2

NATALIE CHECKED HER WATCH. 11:55 P.M. She was supposed to pick up Sam at midnight. She smiled. For once she was on time.

He was waiting for her at the bottom of the hill near his house. They hadn't wanted to risk having her drive any closer as the *putt-putt* of her VW was a familiar sound at the Erickson home. Natalie swung onto the shoulder. She waited for Sam to open the door. When he didn't, she leaned over the seat and opened it for him.

"Don't just stand there, get in!" That was when she noticed that Sam didn't have any luggage. He peered in at her. "What's going on?" she asked.

"I'm not going with you."

"You're not—"

He shook his head. "I can't do it, Natty. This is your adventure, not mine."

"But I've invited you to come along. I want you with me."

He scuffed a shoe on the curb. "Can't happen."

"It *can* happen," she said. "It's a choice you can make."

He met her gaze. "It's a choice I already made."

Natalie felt a wave of anger wash over her disappointment. *Coward, traitor, stick-in-the-mud.* "That's it then?"

"That's it."

The transmission grinded as she shifted into first. "Then I'd appreciate you getting out of the way so I can move on."

"Natty—"

"Bye, Sam. Have a nice life."

96

"Natty, it's just an invitation."

She glared at him, then sighed. "It's more than that, Sam. Somehow I know it's more than that. It's my life."

"No!" Natalie yelled, hitting the steering wheel with her hand. "This can't be happening."

The tire thump-thumped against the pavement. She turned off the engine. The silence was deafening.

She looked toward the highway as a car zoomed past. *I need help.* But Natalie wasn't sure she wanted anyone to stop. It was two-thirty in the morning. What kind of person would be driving through eastern Colorado at 2:30 A.M.?

Natalie opened the car door and the interior light became an uncomfortable beacon in the night. She pulled out the bottom panel of the trunk. There was a spare. A flat spare.

A coyote howled. A car whizzed by and the bass beat of heavy music cut through the silence. Watching it, Natalie shivered. *Something doesn't feel right. There's something out there....It's dark. It's evil. It's—*

She looked away, staring into the dark. The red taillights of the booming music car shrank like the eyes of a retreating animal. There were no headlights on either side of the interstate. The shadows of rolling prairie were layer upon layer of inky darkness. The moon had stayed behind in Estes.

She held her breath as she realized there were no sounds. None. No crickets. No traffic. No wind. No birds. Not even the coyote.

With a sudden motion, Natalie hurried back to her car. She locked both doors and rolled up the windows. Her hands shook.

"It's out there," she whispered.

She held her breath. Her skin tingled. *Something's there. It's dark. It's moving.*

But there was nothing there. Only the darkness.

Then she saw a lone set of headlights in the rearview mirror. She put on her own headlights, then jumped out, waving her arms to flag the vehicle down. Any person was better than being alone with the unknown prowling in the dark.

A pickup turned onto the shoulder and slowed, then stopped behind the VW.

Natalie's stomach lurched as she realized she might have traded her imagined evil for the real thing. "Please," she whispered. "Keep me safe."

The door to the pickup opened. The silhouette of the driver moved from the driver's seat to the road. With the headlights shining, Natalie couldn't see anything except a figure.

Friend or foe? she wanted to ask. She took a step toward the back of the VW and tried to act confident and assured.

"Need some help?" the figure asked.

It was a down-home voice. Friendly.

"I've got a flat."

When the man stepped in front of the headlights, Natalie saw the details of his face. Fifty. The leathery skin of a farmer. A Colorado Rockies baseball cap perched on his head. He held out his hand. "John Crawford."

"Natalie Pasternak."

John walked around the car looking at the tires. He stopped at the right front.

"Got a spare, I see," he said, picking it up. "A flat spare."

"I've never had to use it."

The man turned the spare over in his hands. "That's the way it is with spares. Never think of them till you have to use them, and then you always wished you'd thought of them a heap of a lot more."

"Is there a gas station around here?" she asked.

"Nope. Not exactly around. Ten miles up. But this looks fixable, just got tired of holding its breath, that's all." He rummaged around in the trunk of the VW and found a jack Natalie didn't even know was there. "Let's get the flat one off and we'll get 'em both fixed. Got a flashlight?"

Natalie nodded, relieved there was something she could

contribute. She held it while John worked, watching carefully, filing the how-tos of changing a tire for future reference.

John stood and wiped his hands on his jeans. "Tire off. Now I'll take them both up the road and make them useful." He picked up the tire and motioned with his head for Natalie to bring the spare. They tossed them in the back of his pickup.

"You want to come along or stay here?" John asked, getting in his truck. "Like I said, gas station's ten miles up. I should be back in forty-five minutes."

Riding with a stranger was against everything Natalie had learned. Although John seemed nice…"I think I'll stay here with the car," she said.

"I understand," John said. "You rest and enjoy the stars. And don't worry about anything. God's angels are looking down on you."

When John pulled out, he tooted his horn. As his taillights moved away, Natalie got in the car. She hoped he'd be back.

Natalie looked toward the interstate as a Ryder truck drove by. A widely spaced but constant stream of headlights could be seen coming from either direction.

Where had all the traffic come from?

She shrugged it off. "I'll be fine. Everything will be all right." As if to prove it to herself, she rolled down her window, leaned her head outside, and looked up at the stars. *What if each one was an angel, watching over the world…?*

She smiled and started to sing, "Twinkle, twinkle, little star. How I wonder *what* you are?"

Natalie awoke when the headlights from John's truck lit her car. She looked at her watch. It had been forty-five minutes on the dot.

She grabbed the flashlight and went to help him.

"We should have you fixed up in a jiffy," John said.

"You got them both fixed?" Natalie looked at him, incredulous.

"Friend of mine runs the station. He's good."

"Yeah, he is." She placed the spare in the trunk.

John knelt by the jack and busied himself with the tire. "I got you some snacks. Thought you might be hungry. They're on the front seat of the truck. Help yourself."

"Thanks, that's nice of you." She walked toward the truck, pulled the door open, and froze. Sitting on the seat were a bag of Corn Nuts and a root beer. She was suddenly cold. She glanced at the stars, then at John.

How did he know my favorite snacks?

"Find them, Natalie?"

She grabbed the snacks and closed the door. "I found them. Thanks, John."

He grunted as he tightened the lug nuts. "Where you headed?"

"Nebraska."

"Where abouts in Nebraska?"

Why not say it? "Haven," Natalie said. "Haven, Nebraska."

John smiled. "I know of it. A good place. Very good."

"Then tell—"

John stood, his work done. "That about does it. You can be on your way. Wouldn't want you to be late."

Natalie reached in her pocket and pulled out a wad of crumpled bills. She knew it was less than twenty dollars, but it was all the cash she had. "Here," she said. "If it's more than this, I can write you a check."

John pressed the cash into her hand. "There's no charge for kindness, Natalie."

"But you saved me. You drove all the way to the gas station and had the tires fixed. Surely they charged you something. And the snacks...how did you ever know that Corn Nuts and root beer are my—"

He put up a hand. "There's a verse that comes to mind at times like these. 'Do not forget to entertain strangers, for by so doing some people have entertained angels without knowing it.'" He cocked his head. "You aren't an angel, are you?"

Natalie laughed. "Hardly."

John packed the jack away in the trunk and shut it soundly. "You never know."

She shook John's hand and thanked him again, then waved as he pulled away.

Sliding onto the seat, she started up the car and pulled onto the road. As she ate her Corn Nuts and sipped her drink, she thanked God that John Crawford was the kind of person out driving around at two-thirty in the morning.

After she had gone ten miles she noted the approaching exit. *That must be where he went to fix the tires.* As she drove past, Natalie looked toward the lone gas station. Its lights were out. Not a car sat in the parking lot.

It was closed.

She began to argue with herself.

Maybe they just shut it down for the night.

"At 3:45 in the morning?"

Then how did he fix the tires if it was closed?

She turned her head to check the other side of the interchange. "There's nothing else here."

Maybe he saw it was closed and went up the road a few miles.

Natalie shook her head. "I just saw a sign that said the next exit is twenty-eight miles away. He didn't have time to go that far and back in forty-five minutes."

She rode in silence, pondering—then she put her hand to her mouth, stunned, as the verse John had quoted ran through her mind. Natalie took a deep breath as she understood what had just happened.

He was the angel. John Crawford was the angel.

Eight

Then Jesus said, "He who has ears to hear, let him hear."
MARK 4:9

"I'LL MISS YOU," Edward told Julia.

She tugged his tie. "Why don't you come with me? Your research for the historical society can wait. The immigration records have been there for over a hundred years, they'll be there a few more days."

"You need to go alone, Julia."

"Who says?"

He shrugged. "I say, your invitation says, the finger of God says."

"It appears I'm outnumbered." He put her suitcase in the trunk of their silver Intrepid. "If I were a good wife I would've made you all sorts of casseroles to heat up while I'm gone."

"Because you *are* a good wife, you didn't."

"You're not nice."

"But I'm honest."

She pulled him toward the driver's door using his tie as a leash. "I can't be good at everything," she said, kissing his nose.

"You come pretty close."

She got in the car. "You do make it hard to leave."

"That's my plan." He leaned over and kissed her. "Drive carefully. And call as soon as you can. I want to know all about your adventures in Haven."

She closed the door and smiled through the open window. "If aliens abduct me, wave at the third star from the right, and I'll wave back."

"It's a deal."

She started the car. "I love you."

He blew her a kiss.

The miles flew by until Julia connected with Interstate 29 at Sioux City. She planned on staying overnight in Lincoln, Nebraska, and leaving at six the next morning to arrive outside of Haven in time to meet Walter Prescott and the others. She figured Lincoln was three more hours of steady driving. A long way for someone who was used to taking turns with Edward.

At a rest stop, she plunked her quarters into a machine and got a Mountain Dew and M&Ms. Caffeine city. She listened to Doctor Laura on the radio and reveled in the common sense the doctor touted. She sang with her CD of *Les Miserables* (singing the part of Cosette an octave lower). But outside of Omaha, on the one hour of Interstate 80 linking it to the capital city of Lincoln, she began to doze.

She attacked the first tug of sleep with fidgeting, moving her behind, tapping her hands against the steering wheel, and making faces, all in an attempt to force her body into wakefulness. No good. She turned to deep breaths, an opened window, and a vague rendition of "God Bless America."

By eight o'clock, her mind had made a choice. It was going to sleep. No matter what. All other emotions, thoughts, or logic were handily shunned as sleep commandeered her body. Her breathing slowed. Her eyelids sagged like shades being drawn for the night. Her chin sought the comfort of her chest.

It's so comfortable, so cozy, just a few minutes. It can't hurt to sleep just a few minutes....

HONK!

Julia's eyes jerked open. Gravel. The rumble of tires. *Bump.* Swerve! Straighten.

The rush of adrenaline made her gasp for breath.

She'd come within inches of driving off the shoulder into a ravine. Two tires had negotiated the hump from shoulder to grass when the sound of the semi's horn—

Julia gripped the steering wheel, realizing how close she'd

come to letting go of this tenuous lifeline. She concentrated on the road, her shoulders tense. She forced herself to breathe in and out. Controlled. Strong.

If it weren't for that semi honking at me, I'd be—

Julia scanned the road. On the stretch of flat prairie she could see for miles. There were no vehicles in front of her. She checked the mirror. Only one car shone as a spot on the rear horizon.

There were no semis in sight.

"But the horn," Julia told herself. "I woke up because of a truck's horn. It was loud, distinctive. Those horns don't sound like anything else."

But there were no trucks. Hence, there were no horns.

A shiver passed up and down her spine. "Thank you, God," she said. "I don't know how you did it, but thanks."

Julia made her hands ease their grip on the wheel. She let her shoulders relax. A sign for Lincoln came into view. In just a few minutes she'd be stopping for the night. Everything was all right.

Thank God.

Nine

*Therefore, as we have opportunity, let us do good to all people,
especially to those who belong to the family of believers.*
GALATIANS 6:10

WALTER PULLED INTO the motel parking lot next to a silver
Intrepid. He shut off the van and turned toward Del. "I assume
you want a nonsmoking room since you've bugged me inces-
santly about my nasty habit?"

Del shook his head. "Don't waste your money on a room for
me," he said. "That backseat is plenty comfortable."

"You are not sleeping in the van."

"Why not?"

"Because it's not…appropriate."

Del made a show of looking around the parking lot. "So
who's judging what's appropriate? Is Emily Post lurking behind
the Dumpster?"

"You know what I mean."

Del crossed his arms defiantly. "I gave up my rights to an
appropriate life years ago."

"You're too hard on your—"

Del held up a hand. "Nothing you can say will make me
take advantage of your kindness."

Walter opened his door and got out. He stuck his head
back in. "And stowing away in my van wasn't taking advantage
of my kindness?"

"That was unavoidable. A last resort as it were."

"Your *only* resort."

Del held up a finger, conceding the point. Walter shut the
door and went into the motel office.

Del rolled down his window, preferring the circulating heat of outside over the stagnant air of the smoky van.

A woman with streaks of silver in her hair came out of the office carrying a key. She walked toward the space between the van and the Intrepid.

"That your car?" Del asked her.

She looked up, her sharp eyes showing a weary intelligence. "Sure is."

"It matches your hair," Del said, pointing to her head.

She touched the nape of her neck, looked at the car, and smiled. "I guess you're right." She unlocked the car door and got in.

"It looks good on you," Del said.

"The hair or the car?"

"Both."

She closed the door, waved, and pulled away to the far end of the parking lot.

Walter returned. He got in the van.

"I met a nice lady," Del said.

Walter started the engine and backed up. "You engaged yet?"

"I'm not the marrying kind. Are you?"

"My girlfriend thinks so," Walter said. He pulled into a parking spot in front of Room 23. He took his suitcase out of the van. "At least come in my room and cool off."

Del shrugged and did as Walter asked. He stood by the door to Room 23 while Walter used the key. "Go on in, I forgot something in the van," Walter said.

Del went inside and made a beeline for the air conditioner. He stood in front of the blower and opened his arms wide. "The fluttering of a thousand angel's wings."

Walter called from outside. "You say something?"

"Only, ahhhh."

Walter smiled and stepped inside the room. He tossed a key on the bed. "This room is yours. I'm next door."

"What—"

"This is your room."

"I told you I'd sleep in the van."

"The van's locked, Del old boy. And the room's paid for."
Walter grinned. "If you don't take it you'll hurt my feelings and
it will be a terrible waste of money. And I hate wasting money."

Del stood by the bed, mute.

Walter pulled the door shut. "Night. I'll see you at 6:00 A.M."

Del heard Walter's contented laugh, then the click of another
door. A few moments later, he heard the muffled sound of a
television.

Turning in a slow circle, Del looked around, taking it all in.
A bed with a gray-and-mauve quilted bedspread and two pillows. The glowing red numbers of a clock radio. A television
with remote control. A bathroom he didn't have to share.
Comfort. Security. Safety.

Del fell to his knees and cried.

⁓

Walter lay on his bed and studied the ceiling. He smiled at the
air. He felt great. And for the first time in forever, he didn't
need a cigarette.

⁓

Del didn't want to sleep. The simple joys of having his own
space brought back memories of before. Maybe he could lead a
normal life again. Maybe he could be forgiven.

No. Not yet. He was being tempted by one night's normalcy.

Del lingered in his bath, washing his long hair and soaping
his underwear, socks, and shirt with a little bottle of shampoo
he'd found on the counter. He took a shower to rinse and was
appalled when he found himself singing "Copacabana." He
wrapped himself in a towel and draped the clothes over a chair
in front of the air conditioner, which was still running full
blast. It felt great to be cool again. Even cold. He pulled back

107

the covers and climbed in bed, fluffing the pillows until they formed a backrest. He turned on the television and flipped channels, not caring what he was watching, reveling in the fact that he *was* watching. A baseball game confirmed this was heaven. He set the clock radio to wake him at 5:45. If only he could stay awake, forever wallowing in the comfort.

Del woke to the dual sounds of the morning news on the television and Shania Twain on the radio. The rosy glow of the sun cracked through the curtains.

He let an arm venture outside his covers to turn off the radio but quickly tucked it back in. The air-conditioning had turned the room to ice. His shirt billowed in the arctic breeze.

Wrapping the bedspread around himself, he stumbled out of bed and went to hit the OFF button on the air conditioner. He felt his clothes. Cold, but dry.

"Get a little carried away last night, Del?" He shuffled to the bathroom.

There was a knock on the door, and he looked out the peephole to see Walter holding a razor, toothbrush, and deodorant.

"I gave at the office," Del said through the door.

Walter turned to walk away. "If you don't want—"

Del opened the door. "You think of everything, don't you?"

"It's for my own benefit," Walter said, handing the toiletries to him. "I don't want to look at your ragged mug and smell your ragged*er* breath and body."

"You ready to leave?" Del asked.

Walter walked toward his door. "Ten minutes. They've got rolls and coffee in the lobby so hurry if you want to eat."

Del was ready with five minutes to spare. He paused at the door to his room and looked back inside. He would never forget his one-night detour into normalcy.

Walter was putting his suitcase in the back of the van.

"Sleep good?" he asked.

Del nodded. "I want to thank—"

"No need," Walter said, heading to the motel office. "As my grandma used to say, 'Pass it on.'"

"Smart grandma."

The smell of coffee made the morning perfect. Bagels, muffins, donuts, and toast all sat waiting along with orange and tomato juice. A chamber orchestra played Chopin over the speakers.

"Morning," a woman said from a table near the coffeepot.

"That's my lady," Del told Walter from behind his hand.

She raised her eyebrows. "*Your* lady?"

Del made a small bow. "No offense intended, milady. I had merely mentioned our meeting to my friend."

The woman nodded. "He liked my car."

"And your matching hair," Del added.

Walter poured two cups of coffee. "Pushy, isn't he?"

Del filled a plate with pastries. "I prefer to consider myself refreshing."

She laughed. "And modest."

She looked at her watch. "Gentlemen, I've got to be going," she said, rising. "It's been nice talking with you. Have a good journey."

"You, too," Walter said.

Del tipped an imaginary hat.

She left. The men ate. Del went back for seconds. And thirds.

"Where are you putting all that food?" Walter asked, still working on his second donut.

Del finished chewing. "I'm storing it for the winter."

Walter made a face.

"Tell me about your girlfriend who thinks you're the marrying kind," Del asked.

"What's to tell?"

"Are you getting married?"

"Someday. Maybe."

"You don't sound very sure of yourself."

"She's sure. She's got her head together. I'm not sure. She makes me feel...unworthy."

"Ah," Del said, nodding. "A good woman."

"You make it sound like a rarity."

"It is."

"How do you know? I don't see anyone hanging on your arm."

Del spread a pad of butter on a muffin. "I'm not meant to be with anyone."

"Why do you say that?"

"A feeling."

"If you're feeling guilty about the hook—the *woman* again, I don't think—"

"It has nothing to do with her."

"Then why would you say such a thing?" Walter lit up a cigarette and blew the smoke over his shoulder.

Del fanned it further away. "Most people—men and women—have dreams about being with a mate. Having children. Going on vacations to Disney World. But I never have. Never."

"So what do you see for yourself?"

Del licked some butter off his finger and looked to the ceiling. "My dreams are hazy. I see other people, lots of other people in fact, and I'm talking to them and there's a good feeling between us. But there's no love—not in the usual sense. No family."

"It's just a dream," Walter said, throwing his paper plate in the trash. "You don't have to be limited by a dream. Change it."

"I can't."

"Of course you can."

"No, I can't." He made a fist near his midsection. "It's rooted too deep. It's in here. It's not for me to change."

Walter headed for the door, and Del stuffed the rest of his muffin in his mouth and followed, toting his cup of coffee.

"You make it sound like everything is predestined," Walter

said, getting in the van. "I don't believe that. I can't believe that."

"Neither do I," Del said, putting on his seat belt. "God is a great believer in free will. If everything were predestined, this world would be a perfect place, set up according to God's plans. The fact it's so messed up is proof that free will prevails."

"Then don't say you can't change your dreams."

"Maybe I don't want to change them."

"That's different," Walter said, pulling onto the highway.

"That's why I need to go to Haven," Del said.

"Because of your dreams?"

"It's a feeling…"

"You're big on feelings, aren't you?"

"It's all I have."

"What I'd like to know is, if you're meant to go to Haven, why didn't you get an invitation?" Walter asked.

"But I did."

"You stole *my* invitation."

"A technicality."

"I hope the host agrees with you."

Del looked out the window as the rosy glow of sunrise turned golden. "So do I."

"What's this Kathy woman look like?" Del asked as they walked into the bus depot in Grand Island, Nebraska.

"I have no idea."

Del threw his arms in the air. "That's brilliant. We travel ten hours to pick up a woman you've never seen."

"I'd never seen you, had I?"

"I didn't give you much choice."

"Neither did she." Walter checked the time schedules, looking for the bus that came in at 8:20. "She has two little kids with her, that's all I—"

The wail of a child sounded: "But Mommy, *I* want to hold the backpack."

Walter and Del turned toward the sound and spotted a

111

young woman with nondescript blond hair. Two small children—a boy and a girl—tugged at her arms. Her skirt and shirt were wrinkled. She looked on the verge of tears.

Walter walked toward her. "Kathy?"

The relief on her face was pitiful. "Walter? I'm so glad to see you. During the night I wondered if I'd dreamt the whole thing and I'd arrive in Grand Island and no one would be here and I'd have to figure out a way to go home, or go on to Hav—" She noticed Del standing a step behind Walter. Her eyes asked the question.

Walter held out his arm, motioning Del forward. "This is Antonio Dela...Delat—"

Del stuck out his hand. "Antonio Delatondo, ma'am. Call me Del."

Kathy extricated her hand from Ryan's grip and shook both men's hands. "Are you going to Haven, too?" she asked. "Walter never said he was picking up someone else."

"Yes, ma'am, I'm going," Del said, passing a look to Walter. "My invitation was...delayed."

"The van's out here," Walter said, taking her suitcase.

Ryan ran ahead, stomping on the automatic door. "Look, Mommy! A van, a van!"

"It's a little beat up," Walter said, noticing the rust along the running board for the first time in ages. He slid open the side door and gawked at the mess. He grabbed sacks of cans and took them around the back to put behind the seat. "I don't know why I didn't clean this thing out before I came."

"I know why you didn't," Del said, lifting Lisa into the van. "If your van had been clean, I never could've stowed away."

"Stowed away?" Kathy asked.

Walter shut the cargo doors. "Nothing. Do you want to sit in front with me or back with the kids?"

"In back," Kathy said, taking Del's hand as an assist. "I hope they'll conk out. They didn't sleep much on the bus."

"It's only an hour's drive," Walter said, starting the van.

112

"Only an hour," repeated Kathy. She shivered. "I don't know whether to be excited or scared."

Del turned around in his seat. "Why scared?"

"Too many things fell into place to let me come here," she said, stroking Lisa's head, which had sought the comfort of her lap. "I have a feeling it's important."

"I *know* it is," Del said.

"How?" Kathy asked. "How do you know?"

Walter waved a hand toward Del, dismissing what he would say. "Del thinks even though he stole the invitation to Haven, some momentous thing is going to happen to—"

"Stole?" Kathy asked. "Whose invitation did you steal?"

They filled her in on the invitation in the trash, Del's stowing away in the van, and ended with their night at the motel and the details of what Del had for breakfast.

"You're homeless?" she asked.

"Temporarily without a humble abode. But I assure you, Ms. Kraus, my intentions are honorable."

Kathy shook her head. "I didn't mean...you know the stereotype."

"Del is hardly a stereotype," Walter said. "His vocabulary puts mine to shame even though words are my business. His elocution and diction are excellent. He'd make a superb news anchor if...if..."

Del shook his head. "If I were an egotistical dilettante."

"See what I mean?" Walter said. "Actually, I was talking about the ponytail."

Del ignored him. "What do you do, Ms. Kraus?"

She spread her hands to take in her sleeping children. "And I paint. Pictures of children, mostly. That's how we got here. I sold four of my paintings."

"Congratulations," Del said. "An artist. I admire you."

"Me?"

He was surprised at her surprise. "Of course, you. I couldn't draw a circle that didn't have a chink in it. Painting is a gift."

He nodded toward her children. "*They* are a gift."

"I agree with you on the second part." She kissed Ryan's head, which was nestled in the crook of her arm. "What do you think is in Haven?"

"Probably lions and tigers and bears," Walter said.

Del shook his head. "Haven will give us the key to our lives."

Kathy and Walter were shocked to silence. Walter wanted to argue, to say something that would dismiss the idea. But he didn't. He couldn't. And he could see from the look in Kathy's eyes that she couldn't, either. And he understood.

How could they argue against their own hope?

*Do not be afraid, for I am with you; I will bring your children
from the east and gather you from the west.*
ISAIAH 43:5

"THIS IS IT," Walter said. "This is the exit."

Kathy clutched her stomach. "I don't feel so good."

"It'll be fine, Kathy," Del said. "We'll meet up with the others and—"

Kathy followed the direction of Del's gaze. "What do you see?"

The interchange had no gas stations—no buildings at all—but as Walter topped the crest of the overpass heading south, two cars came into view.

"It's milady!" Del said, pointing.

A silver Intrepid was parked in a dirt pull-off next to a blue Volkswagen Beetle. An ancient burl oak tree shaded them.

"Well, I'll be," Walter said.

"What?" Kathy asked. "Who's your lady?"

"We met her at the motel in Lincoln last night. We had no idea she was one of us." Del waved excitedly as they pulled alongside the other two cars. The silver-haired woman waved back, shaking her head in clear disbelief.

Walter turned off the van. "Hello again," he told her.

"Small world," she said. "If I'd known you were coming, I'd have baked a cake."

Ryan opened his eyes. "Cake, Mommy?"

Lisa sat up and whined, "Me cake."

Julia peered in Walter's window at the children. "Sorry. I seem to have started something I can't finish."

Del and Walter helped Kathy and the children out of the van. They stood awkwardly for a moment, busy with first impressions.

Julia held out her hand. "I guess it's time we met properly. I'm Julia Carson from Minnesota. And who's my gallant knight?"

"Antonio Delatondo, ma'am," Del said, kissing her hand. "But call me Del."

"I will do no such thing," she said. "Not with a beautiful name like Antonio."

Walter stepped in front of Del. "I'm Walter Prescott from St. Louis. And this—" he stepped aside to let Kathy and the kids come forward—"is Kathy Kraus and Lisa and Brian."

"Ryan!" said the boy.

"We're from Arkansas," Kathy said, shaking Julia's hand.

Julia knelt down to the children's level. "Nice to meet you Lisa. Ryan. And as soon as I'm able, I'll make sure you get some cake. Okay?"

Each child grabbed one of Kathy's legs but nodded.

Julia moved toward the VW where Natalie stood. She motioned her toward the group. "This fine young lady is Natalie Pasternak. She's come all the way from Estes Park, Colorado."

Hands were shook all around. Natalie stepped back, stuffing her hands in her pockets. She squinted one eye and surveyed the group. "So what happens now?"

"Well, personally," Julia said, "I'd like to know the circumstances behind each of you being here today. I know I certainly had a few strange things nudge me in this direction, and I'd like to hear your stories." She looked toward the oak tree. "Why don't we sit in the shade and trade miracles."

Stories were exchanged and marveled over. There was laughter, trembling, tight throats, and arms thrown around shoulders. Most of all there was relief. Relief they were not crazy. Relief they were not alone.

Then Ryan, who was drawing pictures in the dirt with a stick, interrupted. "That policeman car went by, but now it's turning around." He pointed to a white and royal blue police

116

cruiser making a three-point turn at the base of the overpass. "It's coming back."

Walter and Del walked toward the highway, their necks taut, their arms tense at their sides. "Are we doing something wrong?" Del asked Walter.

"Not that I know of."

There was a communal wrenching of stomachs when the patrol car pulled beside the van.

"Morning, folks," said a police officer with graying temples.

Walter and Del walked closer. "Something wrong, Officer?" Walter asked.

"Not a thing. Just checking to see if everyone was here."

Walter and Del exchanged a panicked look. Walter stepped forward. "What do you mean every—"

Del sidestepped in front of him. "Everyone's here," he told the officer.

"Then follow me. Haven's a few miles down the road."

"And who are you?" Del asked.

The man backed up before answering, "I'm police chief Adam Newley. Just plain 'Chief' to most, and mud to some." He cleared his throat. "We best be going."

Del nodded and turned to the others who had migrated to the edge of their cars. "This officer—Chief—will show us the way to Haven."

"How did they know we were here?" Kathy asked, pulling Lisa and Ryan close.

Del shrugged and opened the door of the van for her. "Destiny's grapevine."

The ride to Haven was a silent one. Minds were full of questions—and silent prayers.

The small convoy crossed the Platte River, where a patchwork of sandbars interrupted the flow of water. The highway bisected acres of fertile farmland, green with thriving corn. Rows of irrigation pivots towered like sentinels shooting their

117

ammunition of water over the fields. The air smelled of earth, grass, and hope.

Up ahead, clusters of trees marked a town.

"It doesn't seem very big," Walter said, noting that the edges of the town could be easily distinguished.

"It looks perfect," Del said.

They passed a sign: *Welcome to Haven.*

"We're here," Kathy said. There was reverence in her voice.

"Why are you whispering?" Walter asked.

"Because we're *here,*" she repeated.

Walter followed the police cruiser to a lone stoplight. They turned left onto a main avenue. Neatly kept storefronts lined the street. A café, florist, and hardware store were on one side. On the other side was a grocery store with yellow signs in the windows advertising sale prices. Some one-story offices came next, each with its own flag flapping on a pole out front. A stone church topped the corner, wide steps extending an invitation. Its rugged bell tower rose three stories above the rest of Haven.

The cruiser pulled diagonally in front of the church. Walter pulled beside it. Julia and Natalie followed as though performing a synchronized maneuver.

They were getting out of their vehicles when Natalie said, "Hey people, look at that!"

She pointed to the white parking sign that stood in front of the VW, marking the spot. On it was the name Natalie Pasternak. Julia had her own sign, as did Walter's vehicle, which listed the entire van load: Walter Prescott, Antonio Delatondo, Kathy Kraus, Ryan Kraus, Lisa Kraus.

Walter looked at Chief. "What is this?" He pointed at their names.

Chief eyed the signs, then looked back at Walter. "Those are parking signs. We made them special just for you."

"I can see that," Walter said, moving next to one. "But how did you know Del was coming? And how did you know Kathy was bringing her kids?"

Chief started to walk up the steps of the church but stopped and faced them. "Don't you like them?"

"They're super," Natalie said. "But that doesn't explain how—"

"Come on, folks," he said, opening the door to the right of the main church entrance. "Let's get inside where it's cool."

Del started to protest, but Julia stopped him. "Let's do what he says, people. Why try to explain the unexplainable?"

She walked through the door Chief was holding open. The others followed, single file. Ryan paused to look up at the officer. "I'm thirsty. I want Kool-Aid, please."

Chief ruffled Ryan's hair. "I think that can be arranged, young man. Go on in, folks. This is the bell tower meeting room. Make yourselves comfortable."

The walls of the meeting room were constructed of natural stone, the same as the rest of the church. No mortar held the stones together, just the intricate puzzle work of some long-gone craftsman who spent hours honing each stone to an exact shape to fit next to its neighbors. The tapestries hanging from the walls were like those seen in the great halls of a castle. Large plants added warmth to the cold stone. There were no windows, but three doors: the entrance to the front steps, an open door connecting the room to the church's narthex, and another door directly across the room. It was closed.

"Does that door lead to the bell tower?" Natalie asked.

"Yes, ma'am, it does."

"Can we go up there? The view must be fabulous."

Chief opened his eyes wide enough to fully show the clear brown of his iris. "No, ma'am. No one goes up there."

"They can't or they don't?"

He put on his police chief face. "Same thing."

"Do the bells ring?" Natalie asked.

"Not unless they have good reason to," Chief said.

"Good reason?"

He brushed past them. "Come on folks, take a bit of refreshment and have a seat." He motioned to rows of intricately

119

carved chairs that were lined up facing a podium. A table laden with fresh fruit and beverages stood to the left. Ryan ran to the table and grabbed an apple. Chief followed him and poured a cup of Kool-Aid.

"Grape!" Ryan said. "My favorite."

Walter whispered in Kathy's ear. "Why am I not surprised?"

Chief held out a can of Coke for Walter. "We aim to please."

Walter took the Coke. "Obviously."

Natalie stepped forward, and Chief smiled at her. "What will it be, young lady?"

She eyed Chief suspiciously. "You tell me."

He rummaged in the cooler beneath the table, then pulled out a root beer. "How's this?"

She hesitated. "Don't you have any Corn Nuts?"

"Haven't you had enough Corn Nuts today?" he asked.

Natalie stared at the root beer, then shook her head. "I don't want it."

"Why not?"

"It's too creepy," she said. "This whole thing is creepy."

"We're just trying to make you feel comfortable, Natalie," Chief said.

"You can forget about me feeling comfortable," Natalie replied. "I've never felt so uncomfortable in my life. Haven this, Haven that. There's nothing comfortable about what's happened to me the last few days. And I want out." She turned toward the exit.

"Natalie, don't go," Julia said. "You've come this far, don't leave now."

"You've been chosen, Natalie," Del added. "Don't throw the opportunity away."

Natalie turned around to face Del. Anger, fear, and hope all struggled in her expression. Her voice was quiet, pleading. "What have I been chosen for? What?"

Del put an arm across the younger woman's shoulders. The tension seemed to go out of her body.

"I don't understand any of this either," Del said. "But you can't leave now. Whatever it is that's happening here, I feel it's important—and good."

"Me too," Julia said, joining them.

Walter and Kathy moved toward the group, showing their unity.

Chief nodded. "It begins."

He walked to the podium, motioning them to the chairs. "Gather round, folks. Take a seat and let's get started."

The group gathered, taking their drinks and fruit. Several glanced around as if they wished they could stand at the back of the room.

"No need to be wary, folks. I don't bite."

Ryan and Lisa ran to the seven chairs and climbed onto the ones directly in front of Chief.

"'And a little child will lead them,'" he said, smiling down at the children.

Shamed, the adults filled in the rest of the seats.

Chief leaned his forearms on the podium and scanned the group. "Welcome," he said. "Welcome to Haven."

"Why were we brought here?" Walter asked.

"You were not *brought* here," Chief said. "You came of your own free will. That is a very important distinction."

"Semantics."

"The truth."

Julia took a turn. "So why were we invited here?"

Chief nodded his approval at her choice of words. "You were invited to Haven because of your potential."

"Potential what?" Natalie asked.

"Your talents. Your gifts."

Ryan looked at his mother. "Are there going to be presents, Mommy?"

Kathy put a finger to her lips.

Chief smiled. "Not those kind of gifts, Ryan. I'm talking about inner gifts."

121

"I don't have any special gifts," Kathy said, running a finger around the rim of her coffee cup. Then she looked up. "You mean my painting?"

Chief spread his arms. "And so much more."

Kathy shook her head. "I don't have any more. And my paintings aren't anything special."

"That's not for you to judge," Chief said.

Walter raised a hand. "What about Del? *He* wasn't invited."

"But he was."

"No, he wasn't," Walter said. "I was the one who got the invitation, Del stowed away in my van."

Chief shrugged. "As you wish."

Walter raised a hand. "As you wish? What's this 'as you wish' business? All of us have put our lives on hold and taken a big chance coming here. We have a right to get some concrete answers. 'As you wish' doesn't cut it."

"By the end of your stay, all will be revealed. 'And the truth will set you free.'"

"That's a Bible verse, isn't it?" Walter asked. "Even I've heard that one. There was a Bible verse on the invitation, too. And now we're sitting in a church. Does Haven have something to do with…you know…God?"

Chief smiled. "Yes, I do know God. Every place in the universe has something to do with God."

Walter threw his hands in the air. Julia took a turn. "Have we been invited by a church, by some religious sect?"

"The people of Haven belong to the church of believers. That is our sect."

"You're talking in circles, Chief," Julia said. "We'd like some straight answers."

Chief looked confused. "There is nothing straighter than the truth, Ms. Carson."

"Your version of the truth is—"

"This is ridiculous. We come all this way to have—"

"I should have known the invitation was phony—"

"Mommy, why is everyone so loud?"

Del stood and raised his hands to quiet them. "Perhaps our confusion arises from the fact that we haven't asked the right question. You want straight answers, ask straight questions."

Walter crossed his arms. "Be my guest."

Del nodded and faced Chief. "Is the *person* who invited us to Haven—" He held up a hand. "Let me rephrase that." Del straightened his back and lifted his chin. "Is our host God?"

Chief beamed. "Of course."

Amid the bedlam that followed, Kathy raised her face to the sky. "I knew it!"

~~~~~

The motel was a block off Main Street. There were five units. Just enough.

Natalie's room was unlike any motel room she'd ever seen. It was bathed in jewel tones: teal, fuchsia, and goldenrod. An overstuffed comforter with a geometric design graced a black lacquer bed. A fuchsia beanbag chair sat next to an arching black lamp. A simple black table and two chairs sat by the window. The black lacquer dresser was topped with vivid bottles shaped like triangles, squares, and ovals. There was even a CD player and CDs of Reba, Garth, and the Nylons.

As Natalie turned one of the bottles over in her hands she shook her head. *It's like this room is made especially for me.*

The thought was so pronounced she strode outside and knocked on the door to the next room.

Julia answered. "Hello, Natalie. How is your—"

Before Julia could finish the sentence, Natalie had walked past her. She did a quick scan of the room. It didn't take long to realize Julia's room was very, very different from her own.

Natalie fingered a lace doily on a carved walnut table. "You must like antiques."

"I adore them," Julia said. She walked to the bed and stroked one of the four posters. "This bed is turn-of-the-century.

123

Hand carved. And the coverlet is tatted. Such exquisite hand—"

"What's your favorite music?"

"Broadway tunes," Julia said. "I love music that tells a story."

Natalie went over to the stereo cabinet and opened it. She scanned the titles inside. "How about *Les Miserables, Cats, Phantom of the Opera,* and *Oklahoma?*"

Julia looked for herself, her eyes widening. "These are my favorites."

Natalie sat in the rocker. "My room is modern and full of the bright colors I love. And yours is perfect for you."

Julia put the CDs down. "Chief said they wanted us to be comfortable."

"They're doing a good job of ensuring that," Natalie said. "Let's go see the other rooms."

The next room was Kathy's. She answered the door with a huge smile on her face.

"You look pleased," Julia said.

Kathy shook her head incredulously. "I will never be able to get the kids out of this room. They have all the toys they've always wanted but we couldn't afford. Come in and see."

Kathy's room was extra large, half again as big as the other rooms. Near the door was a white round table with three slatted chairs. A bowl of fruit sat in the middle. The furniture was white wicker. Kathy's bed was covered in a patchwork quilt of red and navy gingham. Two smaller beds were nearby, one with white eyelet decorating the bed ruffle, the other with a corded bedspread sporting the logo of the Arkansas Razorbacks. The clear voice of Sandi Patty filled the room.

"It's like a dream," Kathy said. "It's like everything I've ever thought of, but couldn't have. It's—"

"Perfect?" Natalie said.

She looked at her, curious. "Exactly."

"Come with us," Julia said.

Kathy told the kids she'd be right back, and the three moved on to Walter's room. Julia knocked.

"Door's open."

Inside, they found a room bathed in neutral colors, the furniture a pickled oak; the table, glass-topped. Walter's suitcase sat atop a huge ottoman on wheels. Crowning the armoire were leather-bound books held in place by a replica statue of "The Thinker." The sounds of Barry Manilow drifted through the room.

"Isn't this great?" Walter said, tapping his feet to the music, his hands clasped behind his head.

"Make yourself at home. Stay awhile," Julia said.

"I think I will."

Natalie set the suitcase on the floor and sat on the ottoman. "All our rooms are different," she told Walter. "Each one is decorated according to our own tastes."

Walter looked around the room. "Yeah, they got me down. I wouldn't change a thing. I wonder what Del's room looks like?" he asked. "Early trash can?"

Kathy flicked a hand at his foot. "That wasn't nice."

Natalie sprang off the ottoman. "Only one way to find out." She led them outside.

She knocked on Del's door. There was no answer. She knocked again and added, "Knock, knock? Del? It's just us."

A faint, "Just a minute."

"He sounds upset," Julia said. "I wonder if he's all right."

Walter tried the door. It was locked. "Del? Answer the door. It's me, Walter."

The doorknob turned, giving them access. They pushed the door open. Del walked toward the bed, dabbing at his eyes.

"What's wrong?" Julia said, going to his side.

He flipped a hand in the air and blew his nose.

"But you're crying," Kathy said, getting him a fresh tissue. "You shouldn't be crying, this is a gorgeous room. Simple, but gorgeous."

The room was decorated with furniture in sleek lines, including a maple headboard, a dresser, and a single chair by a table. There was a hand-stitched quilt and a vase of marigolds. A crucifix hung over the bed.

"You feeling all right, Del?" Walter asked. "Get him a drink of water, Natalie."

Del shook their intentions away and took a deep breath. He managed a smile. "I'm not crying because I'm upset or sad, I'm crying because I'm happy. This reminds me of the house I grew up in." He pointed to the quilt. "If I didn't know better, I'd say that's the same quilt that was on my bed as a child."

Impulsively, he went to the foot of the bed and pulled up the corner of the quilt. He sighed with relief. "It's not there. My quilt had Mother's initials embroidered on the corner. Eleanor Beatrice Delatondo."

"Now, *that* would be creepy," Natalie said.

"And the crucifix," Del said, gazing at the Christ affectionately, "looks like the one that hung over the couch in our living room."

He sat on the bed and put his head in his hands. "How did they know?"

Walter cleared his throat. He checked his watch. "We've got an hour before they want us back at the meeting room to...do whatever it is they want us to do. Why don't we all go back to our rooms and rest until then."

"Rest," Natalie snickered. "Just make yourself at home."

"Exactly," Walter said.

Natalie headed for the door. "But remember, everyone, no matter how good they make it, this isn't home."

⁓

Del pulled back the quilt and got in bed on top of the sheets. He didn't plan to sleep. He wanted to stay awake so he could immerse himself in the feelings this room stirred. He fluffed the pillows and pulled the quilt over himself.

Turning on his side, he looked at the table and the flowers in the vase. Marigolds were his mother's favorite. Every spring she'd plant trays of tiny seeds in the window boxes outside the kitchen window.

"*You'll see how beautiful they grow, Tony,*" she'd say. "*And such a beautiful name for such a beautiful flower. Marigold. The Holy Mother herself must have named these. Perhaps they made her happy.*"

His mother had made *him* happy. He should call her. Ever since the…incident Del had shunned his parents. He had shunned the world. It was only right. It was his penance for his arrogance. His selfishness. His—

Del sighed and turned his back to the flowers. He adjusted the quilt, tucking it around—

All breath left him.

He held up the corner of the quilt. The embroidered initials EBD stared back at him, the black stitching worn but still decipherable.

Del pulled the covers around his chin, drawing his knees toward his chest.

"Our Father, who art in heaven…"

Pay attention and listen to the sayings of the wise;
apply your heart to what I teach.
PROVERBS 22:17

EVERYONE WAS BACK in the church meeting room at the base of the bell tower. As the adults sat down, Lisa and Ryan played in a corner, absorbed in the baby doll and Hot Wheels cars Kathy had allowed them to bring from the motel.

Walter leaned forward to tap Julia on the shoulder. "Where are the Haven people?" he asked. "Chief's the only one here. I thought there'd be others."

Julia nodded thoughtfully. The same thought had occurred to her. "So did I. I envisioned us walking into a room full of people."

"You were expecting applause?" Del asked from two seats down.

"Maybe." Julia smiled. "Just a little."

Del held up a finger. "'Pride goes before destruction, a haughty spirit before a fall.'"

"Now they've got you doing it," Julia said.

"I say what I see."

Julia felt a flash of irritation and leaned on the chair between them. "Are you suggesting I am prideful and I'm going to be destroyed?"

Del put a calming hand on hers. "A defensive nature does not suit you, milady." He gave her hand a pat. "Personally, I was hoping for a brass band."

"With piccolos," Julia added, smiling again. Clearly she needed to relax. She was taking things way too seriously.

"And two tubas."

Walter fingered the dials of his camera. "You two deserve

each other. Actually, I'd settle for a bit of action. I can't tolerate sitting around doing—"

"Folks?" Chief moved to the podium and raised a hand to get their attention. "It's time we begin."

"It's about time," Walter mumbled. Chief gave him a look, and Julia smiled at the red that suddenly tinted Walter's cheeks. He covered his embarrassment by huffing on the camera lens, then wiping it with his shirt.

"We have some special people in Haven who have eagerly awaited your arrival. Each one of you will be bound—"

"Bound?" Natalie called out. "I'm not going to be bound to anyone."

"You are misinterpreting our intentions, Ms. Pasternak," Chief said.

A voice came from the doorway. "Perhaps Natalie would feel more at ease if she saw the face of a friend."

Everyone turned around to see a fiftyish man with sun-baked skin and broad shoulders. He removed his Colorado Rockies cap and held it to his chest.

"John?" Natalie said, eyes wide. She paled and rubbed her forehead with both hands. "I don't believe this."

"John who?" Kathy asked her.

"John Crawford. He helped me with a flat tire in the middle of the night." She shook her head. "He brought me root beer and Corn Nuts—"

John moved to the front of the room and stood next to Chief.

Natalie glared at him. "He took my tires to a gas station that wasn't even open." She pointed at John. "Will you explain how you fixed my tires in the middle of nowhere?"

"In time, Ms. Pasternak," Chief said from the podium. "But let's get down to business. I'd like to introduce you to your mentors."

Mentors? Julia looked around. *Mentors for what?*

"As Ms. Pasternak has said, this is John Crawford. He is our resident fix-it man. Whatever needs done, he does. In more ways than one." They exchanged knowing smiles. "John has been assigned to Mr. Delatondo."

Del looked up, clearly surprised. "Me?"

"Yes sir," John said.

"Why is he first?" Walter demanded. "Shouldn't the rest of us who were properly invited be—"

"'For God does not show favoritism,'" Chief said.

"Maybe he should," Walter muttered, and Julia reached out to put a calming hand on his arm.

"Wait," she said quietly, and he nodded.

John stepped toward Del. "I look forward to getting to know you." He nodded to Chief and moved to stand against the wall.

Chief turned to Kathy. "Ms. Kraus—"

"I'm next?" she asked, a hand to her chest.

"Yes, indeed," Chief said. "Your mentor is well trained to help you with your children. She's a mother herself. During the school year, she's a counselor at the high school. Anne. My wife."

Kathy turned toward the door. A woman with flashing blue eyes and blond hair pulled into a ballerina's bun smiled at them. "Anne, from the grocery store!" Kathy said, getting up to greet her. "You're the one who gave Ryan my invitation."

"I'm the one," the woman said.

Kathy put her arms around Anne and gave her a hug. "I've been wanting to do this ever since! Thank you."

Anne smiled, though Julia thought she seemed a bit startled at Kathy's display of affection. "You're welcome," she said. "I didn't expect such a warm welcome."

"Don't expect me to hug anyone," Walter mumbled, shaking his head.

"If they know us as well as they seem to," Julia said, "I sincerely doubt they'll expect anything of the sort."

Chief laughed. "Absolutely not. Hugging is optional."

"Good," Walter replied with a snort.

"But since you've spoken up, I believe we'll do you next."

"Oh, do me, do me," Walter said, sarcastically. "I need a cigarette."

"No you don't," said a voice from the doorway.

Walter turned toward it. "Don't tell me what I do and don't—" Walter stopped midsentence and his eyes widened.

The man who had spoken came in the room. "Hello, Walter."

"You."

"Ah yes. Me."

Walter turned toward Chief. "Can I get somebody else? This guy isn't on my best side since he finagled his way into my office using a friend's name. Then he tells me the real Gabe Thompson is well, and I find out Gabe's dead. Not the most auspicious beginning. I want someone else."

Gabe stood by the podium, his hands clasped in front of his body, his feet spread like a retired Secret Service agent on the alert. "I'm for you, and you're for me, and that's the way it's going to be."

"Oh, joy. He's a pest *and* a poet."

Julia nudged Walter's knee. "Behave yourself."

Walter shrugged.

"Ms. Carson," Chief said. "I believe we'll match you with a mentor next."

"Believe it or not," Julia said, "I'm excited to see who it is."

"I believe you will be pleased. Louise Loy is the mayor of Haven, and a good mayor she is. Mayor Loy?"

Julia turned toward the door expecting to see a woman in a tailored business suit. Instead she saw a woman wearing a rumpled skirt and blouse, a wisp of black hair pointing left when it should have pointed right—

"The woman in the Book Bus," she whispered.

Mayor Loy held out her hand. "Nice to formally meet you, Julia."

"Let's move on, folks," Chief said. "You'll have plenty of time

131

to talk with your mentors once we get—"

"You can forget me, if you want," Natalie said. "I'm not sure I want to be a part of this gobbledygook."

"Gobbledygook," Chief said, weighing the word. "An interesting play on the situation. We have saved you for last, Ms. Pasternak."

He waved a hand toward the door. A striking woman in her early thirties walked in and made a beeline for Natalie, flipping her red hair behind her shoulders. She held out a hand.

"Hideeho, Natty-Jo. Fran Pendleton, at your service."

"You're the ranger on the trail."

"Indeed I am," Fran said. "Although those uniforms hardly do me justice."

Natalie shook the woman's hand. "What do you do here in Haven?"

"Drive people crazy."

"You two seem perfect for each other," Walter said.

"Fran runs the Fillerup Café," Chief said. "And she not only serves ham, she *is* one." The others laughed.

"Ham is good as long as it's lean and salty," Fran said. "The lean I gave up long ago, but the salty…"

"We're going to get along great," Natalie said. "I just know it."

Everyone looked at her. "Do I detect a change of heart?" Chief asked.

Natalie shrugged. "Sorry I was such a pain before. Facing the unknown makes me testy."

"Apology accepted and point taken. Now then." Chief drew the mentors close, putting a hand on Fran's shoulder. Walter raised the camera and took a picture. "There you have it, folks," Chief said. "Your job here in Haven is to spend time with your mentors. The rest will come."

"What 'rest'?" Walter asked. "You haven't explained anything."

Chief gathered up his notes as he prepared to leave. "'The

discerning heart seeks knowledge, but the mouth of a fool feeds on folly.'"

Chief walked out of the room, leaving Walter to ask Julia, "Did he just call me a fool?"

She laughed. "Take a picture of yourself, Walter. You already have your caption."

~~~~~

Art Graham cruised into Haven driving a '66 baby blue Mustang in mint condition. The original owner, who believed in regular maintenance and weekly car washes, had babied the car. Technically, the original owner still owned the car...but that was a technicality Art preferred to forget. He had... *acquired* the car in Sterling, Colorado just a few blocks from the apartment he shared—or, more accurately, used to share—with his girlfriend. He had no destination except away. He'd go and go until something stopped him. He'd hoped to travel all night and had played music loud enough to keep God awake, but he'd grown groggy and had been forced to sleep at a rest stop in eastern Colorado. Now he had the feeling he was late for something. Which was, of course, absurd.

He'd turned off Interstate 80 in desperate need of gas. He'd wanted to hold out until the Grand Island exit, but the gas gauge hadn't cooperated. So what else was new? By the time he'd pulled off and seen there was nothing at the interchange except an old oak tree, the red pointer was bisecting the E. That's when he noticed the faintest hint of trees on the horizon and headed in that direction. Looked like a town to him. Surely they'd have a gas station. If not...well, though he'd grown fond of the car, he'd ditch it and...he shook his head. He'd worry about that later.

Right past the town sign, Art saw a Pump 'n' Eat. He smiled and muttered to the place as he pulled in, "You just saved one of the citizens of Haven, Nebraska from having his car stolen."

Luckily it was self-service. He hated telling an attendant to give him two or three dollars' worth of gas. Only teenagers and people without money did that.

The place was busy. He had to wait behind a farmer who was gassing a beat-up truck.

Come on, Gramps. You can do it.

The farmer squinted an eye at Art, then the Mustang, then he looked away.

Don't you think I deserve a nice car like this? I do, old man. And I take what I deserve.

Art dug his hand in his pocket and pulled out a wad of one-dollar bills. He separated two and stuffed the rest in his pocket. When gramps pulled away, Art pumped two dollars' worth of gas and went inside to pay. He wandered the aisles, surreptitiously looking for cameras or other security devices. Nothing.

Dumb hicks. Won't be nothing at all to rob the place.

He ran a hand over his head—the hair was starting to grow back, but it was agonizingly slow. He and a bunch of his friends had shaved their heads one night when they were drunk. All he had left was a tiny braid at the nape of his neck. They'd thought it was cool—until they realized it made them stand out. That was something best avoided when you were someone who was often forced to do things you shouldn't. Art's fingers skimmed the scar across his cheek, the result of another drunken night that had ended in a fight.

Art waited until there was no one in line to pay. A young teenage girl—her face displaying a scattering of pimples—ran the cash register.

Probably a summer job. Doesn't she know working for five bucks an hour won't get you nowhere?

"Have a nice day," the girl said, closing the cash register after taking Art's two dollars. Her eyes skimmed his head and the scar, then met his gaze for a brief instant.

"I certainly will," Art said. "Maybe I'll see you sometime."

The girl's smile wavered. She looked away.

Art strutted to the car, humming. "I'll be seeing you all right," he said as he started the engine. "And I'll introduce you to my buddy."

He reached under the seat and touched the cold, comforting metal of his gun.

Twelve

A friend loves at all times, and a brother is born for adversity.
PROVERBS 17:17

KATHY'S MENTOR, ANNE, gathered Kathy and the kids into her car and drove toward her house.

"I need to stop at home to pick up my six-year-old, Donnie. Then we'll go to Fran's café for burgers and French fries. How does that sound?"

"Fench fies!" Lisa crowed.

Anne laughed. "Lisa's vote is clear."

Anne's home was a fifties-style ranch with a hip roof and a two-stall garage. The siding was light blue, the trim white. Red geraniums lined the sidewalk to the door. A pinwheel in the shape of a Canadian goose adorned the front yard, its wings rotating in the summer breeze. She pulled her car into the garage and came within inches of hitting a chest freezer at the far end.

"Don't mind the mess," Anne said, opening the kitchen door for Kathy and the kids. "I'm great with people, awful with dishes." Anne set her purse on a counter next to the morning's newspaper. "Let me run next door and get Donnie. I dropped him off at the neighbor's before I went to meet you."

She left through the garage. Ryan climbed on a stool by the counter. "Are we eating lunch here, Mommy?"

"Fench fies?" Lisa asked.

"We're stopping so Anne can get her son. Then we'll go eat at a restaurant."

Ryan nodded and twisted back and forth on the stool. "Where's Daddy? Is Daddy going to come be with us?"

Kathy lifted Lisa onto the other stool before she fell trying to climb it. "Daddy isn't coming. He wasn't invited."

"That Del-man wasn't invited. And we weren't invited, either, but you brought us."

"It's not the same," Kathy said, hoping the next question wouldn't be—

"Why not?"

Why not, indeed? Out of habit Kathy folded the newspapers. She stacked the scattered dishes next to the sink. *Maybe I should have brought Lenny. Maybe my stomach wouldn't be full of knots if we'd come together or if I'd told him I was going instead of sneaking off—*

"I want to talk to Daddy," Ryan said. "I want to say hi."

The kitchen door opened, and Anne came in behind a tow-headed six-year-old with eyes that matched hers.

"Daddy!" Lisa whined.

Anne shut the door. "They want their father?"

"No…yes," Kathy stammered. "We were just talking, and they want to say hi to their dad."

"I think that's a grand idea," she said, pointing Donnie in the direction of the other stool. The boy climbed up. The children eyed each other.

"He won't be home," Kathy said. "He's a salesman. He's on the road."

"You can leave a message, can't you? Doesn't he check in with a main office?"

"Well, yes…"

Anne handed the phone to Kathy. "Call and leave a message. You can give him this number," she wrote it down on a memo pad, "or the number of the motel. I'll look it up for you while you're dialing."

"I don't know…." Kathy said. She didn't want to speak to Lenny. If they talked, they'd argue. But maybe if she just left a message to say that she and the kids were all right…

"Call, Mommy," Ryan said.

Kathy dialed Lenny's office and was referred to his voice mail. Anne shoved the motel's phone number toward her. Kathy cleared her throat.

"Lenny, this is Kathy. The kids and I are fine. We're in Haven—that town I was invited to. Everything's fine. I'm sorry to leave like that…here are two numbers where you can reach us." She gave him the numbers. "I…bye, Lenny."

"There, doesn't that feel better?" Anne asked.

"But I didn't get to talk!" Ryan said.

"I'm sorry, sweetie," Kathy said, having completely forgotten him. "When—if—Daddy calls back, you can talk to him then."

Anne slapped her hands on the counter. "It's time for fench fies."

⌒

The blue Mustang turned into the church parking lot. The man inside eyed the Fillerup Café across the street. There was a parking place out front, but he avoided it. He didn't want people to notice his car. Or him.

"I'm hungry for some fries," he said to the silence around him.

⌒

The Fillerup Café sat on the corner of the highway and Main Street. The large glass front let potential customers see in and satisfied customers see out. The bright yellow door opened and closed often, letting out the enticing aroma of hamburgers, broasted chicken, and coffee.

Anne pulled the car into a parking space in front. "We came at the right time. An hour ago, we would've had to park down at the hardware store."

"Busy place?" Kathy said, helping Lisa out of her seat belt.

"Good place."

Fifties rock 'n' roll greeted them. Pink vinyl booths sat on a black-and-white checkered floor. A waitress wearing a gray poodle skirt and saddle shoes took an order. Fran waved from behind the cash register. Natalie was handing a menu to a man whose hair was growing out from a military buzz cut.

Natalie bounced to their side. "May I help you?"

"You fit right in," Kathy said. "Making some new friends?"

"Tons. This place is super. The couple in the corner are going on a vacation in Colorado next month so I gave them the spiel on Estes Park, and the two girls by the window both like the same guy—though Tina doesn't know Mary likes him." She nodded toward the other corner where a muscled hunk pretended not to watch the girls watching him. "But I told them not to trust any guy who takes the pickles off his hamburger. Too picky." Natalie indicated a farmer-type at the counter. He saw her and waved. She waved back. "That's Marv. He's got six kids and eleven grandkids. He wants his oldest son to take over the farm. The kid isn't keen on the idea. But the daughter is, so I told Marv to get with the program and quit barking up the wrong—"

"You got all that information while you were taking their orders?"

Natalie shrugged. "I like people. They talk to me."

"Obviously."

"We need a table for five," Kathy said. "One high chair and one booster."

Natalie glanced at Fran, who pointed at the high chairs in the corner. Natalie nodded.

"Right this way, please," she said.

They got the children settled, and Natalie began to hand out menus. Anne raised a hand. "If I may?" She looked to Kathy, who nodded. "We want two hamburgers and fries with chocolate malts. And for the kids..." She looked at them. "Hamburgers or hot dogs?"

"Hot dogs!" they said together.

"Three kids' meals with hot dogs."

"You guys are easy," Natalie said. "I'll be right back."

"I like her," Anne said, after she'd left.

"I do, too," Kathy said. "She bubbles over. And she sees details the rest of us miss."

Natalie brought the kids coloring sheets and crayons. She stroked a blond curl away from Lisa's eyes. "I love babies," she said.

"Big girl!" Lisa said, frowning.

"Well, pardon me," Natalie said. "I love big girls, too."

"Have a seat," Anne said. "Join us."

Natalie looked around, and Kathy followed her gaze, impressed by the girl's responsible attitude. The lunch rush was over. The waitress, Susan, was handling everything just fine. With a nod, Natalie borrowed a chair from another table.

"I'm having such a good time," Natalie said. "Fran is the neatest lady."

"And bright and beautiful and brilliant," Fran said, coming up behind her. She put her hands on Natalie's shoulders. "See this girl?" she asked the group. "She's a doer, this one is. Came in here and started helping without me even asking."

Susan came by with the coffeepot and stuck her head in the conversation. "Old Oscar Norris gave her a dollar tip. The biggest tip I've ever gotten from Oscar was a tip of his John Deere cap."

"And Emma Larkins said you were a breath of fresh air," Fran said.

"My boyfriend back home calls me a breath of *hot* air," Natalie said, blushing.

Kathy reached forward and patted Natalie's hand. "He's a man."

"Now that's a broad statement," Anne said, laughing.

"You know what I mean," Kathy said. "Men don't always appreciate the attributes of the women they love."

"Love?" Natalie said. "You think he loves me?"

The other three women exchanged a look. "Doesn't he?" Fran asked.

Natalie helped Lisa color the clown's nose on her placemat. "He loves me as a friend. He's told me that."

"But you want more?" Kathy asked.

140

Natalie tucked in her lips as if holding in the words. Her forehead showed a new wrinkle.

"Whoop!" Fran said, breaking the spell. "I smell hamburgers burning." She hurried to the kitchen. "What're you doing in there, Robert? Testing the smoke alarms?"

Natalie stood. "I'll go help," she said, following after Fran.

"Unrequited love," Anne said, sighing. "There's nothing more heartbreaking."

Kathy looked after Natalie thoughtfully. "I think there's more to it than that."

Art bit into a French fry. He glared at the table of laughing women and kids in the corner. The two boys were fighting a sword duel with their French fries, dropping most of them on the floor. Their hot dogs were half eaten. If Art had his way, he'd clean their plates.

He coated another fry with catsup. The extra calories from the condiment would get him a little further in the day before the hunger pangs set in. The waitress who wasn't wearing the dopey costume came to his table, refilling his water.

"Sure you don't want a hamburger to go with those fries?" she asked. "I've heard Robert makes the best."

"I'm sure," Art mumbled.

The girl hesitated, but nodded and left. Art saw her talk to the lady at the cash register. They looked his way. He looked at his plate, fidgeting. Maybe he'd better leave—

"Sir?"

Art looked up to see the waitress, holding a heaping plate of French fries.

"I didn't order those," he said.

"Oh, I know, but Robert—he's the cook—he made too many and the lunch crowd's dying out, and he told me if I didn't help get rid of them, he'd make me eat the whole batch myself. And I can't do that. I'd simply burst." She shrugged. "I thought maybe you'd help me out since you like fries."

Art knew none of what she was saying was true, but the thought of another order of French fries made him set his pride aside. He moved his half-empty plate to the side, leaving room for the new plate.

"Thanks so much," Natalie said. "That'll get Robert off my back."

"Anytime," Art mumbled, avoiding her face.

She bounced on her heels a few times, then walked away.

High and mighty do-gooder.

He ate every last fry.

Thirteen

You are the light of the world. A city on a hill cannot be hidden.
Neither do people light a lamp and put it under a bowl.
MATTHEW 5:14–15

"I'M HAVING MY SECRETARY run across the street and get us a couple salads from the café," Mayor Loy told Julia. "We'll eat in if that's okay with you."

"Fine with me," Julia said, following Louise into her office.

Louise swept a hand across the room. "Well, this is it," she said. "Not anything as fancy as the governor's mansion. The perks of being a small-town mayor are few."

Julia scanned the office. It didn't take very long. An ancient oak desk, which would be worth a lot if someone took the time to refinish it, dominated the room. A tan four-drawer file stood in the corner, and there were only two chairs—one for the mayor and one for a visitor. A window air conditioner struggled to keep up with the August heat.

It was all excruciatingly normal. But what was far from normal, and what caught Julia's eye and held it, was a framed laser-cutting of the Lord's prayer hanging behind Louise's desk.

"What happened to separation of church and state?" Julia asked, sitting down in a cracked leather side chair.

"I am not a church, I am a person."

"But you can't have religious items in your office. Can you?"

Louise opened the bottom drawer of the file cabinet and retrieved her purse. She got out her wallet and dumped the change onto the desk. A quarter rolled to the floor at Julia's feet.

"Read it," Louise said.

"The quarter?"

"Read it."

Julia didn't need to look at the coin. "I know what it says, Louise, but I—"

"What does it say, Julia?"

Julia lay the quarter on the desk. "It says, 'In God We Trust.'"

"So saith the government."

"But—"

Louise raised her hand as if she were taking an oath. "I pledge allegiance to the flag of the United States of America. And to the republic, for which it stands, one nation, *under God...*"

"I know all this, I really do," Julia said. "And I concede."

Louise cleared away the change and sat in her chair. "I don't want you to concede, Julia. I want you to connect."

"With what?"

"With the people. With your own beliefs."

"I am very comfortable with my beliefs, thank you," Julia said, crossing her legs. "And with the people."

"Is that why you ignore them?"

"Ignore whom?"

"The people. The citizens who are desperate for someone to speak up for them, to say what they are afraid to say...."

"And what might that be?"

"We want God back in our lives."

"I tried to promote basic values when I was governor—"

"You're a coward."

Julia felt the heat fill her face and then drain from it, leaving her feeling pale with anger. She leaned toward the desk, tapping a finger on the wood to make her point. "A coward, am I? I'm the woman who ran for governor of Minnesota—and won—when there'd never been a woman in that office."

"How did you win?"

"In the usual way. By getting the most votes."

Louise shook her head. "No, not that. *How* did you win?"

Julia's anger turned up a notch. "Are you implying my campaign wasn't on the up and up?"

Louise rocked some more, tenting her fingers under her lower lip. "Describe the stereotype of a politician."

Annoyed, Julia scooted back in her chair. She calmed herself by smoothing the crease of her pants between her fingers. "I suppose the stereotype of a politician is a fast-talking opportunist who says whatever it takes to get elected."

Louise held her gaze.

"What?" Julia asked. "You think that's me?"

Louise rocked some more.

"I may be fast-talking in the literal form of the phrase, and I've never been afraid to take advantage of any opportunities that are laid in front of me, but I do not, and have never said whatever it takes to get elected."

"Are you a Christian?"

"Am I a…of course, I am."

"Do you acknowledge that Jesus died so you can be forgiven of your sins?"

"I…I rarely hear it put so bluntly, but yes, I believe that. It's a fact."

"Have you ever—while you were running for governor or otherwise—shared your religious beliefs with anyone?"

Julia recrossed her legs. "Well, no…not exactly. But people know what I believe." She got a new thought and sat up straighter. "They know what I believe because of how I act."

"You show them your beliefs by example."

Julia nodded smugly. "You betcha."

Louise leaned forward and pulled the chain on her desk lamp, making the bulb glow. Then she took the wastebasket beside her desk and placed it over the lamp.

"What *are* you doing?"

"Can you see the light?"

"No," Julia said. "Of course I can't. You covered it up."

"Is it a bright light?"

"I suppose."

"But you can't tell, can you?"

"Not with a wastebasket covering it."

"But it's still glowing, isn't it?"

"Sure. But it isn't doing a lot of good hidden under—" Julia stopped herself.

Louise nodded.

Julia pointed to the lamp and wastebasket. "That's me?"

Louise nodded.

"I may be glowing, but—"

"Your light is dimmed because you keep it hidden."

"Hiding my light under a basket?"

"Exactly." Louise's voice softened. "And it's not just *your* light, Julia." She removed the wastebasket and returned it to the floor.

Julia squinted at the brightness of the light. Louise reached for the lamp. She gave Julia a steady look. "If no one can see the light, you might as well turn it off."

Louise pulled the chain, extinguishing the glow.

⌒

"Is your name really Gabe Thompson?" Walter asked as they drove the two blocks to the *Haven Sentinel* offices.

"Actually, it's Gabriel."

"But it's Gabriel Thompson?"

"At your service."

"It's so strange you have the same name as someone I know. Knew. It *was* convenient for your purposes, wasn't it?"

"Tailor-made." Gabe chuckled.

"Did I say something funny?"

"No," Gabe said. "It's an inside joke."

"I don't like inside jokes." Walter pulled in front of the offices. He shoved the van into park. "In fact, I detest inside jokes."

Gabe got out of the van. "We'll keep that in mind."

Walter grabbed his camera and burst out of the van, meeting Gabe at the curb. "*We?* What's this *we* business? Are you and your Haven cronies enjoying a joke at my expense?"

"I assure you, this is no joke."

"Maybe that's why I'm not laughing."

Gabe opened the door to the office and held it for Walter. "You might try laughing a bit more, Walter. It's good for the soul."

"Ha ha."

The offices of the *Sentinel* were a study in disorder. Every flat surface held a file folder or pile of papers. Winter coats hung from the hat rack, while the air conditioner fluttered the stacks of papers. There were two metal desks out front, one of which was missing a leg. A leaning stack of aging Penney's catalogs substituted for the missing appendage.

A young man looked up from one of the desks, a budding Jimmy Olson looking to Gabe as Superman. The kid tapped the papers he was working on into a neat line and stood.

"Here you go, Mr. Thompson," he said. "The Honor Roll is done, but I didn't have time—"

"Honor roll?" Walter asked.

Gabe ignored Walter's question. "Thank you, Stanley. Walter and I will finish it up." He put a hand behind Walter's back. "Walter Prescott, I would like you to meet the *Sentinel's* do-all, be-all, Stanley Bishop. Stanley, Walter Prescott."

Stanley shook Walter's hand enthusiastically. "I've heard so much about you. You should feel so honored. I mean, to be chosen and—"

Gabe interrupted. "Why don't you run down to Fran's and let them proof their ad for the Honor Roll?"

"Yes, sir, Mr. Thompson." Stanley shuffled papers on his desk and found the layout for an ad. "Nice to meet you, Mr. Prescott."

Gabe walked into a back office that made the main office look clean. On a table near the window sat an old percolator coffeemaker, a stack of stained mugs, and a Crock Pot. Gabe lifted the lid and stirred the concoction inside. He licked the spoon.

"Perfect," he said.

"Is that chili I smell?"

"It is. I make the best chili in Haven."

"Don't people generally make chili when it's cold outside? Not August."

"I make it then, too," Gabe said, wiping out two bowls with a paper napkin. "It's the only thing I *can* make."

"You have chili every day?"

"Not on Sundays. After church I eat a proper dinner at Fran's." He took the lid off a blue Tupperware canister. "Oyster?"

"Pardon me?"

Gabe grabbed a handful of oyster crackers, lifted them above the canister, and sprinkled them back inside like salty gems in a treasure chest.

"Sure," Walter said.

Gabe cleared an empty space on his desk for Walter's chili bowl. He poured coffee in a mug that said, "I look 30, act 20, feel like 60, I must be 40." It had a chipped handle.

"Have a seat," he said, pulling out a chair like a solicitous maitre d'.

"Such ambiance, such presentation," Walter said.

"Don't knock it." Gabe took his place behind the desk. He covered the chili with oyster crackers, making them look like stepping stones strewn across a murky pond. Using the back of his spoon he dunked them under, then blew on a spoonful. "Mmm. You want more chili powder, there's the shaker."

Walter had already taken his first bite and found the concoction surprisingly good. "This is fine," he said. "Amazingly fine."

"Don't judge a Crock Pot by its cover, Walter."

"Gee, did you make that up all by yourself?"

"Your sarcasm stings."

"Wait till I get warmed up."

"What makes you so bitter, Walter Prescott?"

"I'm not bitter, I'm realistic."

"You're bitter. Is life so hard at the top?"

"Top, you say?" Walter snickered. "I'm hardly at the top. Wallowing around in mediocrity is more like it. And who knows how long that will last."

"Meaning?"

Walter shrugged and coughed. He always coughed when he thought about the upcoming biopsy. "I've got a medical problem."

"I know."

Walter slapped a hand on Gabe's desk. "How do you know? Tell me."

"No."

Walter's anger was cut short by Gabe's blunt answer. He shook his head. "Can I have you around for staff meetings? You certainly know how to squash an inquiry."

Gabe fingered the corner of the papers Stanley had given him. "Don't worry so much, Walter. It's out of your control."

"Oh, that makes me feel *scads* better."

Gabe shrugged. "Since that's the way it is, you need to give it up. Let God handle it."

"Easy for you to say. You're not courting cancer."

"Maybe you're not, either."

Walter sat forward. "You know something I don't?"

"Perhaps."

"Then tell me!"

Gabe leaned toward him. "I know God will take care of you."

Walter snickered. "Is that all?"

"That's quite a lot."

"If God wants to take care of me like I want to be taken care of, it's great. But what if he wants to 'call me home,' as you people say."

"That *is* his choice."

Walter stared at him. "Don't go into counseling, Gabe. Stick to the news." He turned away. He didn't want to talk about it anymore. He tried not to even think. Period. His eyes scanned the mess on top of Gabe's desk, and he held up his camera. "May I? It's proof my desk isn't so bad."

Gabe nodded, and Walter snapped the picture. Then he noticed the papers Stanley had handed in.

"What's this honor roll business?" Walter asked.

"The Haven Honor Roll."

"But school's out. What kind of—"

Gabe held up a hand. "Not that kind of honor roll." He turned the paper around for Walter to see.

"You list television shows?" Walter asked.

"We single out the shows that shine, the movies that move us, the characters with character."

"Making you an editor with ethics?"

"Ethics and guts," Gabe said, blowing on a spoonful of chili.

"Or gall."

"You don't approve?"

Walter shrugged as he scanned the page. The shows were divided by days and show time. A short description touted each show's story line. The rest of the page was full of ads from local businesses. "At least you aren't too heavy handed, spouting the virtues of one show versus another."

"If a show is listed on the Haven Honor Roll page—and an advertiser has chosen to support it with an ad—a viewer can be assured that the show respects the basic virtues the majority of us hope to emulate in our lives. We're not necessarily saying these shows are great classics, or these advertisers' products are better than the rest, but a reader of the Haven Honor Roll can be assured the shows *and* the advertisers respect family values."

"Isn't that trouncing on someone's constitutional rights?"

"I'm not doing what isn't already done, Walter. Movies on cable TV state what the movie contains: nudity, violence, adult situations. They're not rated for fun, but as a warning. They accentuate the negative; we accentuate the positive. And as far as the ads…we have a waiting list of companies wanting to advertise on the Honor Roll page."

"But you're showing favoritism to certain shows, and certain advertisers. Don't you get letters of complaint?"

Gabe opened his bottom drawer. He pulled out a box of opened letters and checked the tally on the side. "So far we have 256 praising the method, 2 against. Have you forgotten that our nation is based on majority rule? Should we bow down to the 2 and compromise the 256?"

"I wish I had your guts."

"You do."

Walter shook his head. "You say I'm bitter. Maybe I am. I hate the programs that are sent to us at KZTV. The bizarre talk shows giving misfits and miscreants airtime. The inane sitcoms that are obsessed with sex or bathroom functions, the depressing dramas where evil outwits the system. Then there's the news, full of the bizarre, the outrageous, or the flashy. But we have so little control over it. As an affiliate, we can only influence a small portion of the programming. We can choose one talk show over another, suggest they put in a positive human-interest story on the news between the weather and sign-off. But we can't change what comes over the airwaves 90 percent of the time."

"Yes, *you* can."

Walter hesitated. "Yes, anyone can, or yes, I, Walter Prescott, can?"

"Both," Gabe said. "But let's talk about you."

"Oh, goody," Walter said, stirring his chili. "I'm not sure I'm going to like this."

"Responsibility has nothing to do with what one likes or dislikes."

"You sound like a father telling a son to grow up."

Gabe pointed an empty spoon across the desk. "Walter, grow up."

"I traveled eleven hours for this?"

"This is only the beginning."

"I can hardly wait."

"You were offered a job at the main station in New York, weren't you?"

"But I decided to stay in St. Louis because…because…"

"You were comfortable there."

"It's not a sin."

"No," Gabe said. "But taking a stand doesn't involve comfort. It can be most *un*comfortable."

"If this is a sales pitch, you're not a very good salesman."

"Yes, I am. I sell the truth."

"Ah, a truth-seller. Nice title."

"Whoever lives by the truth comes into the light."

"Bible words again?"

"The Bible is the book of truth."

"You sound like Bette."

"A good and noble woman."

Walter blinked. "You know her?"

"We can learn from such people."

"So she keeps telling me."

"She loves you."

"She worries too much."

"Worrying over a loved one's salvation is valid."

"I don't need saving."

"Many are invited, few are chosen."

"Ha! There's that word again. Stanley said I was chosen. Are you saying I'm not?"

"You just said you didn't need to be saved."

"I don't need people reminding me of my faults."

"A wise man welcomes reproof."

"I never claimed to be wise."

"That is the wisest thing you've said."

Walter sighed, "You're speaking in circles, Gabe."

"No beginning and no end."

Walter rolled his eyes. "You're impossible."

Gabe smiled. "In God all things are possible."

"I need a cigarette."

"Eat your chili, Walter."

～

"Thanks for helping me rearrange the meeting room for the dinner tonight, Del," John said, walking down the steps of the church. "After lunch I've got to check on the air conditioner. It's been acting up."

"No problem." Del stopped when he reached the sidewalk. "Where to?"

"I feel like pastrami on rye, a pickle, Fritos, and a huge glass of iced tea," John said.

Del slowed his walk.

"What's wrong? You want ham or turkey? That's okay, the deli in the grocery store has all sorts of—"

"I seem to be low on funds," Del said, jingling what was left of the change he'd stolen from Walter's van.

John clapped him on the back. "You're a guest of Haven, Del. Don't worry about money. It's on the house."

"Generous house." Del quickened his pace as they headed toward the grocery store. "Do they have sourdough?"

"I'm sure they—" Suddenly John stopped, and Del had the oddest image of him perking his ears like a doe in the forest. He turned to look behind them. Del followed the direction of his gaze in time to see a young man with a shaved head cross the street from the Fillerup and head for the church parking lot.

"What's wrong?" Del asked.

John shook his head. "It was just a feeling."

"But what did you see?"

John glanced at a boy getting in a blue car. "Nothing," he said. "Nothing that concerns us. Yet."

Art started the Mustang. He burped loudly, enjoying the reverberations. Shifting the car into reverse, he backed out of the parking space.

He pulled onto Main Street and headed west, passing a small strip motel and an open field that separated it from a one-story school building. On a whim he turned left. Within blocks a city park appeared before him. One square block of trees, picnic tables, swing sets, and plenty of grass to lie down on.

He stroked his scar. "Time to lay low, Art my boy. Rest up. Tonight will be a busy night."

Fourteen

"WHAT'S WRONG, NATALIE?" Fran asked, looking up from the pile of lunch receipts.

Natalie rubbed a corner of the counter, making figure eights. "I was thinking about my parents, that's all."

"Do you want to call them and let them know you arrived safely?"

Natalie stopped wiping, then resumed, going in the opposite direction.

"Natalie?"

"They don't know I'm here."

"They don't—" Fran set the receipts aside. "They don't know you're four hundred miles from home?"

"I didn't tell them."

"You just left?"

"I left a note."

Fran grabbed the corner of Natalie's sleeve and pulled her toward the phone. "You call them right now."

Natalie shook her head. "It'll only make things worse."

"So they yell a little?" Fran said. "You deserve it. They deserve to know you're all right."

"I suppose…" Natalie took the receiver, then put it down. "Maybe I'll write them a letter. I'm much better at writing than I am at talk—"

"Chicken."

"I like chicken."

"Natalie…"

"But it's long distance."

Fran rolled her eyes. "Most four-hundred-mile phone calls are. Dial."

Natalie dialed. Her mind was a jumble. She had no idea what she was going to—

"Hello?"

She swallowed. "Hi, Ma."

"Natalie? Where are you? When we found you gone, we called Sam and he said you'd gone to Haven, Nebraska. I've never heard of such a place."

"It has something to do with my writing, Ma."

"Your writing? You haven't joined a writer's colony, have you? Or been taken in by some slick agent who's told you a pack of lies, promising to make you a—"

"It's not like that."

"Then what is—"

Her mother's voice broke off and was replaced by a deeper, angrier voice. Her father. "Natalie! You get back here and help your family! You have a job to do. The shower in the Cochise cabin sprang a leak and flooded the entire bathroom. The sheet vinyl needs to be replaced and—"

"Natalie? It's your mother again. When will you be home?"

"I don't know, Ma. Soon."

She paused. "You're all right, aren't you, Sunshine?"

"I'm fine. I'm learning a lot."

"About what?"

About life. About God. "I'll keep in touch, Ma. I promise. Bye." She hung up, then slumped onto a chair and let the tears fall.

Fran handed her a Kleenex and patted her shoulders. "Where's this coming from? You homesick so soon?"

Natalie shook her head. She blew her nose and held out her hand for another tissue. "Just hearing Ma's voice, you know… she called me Sunshine and she's my…*mom.*"

Fran pulled out a chair and sat. "Mothers are important people, aren't they?"

Natalie nodded. "And I wanted to tell her...I have things to tell her..."

"About Haven."

"That too."

"That too?" Fran asked.

Natalie looked around the café. She could hear Robert in the kitchen, humming as he scraped off the grill before the dinner rush. Fran must have seen her concern, for she rose and went to close the kitchen door. When she returned, she said, "We're alone, Natalie. You can tell me."

"I need to tell someone."

"Tell me."

Natalie took a cleansing breath. "I'm pregnant."

"Oh, Natalie..."

"Sam and I only did it the one time. We've been such good friends, best friends really, and one time we just let it...we wanted to know what it was like." She looked at her lap. "We didn't think about...*this*."

"*This* is a human life, Natalie."

She shook her head. "I'm only eight weeks along."

Fran put a hand on hers. "Your baby's heart is beating, it has brain waves, it has fingerprints. It's alive, Natalie."

Natalie sprang out of the chair. "It can't be! I can't have a baby. Sam doesn't want to marry me. Even if he did, we don't have any money. Besides, I want to be a great writer, go on book tours, be famous. Having a baby now isn't...isn't..."

"Convenient?"

Natalie saw Fran's look of disapproval. She felt the heat rise in her cheeks. "I know. We should have thought of that when we had sex."

Fran nodded. "A first mistake."

"We do love each other."

"Then marry."

"*I* want to. Sort of."

"But Sam doesn't?"

"Sam doesn't want to commit to me and especially not to a baby. Not now."

"There are lots of couples out there aching for a baby, Natalie."

She turned toward her. "Adoption?"

"It's an alternative."

"I couldn't give my baby to someone else. I couldn't—"

"But you could kill it?"

Natalie recoiled as if she'd been slapped. She stormed to the door before facing Fran. "It's *my* baby and I'll do what I want!"

She threw the door open and slammed it on her way out. The rattle of the window followed her as she ran away from the café.

~⌒~

Robert poked his head out from the kitchen.

"Did she decide?"

"No," Fran said. "We need to pray for her."

Robert nodded and went back to scraping the grill. Fran grabbed her car keys and headed after Natalie.

~⌒~

"How about, 'Alabama lawyer with two children defends man and teaches lessons in integrity'?"

"*To Kill a Mockingbird,* right?" Gabe said. "You're getting into writing these descriptions, aren't you?"

Walter took another sip of coffee. "It's okay."

"Uh-huh."

"It's enjoyable."

"Uh-huh."

Walter threw his hands in the air. "All right! It's the most rewarding thing I've ever done in my entire life. It makes my existence complete."

"That's better," Gabe said.

"You're getting a kick out of seeing a crusty newsman like

me write glowing accounts of movies about good people doing good things."

"They're good movies."

"No blood, guts, or sex scenes."

"How will we ever survive without those things?" Gabe asked.

Walter snorted, then reached up to finger the pack of cigarettes in his shirt pocket. He wanted a cigarette. Badly.

He glanced at Gabe and saw the understanding look on his face. Gabe poured two more mugs of coffee, handing one to Walter. With a sigh, Walter left the cigarettes where they were and set the listings aside. "You know this *is* a good idea. I've heard people at Bette's church—"

"Not your church?"

"Bette's church," Walter continued, "complain that they never know what's going to be on television shows. Even some of the ones you think are safe will suddenly spout off a cuss word or delve into a conversation full of sexual innuendo—"

"Just when we have our family tucked on the couch around us."

Walter flipped the subject away. "Personally, I think they're overreacting. Bette says sitcoms are the worst. I think they're funny."

"You still don't get it, do you?" Gabe shook his head.

"Sure, I get it. I just don't approve of censorship. Television isn't that bad. Besides, everyone knows it's not real life. It's just entertainment."

Gabe sighed. "I have an assignment for you."

Walter raised a hand, fending off his next words. "Hold everything. I gave up doing homework years ago. It's never been my forte."

"So you used the 'my dog ate it' excuse?"

"I *created* it. And I didn't even have a dog."

Gabe rocked in his chair. "But now, since your secret has been revealed, you'll have to do the assignment. Or think of a new excuse."

Walter shook his head. "Me and my big mouth."

"Your assignment is to watch some sitcoms tonight. Really watch them, with family values in mind."

"Do I have to take notes? I hate taking—"

"No notes. You can just report to me in the morning."

"Report." Walter shuddered. "I hate reports, too."

"You hate—? You *are* a reporter, Walter," Gabe pointed out. "Or did you forget that?"

"Nah, I remember. I'll do what you said."

"Such enthusiasm."

Walter shrugged. "I'm not getting graded on this, am I?"

Gabe cocked his head as though considering the idea. "Actually, I think you are." He laughed. "Yes, I know for a fact that you are, Walter. And let me remind you that the teacher is tough. Quite the taskmaster." Gabe cackled at his joke.

"Very funny," Walter muttered, pushing himself out of the chair. But he took Gabe's words to heart.

~

"Del, will you get the vice grips out of my truck?" John asked as he took the front off the church's air conditioner.

"Sure thing." Del opened the toolbox in the bed of John's truck and grabbed the tool. That's when he noticed a piece of paper taped to John's door.

That wasn't there a few minutes ago. He pulled it off and read it: *"Mr. John. My Daddy and Mommy had a fight. Can you fix it, please?"*

Del hurried back to John.

"Why are you out of breath?" John asked.

"This was on your door." He handed the note to John, who read it and nodded seriously. "Who's it from? There's no signature."

"I know who it's from," John said, taking the tool and working faster. "Let's finish up here so we can go fix it."

"Fix it?" Del asked. "How can we possibly fix an argument?

Why would we fix an argument? It's none of our business. I know. I've butted into other people's business and it led to no good."

John stopped working and looked at him. "We need to try, Del. Helping those in need is everybody's business."

"Philosophically, I guess."

"Absolutely, without a guess."

Del pointed to the note. "You get many of these?"

"A few a week. A lost cat, a broken skate."

"Do they always leave notes?"

"Most of the time," John said. "It's easier for them, especially when the problem is delicate, like Amy's problem today."

"Amy's the one who sent the note about her parents?"

"Yes, and in just a moment...I'll be free to..." He grunted, battling the air conditioner. "There. Go flip the power on, and let's see how it flies."

Del did as he was told, and the air conditioner sprang to life. John groaned as he got up from his knees. "Now for the important fix-it job." He gathered his tools.

"What are you going to do to help Amy?" Del asked. "Talk to her parents?"

"Nothing like that. You're right, it's not my place to interfere in the personal lives of others—unless they ask for help. It's up to God to intervene in the big ones. I help in subtler ways."

"Like...?"

"Follow me."

They crossed the street to Flo's Flowers. A bell rang when they opened the door.

A woman came out of the back room. The fabric of her smock was an Impressionist's interpretation of her wares, with splashes of blues, corals, and greens. Her blue-black hair added its own brilliant accent.

"John, old man," she said, rolling down her sleeves and moving to greet him. "A dozen roses, carnations, or don't you dare forget-me-nots?"

"How about a dozen pink roses."

"Who's in trouble?"

"It's not polite to ask, Flo."

She waved a hand at him. "Not polite, but worth a try." She opened the cooler and picked a dozen stems. "Are you sure I can't deliver these for you?"

"I'm sure."

She wrapped them in green tissue and tied a pink bow around them. She glanced at Del, a gleam in her eye. "Anything for you, Mr. Delatondo?"

"It's not fair, you know me and I don't know you," Del said, drawing her hand to his lips.

"Ooh, John," Flo cooed. "This one was a good choice. Definitely a good choice."

"Flo—"

She caught his look and stammered, "A good choice for an assistant. He could fix a lot of arguments—or cause a few, I'd imagine."

"No, ma'am," Del said, not missing any of the exchange. "I'm a gentleman. Or rather, I try to be."

She paused a moment and her grin faded into seriousness. "I know you are, Del."

John interrupted the moment, talking too loud. "Give me that vase with the red carnation in it, Flo. And hand me two insert cards."

"What are you going to write?" Del asked.

"The only words that are magic."

"Charge it?" Flo joked.

John leaned on the counter and carefully wrote "I love you, wife" on one card, and "I love you, husband" on the other.

Flo poked his shoulder. "You romantic, you."

He pointed a finger at her. "You keep my secret now."

She crossed her heart. "I always do."

"We're going to deliver them?" Del asked as they left the store.

"You're going to deliver them."

Del stopped in the middle of Main Street. "I'm not the Santa Claus here. You are."

John kept walking, calling over his shoulder. "And I've appointed you my elf."

Del considered this a moment and ran after John. "Can I drive the sleigh?"

"This is it?" Del asked as they pulled up. He looked at the modest ranch home with a half-mowed lawn. The distant roar of a lawn mower filtered around from the far side of the house.

"You take these to Amy's mom."

"How do you know it's her mowing? Maybe it's her husband."

"It's her. Go on."

Del opened the door to the truck and stepped out. He carried the pink roses in the crook of his arm like a beauty queen. He took two steps, then returned to the truck.

"What am I supposed to say to her?"

"How about, 'These are for you'?"

"What if she asks who they're from?"

The sound of the mower got louder. John pointed in its direction.

Del walked toward the sound. He paused at the corner of the house, gauging its location. He didn't want to pop out and scare the woman to death. The sound of the mower receded. Del stepped around the side of the house. Amy's mother was mowing the strip parallel to the house, heading away from him. He stood his ground. She spotted him when she turned. She looked at his face, then the flowers, then his face again. She let go of the accelerator and stood in the sudden silence, waiting for him to come to her.

Del took a few tentative steps. He held out the flowers. "These are for you."

She cocked her head, eyeing him warily. "From who?"

"From someone who loves you very much," Del said, amazed he'd thought of the words.

"Hmph," she said. "Who's that?"

Del placed the flowers in her arms. "They're from your husband."

A bead of sweat ran down her neck and pooled at her collarbone. She ran a forearm across her brow before placing a finger on a delicate bud. "He loves me?" she asked Del.

"He loves you."

"He loves me," she repeated. It was not a question this time. Leaving the mower she headed to the house. Remembering Del, she turned back. "Thank you," she said. "You'll never know how happy—"

Del held up his hand, stopping her. "My pleasure," he said as she headed for the house. He hurried to the truck and yanked open the door, sliding onto the seat. "That was the neatest, most satisfying…can we do it again?"

"The husband's next," John said.

"Well, let's get going," Del said, waving his hand. He glanced back at the house. A little girl came out on the front porch, half hiding behind a pillar. "Look at that, John," he said, pointing. "Is that Amy?"

The little girl waved at John. John waved back. "That's Amy telling me thank you."

Del shook his head. "I feel like I should be thanking her. It's done as much for me as it has for her."

"By George, I think he's got it," John said.

As they drove away, Del began to sing, "Jingle bells, jingle bells…"

⸻

"I appreciate the tour of the city office, Louise," Julia said, arching her back. "But if I don't get some fresh air into these lungs and some long strides logged onto these legs, they both are going to collapse."

"Would you like to take a walk?"

"Absolutely," Julia said.

"You mentioned during lunch that you wanted to call your husband. Would you like to do that first?"

Julia was ashamed she hadn't remembered. Poor Edward. He was probably frantic.

"Use my office," Louise said, getting up to leave.

Julia thanked her and sat at the mayor's desk. Checking her watch, she called Edward's office. With all his research, it was a long shot he was in, but—

"Hello?"

"Edward!"

"Julia? I can't believe you called. I've been thinking of you all day and—"

"I've been thinking of you, too, Edward," she said, fudging. "But I've been so busy—"

"No, Julia, you don't understand. I've been thinking of you all day, but the thoughts haven't been good. I've been getting bad feelings."

"What kind of bad feelings?"

She heard him take a deep breath. "I don't know…it's hard to explain. But my stomach has been churning, acting up like I'm nervous."

"Better lay off the bratwurst, dearest."

"It's not…listen to me, Julia. Ever since eleven o'clock, I've had the feeling something bad was going to happen to you. And then I didn't have any way to get hold of you, and you hadn't called and—"

"I'm perfectly fine, Edward. Haven is a nice little town. There's no one here who would hurt—"

"Maybe you're right. I hope you're right."

Julia stroked the phone as if it were his hand. "I'm fine," she repeated soothingly. "I've been assigned a mentor, the mayor of Haven. A very nice lady named Louise Loy. We've been having some deep discussions about politics, life, that sort of thing."

"So Haven's a normal place?"

Julia glanced at the Lord's Prayer hanging behind her. She remembered the wastebasket placed over the light.

"Perhaps *normal* isn't the word."

"But it's friendly?"

"Yes," Julia said, rocking in the chair. "The natives are friendly."

"When will you be home?"

Good question. "I have no idea. I'm still not exactly sure why we're here."

"They haven't told you?"

"All they'll say is, 'The rest will come.'"

"What does that mean?"

"Who knows?" Julia felt the chill of the air conditioner as it pushed an artificial breeze across the small office. "I've got to go, dear. Louise and I are going for a walk."

"A walk? You be careful, Julia. Don't you go walking alone."

Julia laughed. "Oh, please, Edward. Who would hurt a middle-aged woman like me?"

Fifteen

They will not toil in vain or bear children doomed to misfortune;
for they will be a people blessed by the LORD,
they and their descendants with them.

ISAIAH 65:23

"NOW, THIS IS WHAT I NEED," Julia said, walking down the sidewalk with her long stride in overdrive.

"God grant me longer legs," Louise mumbled, trying to keep up.

Julia slowed down. "I'm sorry." She gave Louise a repentant smile. "I get carried away. Edward threatens to buy a motor scooter to use when he walks with me."

"A Harley would be good," Louise gasped.

"Is that a park up ahead?" Julia asked.

"The city park. That looks like Anne's car. And Fran's."

"They're having a party without us?" Julia said. "We can't have that."

They entered the park and easily found the picnic table near the swings where the women had gathered while the three children played on the playground.

"Hideeho, Mayor," Fran called, waving them over. "Come join us as we discuss life, liberty, and the pursuit of cheesecake."

"I love cheesecake," Louise said, swinging a leg over the bench of the picnic table.

"Then you're welcome here," Fran said.

"Actually," Natalie said, tearing a blade of grass in two, "we're discussing me."

"Gee, do we each get a turn for free analysis?" Julia asked.

"Not today," Anne said, patting Natalie's hand.

Julia glanced from one to the other. "What's going on?"

Natalie tossed the pieces of grass on the ground. "I'm pregnant."

"Oh," Julia said quietly.

"A child," Louise said.

"That pretty much sums it up." Natalie shrugged. "My boyfriend back home—Sam—he's the father, but according to him we're just friends." She shook her head. "I've messed up my life but good. I wish I could turn back time."

"Don't we all." Julia gave Natalie a level stare. "How old *are* you?"

"Eighteen."

"Not much time to turn back, deary."

"It's time enough to make a mistake."

"So take care of it."

"Julia!" Kathy said, her tone mirroring the shock in the other women's faces. "You can't mean—"

"An abortion." Julia looked at them, then dropped her eyes. "Sometimes it's necessary. Sometimes there is no other choice. At least it's legal now—"

"Just because it's legal doesn't make it right," Kathy said.

Julia held up a hand. "I'm not saying the decision is easy. In fact, it's one of the hardest decisions a woman has to make, but...I've struggled too hard in a man's world to let anyone tell me I can't control my own body."

"You want some say-so," Fran said.

"You betcha."

Anne fixed her with a somber look. "What about your child's say-so?"

"Well...I—"

"You don't want to be dependent on someone else making your decision for you."

"Absolutely."

"And yet the child is dependent on the mother for growth and survival. He or she doesn't have a choice."

"Yes, but—"

"What about the others who are dependent on us to take care of them?" Kathy said. "My grandma is ninety-two and can't live alone anymore. She's dependent on the nursing home for help and on us to love her and care for her. And what about Lisa, Ryan, and Donnie?" She pointed to the children. "They're totally dependent on us to provide for them, to keep them safe and healthy. I couldn't do anything to hurt any of them."

"Neither could I," Julia said. "It's not the same."

Kathy slapped her hands on the picnic table. "Why not? If I made the choice to kill my children now, all society would condemn me. I would belong in jail. And yet when a mother chooses to kill her unborn child, it's all right? That doesn't make sense."

"Some don't consider the fetus a baby until—"

Anne held up her hand, cutting Julia off. "'Before I formed you in the womb I knew you, before you were born I set you apart.' God said that to Jeremiah."

Julia slid off the bench. She paced behind the table. "I was just giving Natalie one of the options. A woman should have the freedom to choose."

"I already chose."

A moment passed. Then two.

"There's no hurry, Natalie," Kathy said. "You should talk to Sam. We'll talk to him too if you—"

Julia swung around, pointing at Kathy. "You're afraid she's chosen against you. You're afraid to hear her choice as it is right now."

"I am not afraid—"

"You are! You're scared she's going to choose an abortion so you go on and on, telling her to take her time—"

"You're the one who's going on and on—"

"Only to compete with—"

"Stop!"

Julia and Kathy froze, Julia with a finger in Kathy's face, and Kathy rising from the bench to meet it.

"Sit down!" Natalie said. "Both of you." She waited until they were seated at the table, then went on. "This is not a national debate. Julia, you are not running for president, and Kathy, you are not some radical carrying placards and lying down in front of clinics. Neither one of you will get your point across by yelling at each other."

Fran swept a stray hair away from Natalie's cheek. "You said you'd made a choice, Nat?"

Natalie nodded. "They didn't let me finish. I was trying to make a point. The point being that I already made a choice when I decided to have sex with Sam eight weeks ago." She traced a carved initial on the picnic table. "That wasn't a good decision. Not for him, not for me, and not for the baby."

"As for the other choice?" Louise asked.

She closed her eyes. "I wish this was the plot of one of my stories. I could get the heroine out of it. Easy."

"Life's not as easy as fiction," Anne said.

"I know." Natalie reached out and touched each of their hands. "I hear everything you're saying. This affects both Sam and me. All of us. Forever." She angled a chiding look at them. "But your yelling at each other won't help."

Kathy held out a hand toward Julia. "Truce," she said.

"Truce."

~

What are those women yelling about? Can't a man get any peace around here?

Art turned on his side, resting his head on his arm. He scooted a few inches to the right to stay in the shade as the sun shifted in the afternoon sky. He cracked open one eye and looked at the women across the park. A cute young girl, about his own age. Two blondes: one dishwater blond and another with that white blond hair that reminded him of Sheila Barnes back in high school. If only it were Sheila, he'd show her what

170

happens when you dump Art Graham....He shook his head and studied the other three women. One was a redhead, the other two were older ladies. One short and dumpy, the other kind of classy looking. It was Classy who was doing the yelling. Pacing back and forth, acting loud and obnoxious. Not like a lady at all. Yelling like his mother...

"Shut up," Art mumbled into his arm.

The women were quiet.

He smiled, gloating over his power.

⁓

"I was proud of you, Kathy," Anne said as she emptied the sand out of Donnie's shoes before letting him in the backseat.

"For what?" Kathy asked, doing the same with Ryan's shoes. "Snapping at Julia like a crazed piranha?"

"For speaking up."

"I certainly did that."

"You took a stand. Have you always been so passionate about the pro-life issue?"

Kathy stopped and thought a moment. "Is that what I am?" she said. "I didn't even know I had an opinion until I got here and found out Natalie... The idea that someone I was talking with, someone I could see and touch, would consider an abortion flicked a switch in me. I'd made my choice back when I was expecting Ryan, but I never thought about it much in regard to other people."

"The faceless masses," Anne said, getting in the driver's seat.

"They are easy to ignore."

Anne checked her watch. "We've got an hour before dinner starts. I'll drop you back at your room so you can get cleaned up—with one detour."

"Where to?"

"My school. I want to show you where I work. Home of the faceless masses."

The Haven Junior-Senior High School was a one-story brick building with an empty flagpole out front and an empty parking lot to the side.

"There's the motel, Mommy," Ryan said, pointing to the back of the motel across the football field. "I want to play with my cars."

"Barbie," Lisa said.

"Just a minute, kids," Kathy said, "Anne wants to show me where she works."

Donnie smacked Ryan in the arm. "Race you to the art room."

As soon as Anne unlocked the door to the school, the kids ran down the hall with Donnie in the lead. They added loud screeching noises as they applied their brakes to turn the corner.

"Will they be all right?" Kathy asked.

"Better to ask if the art room will be all right," Anne said with a grin.

Kathy fanned herself with a hand. "Doesn't the school board believe in air-conditioning?"

"Not during the summer," Anne said, flipping the light in the office. "Actually, not at all. The school was built without central air, before people got spoiled into thinking their bodies have to be maintained at seventy-six degrees."

"Guilty," Kathy said.

Anne's office was a small eight-by-eight cubicle with posters reminding her students to Touch the Future and that Fate Finds Persistence Irresistible.

"So this is where the world is changed," Kathy said.

"One pimply-faced adolescent at a time."

"You love it."

"I do," Anne admitted. "It's very rewarding."

"And challenging."

"And heartbreaking." She sighed. "The kids are so vulnerable and aching for guidance...though they'd never admit it." She opened a file drawer and set her hand on top. "There's a lot of confusion in these files, but also a lot of triumph. You'd be surprised—"

"Mom!"

"Uh-oh," Kathy said, turning toward the door.

"It's just Donnie," Anne said. "That's his I'm-not-getting-my-own-way voice. I'll go check it out."

Anne left the room, and Kathy heard her calling, "You'd better not be making a mess, Donnie boy."

Kathy wandered to the open file drawer. Her fingers walked over the tabs of the folders, touching names of children she didn't know. Eileen Brenner, Marty Darda, Kathleen Grady . . .

Kathleen Grady? That's me!

"It must be another Kathleen Grady," she murmured. She let her fingers walk a few files past, then backtracked. She pulled the file from the drawer, opened it, and sucked in her breath. The yearbook picture of her seventeen-year-old face was taped on the inside front cover. Braces, big bangs. There were only two papers in the file. The top one looked familiar. It was a letter written on Garfield stationery in Kathy's rounded cursive.

"Dear Mrs. Robb, I have a problem I need to talk to you about. It's urgent! Can I come by your office after school tomorrow?"

She remembered writing the letter. She'd been sitting in her room, on her bed, with a calendar in her lap. She'd been counting the days. Too many days. She knew she was pregnant.

Kathy flipped to the second page. It was a paper she'd never seen. A handwritten list with two categories: Pros and Cons. It was Mrs. Robb's handwriting. Under the Pros were listed: Supportive family, Christian values, Intelligence, Willingness to do the right thing. Under Cons were listed: Age, Really in love?, Willingness to sacrifice her own dreams.

A note was written across the bottom, summing it up: "Kathy will be fine as a married lady and mother. But by jumping into adult life will she ever gain the confidence she needs to use her many gifts?"

"My many gifts?" Kathy asked.

"Your many gifts," Anne said from the doorway.

Kathy turned to her and asked the question again. "My many gifts?"

"He gave you the file, didn't he?" Anne said, fingering her cross necklace.

"He who?"

"You need to remember your potential, Kathy. You need to know."

"Know what?"

"You need to know you're special. You're worthy. Because of him."

"Worthy of what?"

"Worthy to receive God's instructions."

"He's the one who wanted me to see this file?"

Anne shrugged. "How else did you get it?"

"Does this type of thing happen often?" Kathy asked. "You seem so calm, like you've seen this a million times."

"I have seen it a trillion times," Anne said. "So have you, so have all of us."

"I haven't," Kathy said. "I know for a fact this is absolutely the first time I've ever had God give me anything."

"You know that's not true."

"I mean anything as specific as a file."

Anne looked at her.

Kathy tried again. "Anything so…personal."

"He reaches out to you all the time, Kathy. He tries to reach all his children, but so few are willing to listen."

Kathy stared at the file cabinet, so ordinary with its chipped paint and crammed drawers. Then she looked at the file folder from her youth—the original file folder, brought here especially so she could remember her potential. She held the file against her chest.

"I'm willing," she said, her voice breaking. "I'm willing to listen to it all."

"Soon," Anne said.

Disappointment filled her. Kathy wondered if her heart would break from it. "Why not now?"

"In his time, not ours, Kathy. In his time."

They walked to the art room to get the kids. Ryan and Donnie were painting on easels, their blue and green bands leaving a white void between earth and sky.

"Where's Lisa?" Kathy asked.

Ryan pointed to the corner with his paintbrush. Lisa was curled on the carpeted platform where the subject matter was usually displayed for painting or drawing. Her head rested on one arm, the thumb of her other hand was in her mouth. She was clutching the piece of draping cloth used for still lifes as a surrogate blankie.

"Such an angel," Anne whispered.

"I wish I had my paints," Kathy said wistfully.

"Use ours." Anne pulled another easel close. She opened a cupboard full of watercolor paper and canvases. "Pick your medium." Anne opened another cabinet full of paints.

Excitement took over, and Kathy moved forward. Careful not to make any noise, she attached a piece of watercolor paper to the easel. Taking out a palette, she matched tubes of paint with the hues of her daughter and squeezed a half-dozen tubes onto the palette.

"What's she doing, Mommy?" Donnie asked.

Anne shushed him and pulled the boys out of the way so they could watch. Kathy barely noticed. As her concentration grew, no sounds invaded her ears. No movement distracted her focus. She dipped her brush in water, then color, then water again, her eyes juggling the art of her subject and the art of her hands. As if sensing her mother needed her to be still, Lisa slept on, her only movement the soft rise and fall of her chest and the flutter of one stray piece of hair as her breath moved it up and back.

The picture emerged. Not just a rendering of her daughter

caught in a moment of childhood sleep, but the essence of Lisa's innocence, her serenity and her willingness to be at peace with the world.

The boys sank to the floor, their eyes flitting from Lisa to the painting, their mouths open as they watched the watercolor Lisa appear on the paper. Anne sat on the floor beside them, nodding, smiling, knowing.

As Kathy added more water to the page, the green paint that was the carpet bled and spread as if it were a meadow of spring grass come to life. She rinsed her brush and refined the last few curls of Lisa's hair. Then she stepped back, letting a soft breath of wonder escape her.

She was finished.

Lisa stirred, making soft mews of wakefulness. She extended her legs and stretched, opening her eyes, closing them, opening them once more. She smiled at her mother. "Mama."

Kathy blinked as if surprised her subject had come to life. She knelt down and opened her arms. Lisa filled them, her cozy warmth a blessing in spite of the stifling heat. Lisa noticed the painting.

"Baby," she said.

"Lisa," Kathy replied softly.

Lisa buried her head in Kathy's neck. "Luv you, Mama."

"Now it's time to listen," Anne whispered.

Sixteen

Does not wisdom call out? Does not understanding raise her voice?
On the heights along the way, where the paths meet,
she takes her stand; beside the gates leading into the city,
at the entrances, she cries aloud: "To you, O men, I call out;
I raise my voice to all mankind. You who are simple, gain prudence;
you who are foolish, gain understanding."

PROVERBS 8:1–5

THERE WAS A KNOCK on Natalie's door.

"Hideeho, Natty Jo," Fran said. "Mind if I come in?" At Natalie's nod, she did so, making a tour of the room. "I like these colors. They show life and imagination."

"They keep my mind awake," Natalie said.

"A noble goal." Fran sank into the beanbag chair, her knees at eye level. "Oh, yeah. This is comfortable." She held up her arm, clearly wanting to be rescued.

Natalie laughed and pulled her up. "You have to curl up in a beanbag. You can't sit normal."

Fran gave the chair an accusing look, as though it might try to take her captive. "These muscles don't curl. I'm getting old."

"You are not," Natalie said, pulling out the regular chair by the table. "You can't be over thirty…five."

Fran laughed. "You are so far off…" She waved further discussion away. She set her hands in her lap. "Which leads me to why I'm here. I want to read your book."

Natalie glanced at her bed, where the notebook holding her manuscript pages lay. "I felt a little crazy bringing it," she confessed. She shook her head, picking up the notebook and holding it close to her chest. "The book's not ready.…I won't let anyone read it."

"No one?"

"Well, Sam's read it."

"What does he say?"

"He says it's okay, but he's not into romance much. He doesn't understand." She ran a hand over the pages. "I don't know if I can let anyone else read this."

"It's going to be hard to get it published if you feel that way."

"You know what I mean."

"Yes, I do," Fran said. "And if you want a yes-man telling you it's great and perfect as it is, I'm not your reader. But if you want the truth…" She looked at Natalie, a challenge in her eyes.

"Are you daring me?"

"The truth at twenty paces—or pages, whichever comes first."

With a last wistful look at her manuscript, Natalie handed it to Fran, who retrieved a pair of reading glasses from her pocket. "Age again," she explained. "Why don't you take a long shower while I read? When you come out you'll be fresh and ready to hear my verdict on what I've read."

Natalie looked at her, doubtful. "Are you going to pass sentence, too?"

"Hmm. Passing sentence on the sentences. You must remember, dear one, that needing to revise is not commensurate with the death penalty."

Natalie rummaged through her suitcase for a change of clothes. "I'll try to keep that in mind." She hesitated at the bathroom door. "Go easy on me, all right, Fran?"

"Nat…"

She held up her hands. "Fine. Go for it. Tear me apart."

Fran rubbed her hands together. "This'll be fun."

Natalie closed the bathroom door. "I can hardly wait."

"Can I come out now?" Natalie asked from behind the bathroom door. "I'm turning into a steamed prune."

"The coast is clear. All scissors, red pencils, and erasers have been sheathed."

Natalie cracked the door and peered out. "I don't see any pages flung across the room in utter distaste. That's good."

"I'm not that brutal," Fran said.

Taking a comb from the counter, Natalie moved to the bed. She combed through her wet hair. "Exactly how brutal were you?"

The older woman held up her hands. "Look. No blood."

"That's encouraging."

Fran closed the manuscript in her lap. "I don't want to tear it apart, Natalie. I want to help you build it up."

"Does it need a lot of building?"

The slightest pause. "Yes, it does."

Natalie flung herself back on the bed, her arms splayed. "Give it to me straight. I can take it."

"You don't look like you can take it."

"I'm bracing for total rejection."

"You take things too personally."

"My writing is personal."

"All the more reason to make it the best it can be. You wouldn't want a mediocre manuscript representing you. Would you?"

Natalie reluctantly sat up on her forearms. "I suppose not."

"Then listen to the truth."

Natalie made a face, bracing herself. "All right. I'm ready."

"Being a bit melodramatic, are we?"

Natalie relaxed.

"That's better." Fran cleared her throat and set her glasses on her nose. "There are several small things I think need to be changed—"

"Such as?" Natalie challenged before she could stop herself.

"Such as the title," Fran explained. *Denizen's Desire?* She raised one expressive eyebrow.

Natalie opened her mouth to argue, then clamped it shut. She'd asked for Fran's input, hadn't she? "Fine," Natalie said. "I can change the title."

"But what needs the most work is the subject matter."

"Love."

"Of a sort."

Fran opened the manuscript, hunting for a page. "Here it is: 'Fiona swooned when Kurt came in the room, her heart beating faster.'"

"You don't like *swooned?*"

"Have you ever seen anyone swoon?"

Natalie couldn't answer.

"I thought not. And why does Fiona like Kurt anyway?"

Natalie shrugged. "Because he's a hunk. And he owns a castle."

Fran closed the notebook, studying Natalie. When Natalie started to squirm, she asked, "Tell me why you love Sam."

"What's Sam got to do with this?"

"Tell me."

Natalie cocked her head, thinking. "He feels things deeply. He loves nature...." She felt a smile lift her lips. "You should see him sitting beside a lake way up in the mountains. There's something that comes over his face. A peace. His eyes get darker, like he's absorbing all he sees and keeping it there, deep inside. He's actually very spiritual, but he doesn't know it."

"What else?"

"He listens to me. He's the only one I've told about my dreams, what I'd really like to have happen with my writing. And he doesn't laugh. Not much, anyway." She held up a finger, thinking of something else. "And he's talented. And brave. He doesn't like the same kind of music other kids our age like. He likes what *he* likes. And he writes the kind of music that touches him. And I just know it will touch other people someday. I know it."

"So he's not a hunk."

Natalie laughed. "Sam?"

"And he doesn't own a castle?"

She bit her lip. Fran had a point. "My characters aren't very deep, are they?"

"They aren't very real."

Natalie started to argue, but Fran raised a hand to stop her. "Just tell me this: How would Kurt react to a mountain lake?"

"Well…I don't—"

"Is he spiritual? Does Kurt listen to Fiona's dreams? What are his talents?"

Natalie plucked at the stitching in the bedspread. "I don't know."

Fran set the notebook on the table and sat beside her. "When you helped me at the café today, I saw you talk to people, learn about them. You're a great observer, Nat. You noticed the love triangle between Tina, Mary, and Billy. You caught on that Marv's daughter would be the perfect choice to take over the family farm. You sensed the hunger in that boy eating the french fries and got him more, all the while being mindful of his pride. Those are real people, Nat. Those are people with complex emotions, interesting pasts, and uncertain futures."

"But books like mine are popular," Natalie said. "There are tons of them in the bookstores."

"A pyramid gets smaller as it reaches the top."

"What?"

"Rise above the rest, Nat. There will always be masses of the mediocre. You can aim higher than that."

"Maybe, but will I hit anything?"

"You won't know until you try."

After Fran left, Natalie plopped on the middle of her bed and opened the notebook containing her manuscript…the manuscript that was supposed to attract an agent—hopefully, a New York agent who would lavish her with praise and auction it off for six figures. Then she'd quit her job at her parents' resort and travel the world on book tours where she'd get to stay in fancy hotels and have people fawn all over her.

Natalie stretched on her stomach with her head at the foot of the bed. She chewed the tip of the pen, jump-starting her thoughts by reading the last page she'd written: "Fiona's raven hair fell in a tumble on her shoulders. When she moved, the gentle swish of it across her bare skin was like the fingers of the lover she longed for. Kurt. If only he'd burst through her bedroom door and rescue her from her own desires, sweeping her into his—"

She broke away from the words and shoved the notebook off the foot of the bed. She rolled over onto her back and threw the pen. It made a slow arc across the room, bouncing off the wall behind her. She extended her arms and groaned miserably. "Fran's right. Why do I write this bunkum tribble?" She laughed at her own words. "Now, *that's* good vocabulary."

Fran's reaction had changed everything. She had so much work to do. So much…

With a sigh, Natalie closed her eyes and called up her fantasy. Her Fame Fantasy.

She'd be coming inside from repairing some wayward toilet when her mother would hand her the phone. "It's for you," she'd say. Natalie's stomach would tighten. She'd *know* this was it. Her big break. It would be an agent calling from a sleek Manhattan office with a view of the Empire State Building. "Is this *the* Natalie Pasternak?" they'd ask. She'd assure them it was. They'd continue, "I've just sold *Denizen's Desire* to Hollywood. Demi Moore and Brad Pitt have agreed to star. We'll be sending you a check for your advance on the book. Will nine hundred thousand dollars be agreeable?"

Natalie laughed out loud. "Make it a million and we'll talk," she told her empty room.

She rolled off her bed, grabbed a book off the bedside table, and moved to the mirror above the sink. She flipped on the light, then held the book near her right ear, displaying it for all the world to see and appreciate. She raised a hand, fending off the flashbulbs of the press, all the while smiling her celebrity smile.

"Thank you, thank you," she told the mirror. "You have been so *terribly* kind. But I only have time to autograph three—no, make that four—more books before I'm off to Paris for the European premiere of my masterpiece." Natalie looked behind her. "Oh, there's my limousine now. Ta ta."

She waved her good-byes to the mirror, but her smile faded as her gaze drifted to her midsection. She cupped a hand over her abdomen, shaking her head. "You don't fit into my fantasies, little one. I want to do the right thing, but giving up all my dreams isn't right. Is it?"

Natalie drew the book to her chest and glanced in the mirror. Ǝ⅃ᗺIᗺ Y⅃OH, the reflected title read. She cocked her head, reading it again, backwards.

"Holy Bible," she said, and a jolt ran through her. She tossed the book on the counter as if it were hot, backing away from her reflection.

From the book's reflection.

"But I don't want a baby," she told it. "And I don't have to have a baby." She leaned forward and shut off the light. The reflection of her fantasy fell into darkness.

Relieved, she moved toward the bed, only to pause in confusion when she spotted the Bible there, on her bedstand. "What...?" She rubbed her eyes, looking from the bathroom to the nightstand and back again. She could see the shadow of the Bible in the bathroom.

But hadn't she taken it from the nightstand...?

Nervously, she pointed a finger at the second Bible. "But I don't want to do the right thing! A baby will ruin everything."

The Bible lay there, seemingly unaffected by her words.

Natalie scrambled over the mattress on her hands and knees, needing to get away from the Bibles. She snatched a pillow, turned it the long way and wrapped herself around it. She rubbed her cheek against the cotton fabric. "I don't know what to do," she moaned. "I just don't know."

She kept her back to the Bibles, afraid of the power she sensed but didn't quite understand.

Four doors down, Walter sat on his tan-and-white striped bedspread and stared at his phone. A cigarette burned in his hand, the length of ash reaching the point where gravity would soon take over.

It fell on Walter's shirt.

"Aw, man," he said, snuffing the cigarette in the ashtray. He brushed the ashes onto his hand and disposed of them. "Get your mind in gear, Walter. You can't sit here smoking while you worry about a biopsy and Bette. You're digging your grave either way. If the cigarettes don't get you, the worry will."

He dialed Bette's number; she answered on the second ring.

"Walter, I've been so worried. Why didn't you leave me a message? Why did I have to find out you went out of town from Dave at work? You obviously didn't tell him about Haven, but I put two and two together—"

"It was a last minute decision, Bette."

"But I saw you throw the invitation away. What made you change your mind?"

Phone numbers appearing out of nowhere, voices at the end of the line who understood. A homeless man...

"As I recall, you regularly use the excuse of 'it's my prerogative,' so I'm going to follow suit."

"You're not telling me anything, Walter," she said. "Don't I deserve—"

"I love you, Bette," he said. "For whatever reason, I decided to go to Haven, and I didn't want to talk to you and risk being talked out of it. Leaving like I did was totally out of character for me and it wouldn't have taken much to put the brakes on my momentum."

"What's there, Walter?" she asked. "What's in Haven?"

"A town. People. We've each been assigned a mentor—"

"We?"

"Four of us received invitations, but there are five of us here. We're—"

"You're there to do what?"

He looked at the cigarette longingly. "That's a tough one. The people here are very nice, but they aren't great with the straight answers."

"But you're a newsman. Ask the right questions."

"Maybe I don't want to know the answers. Yet."

"Dave is suspicious. He thinks you've gone over the edge. What with that Gabe character showing up, and you darting out of the office afterwards and then asking for emergency time off. You really should call him. For your job's sake."

"I'm not sure I care about my job anymore."

"What?"

The statement surprised Walter as much as Bette. *What am I saying?* "My mentor is Gabe Thompson."

"*The* Gabe Thompson? The one who brought you the invitation?"

"The same. He's a newspaper man here. And he's got some opinions…you'd like him."

"Why?"

"He's disgusted about what's on the air, just like you are. And he's not afraid to say so and do something about it."

"Take a lesson, Walter."

"Yeah. I think that's why I'm here. To take a lesson."

"You don't sound too pleased."

"It's not easy for me. You know I'm not a mover and shaker. I like power but I don't like to blaze new trails. I do my job well and let everyone else do theirs."

"Maybe you haven't been doing your job well."

"Thanks a lot."

"Maybe by remaining silent, you've added to the problem."

"You and Gabe should get together to coordinate your strategy."

There was a moment of silence between them, then Bette

said, "The hospital called, Walter. About the biopsy."

He ran a hand over his forehead. "I don't want to think about it."

"They want to move it up one day."

"Great," he said. "One less day of peace of mind."

"You call what you're going through now peace of mind?"

"No, but…what if it's cancer, Bette? What if I'm going to die?"

"We're all going to die."

"Don't give me that—"

"I'm sorry," she said. "A pat answer is not what you need to hear."

"What do I need to hear?"

"You need to hear that I love you and will be with you through it all—whatever it is. You need to know that God will be with you through it all." She took a long breath. "Don't think the worst, Walter. It may happen, but it's not inevitable. Give your worries to God and let him create a miracle."

"I don't think God would waste a miracle on me."

"Why not?"

"Why bother?"

"You are the most egotistical, self-denigrating—"

"I can't be both."

"Somehow you manage."

"It's a gift."

"Don't give in to it, Walter. If this Haven business is God giving you another chance—if he's inviting you there to teach you something—he certainly doesn't want you to die in the near future. He has plans for you."

"'News of my demise has been greatly exaggerated'?"

"I certainly hope so."

"I do love you, Bette."

"Then take care of yourself. *All* of yourself. Your physical, mental, emotional, and spiritual self."

"You don't ask for much, do you?"

"I ask for the world."

"Do you get it?"

"I'm working on it. Bye, Walter."

He hung up and sat in the silence. He picked up a cigarette and started to light it, then abruptly clicked the lighter shut. He snapped the cigarette in two, then picked up the ashtray and gathered all the cigarettes from the room. He took them outside to a trash can. When he returned to his room, he gave his reflection in the mirror a satisfied smile.

"How's that for cleaning my 'self'?"

⁓

Everyone gathered at the bell-tower meeting room for dinner. Two round tables were set with fourteen places. Besides the mentors, Anne's husband, Chief, and little Donnie were added guests. Susan and Robert from the Fillerup put the finishing touches on the buffet table. The three children scoped out the food, their eyes coming to rest on the bowl of lime Jell-O, the macaroni and cheese, and the chocolate cake.

"Dinner is served," Fran called. "Come help yourselves. We tried to accommodate all of your tastes."

Walter noticed the prime rib. He nudged Julia in the side. "I won't even ask how they know what our tastes are."

Julia waved a hand in the air. "I no longer care to know." She took a heaping spoonful of scalloped potatoes. "As long as I get my potatoes, bread, and butter, I'm a happy camper."

"Starch city," Walter said.

"I'll take my starch over your cholesterol, Mr. Prescott."

They chose their places, instinctively sitting next to their mentors. Chief and Donnie were added to the table with Kathy and her kids. Del and John joined them.

The first ten minutes of dinner were spent oohing and ahhing over the tastes and smells of everyone's favorite foods. Real conversation didn't start until second helpings were heaped on plates.

"I've been wondering something, Anne," Walter said, leaning

toward the other table. "You seem to be the only mentor who's married and has a family. John's single, Fran, Gabe, and Louise are all here alone. Why is that?"

Anne and Chief exchanged a look. "We're the lucky ones, I guess."

"But don't you think that's strange?" Walter persisted. "Especially in a small town where family is so important." He turned to Gabe. "Why aren't you married?"

Gabe finished chewing a piece of broccoli. "You might say I'm married to my work."

Walter considered this a moment, a crease forming between his eyebrows. Then he wiped the corner of his mouth and pushed away from the table. He tapped his glass with a spoon. "People?" he said. "I was thinking it's only fair that our mentors tell us a bit about themselves. They seem to know so much about us. I'd like each one of them to stand and tell us about their life and their family."

Gabe spoke up. "I don't think that's appropriate, Walter. Our lives are of little consequence. You are the ones who are important."

"I disagree. Wouldn't the rest of you like to know?"

"I would," Julia said.

"So would I," Natalie echoed.

Suddenly John stood. "May I see all the mentors outside for a moment, please?"

Before anyone could object or ask why, the mentors—plus Chief and Donnie—fled the tables and went out onto the front steps of the church. They closed the door behind them.

"What's all that about?" Del asked.

Walter fingered his pocket for a cigarette. "I don't know, but they'd better come back with some answers."

"Maybe it's none of our business," Kathy said, wiping cake crumbs from Lisa's chin. "They're nice people. Leave them alone."

"They're nice people who want to know—or *already* know—everything about us," Walter said. "If you've been having the same type of experience I've been having, they've asked some very personal questions, delving into areas no stranger would dare delve into."

"They care about us," Natalie said. "At least, Fran cares about me, I know she does."

"I agree with you," Del said. "But I also agree with Walter. There's something odd going on here, and I wouldn't mind finding out what it is."

Kathy raised her hand tentatively. "I saw my high school file this afternoon. At the school. With letters in it from my senior year. They were the originals. I *was* wondering…how did they get them?"

"And the quilt in my room is the quilt my mother made," Del said. "It isn't just *like* my mother's quilt. It *is* her quilt. It has her initials embroidered on the corner."

"So, they're thorough," Julia said. "But they haven't used these things to harm us in any way. Have they?"

"Well, no," Kathy said. "Actually, seeing the file made me feel better about myself."

"And the quilt?" Julia asked Del.

"It made me feel at home."

"So why pry? Why not just leave them to what they do best and enjoy ourselves."

Kathy raised her hand again.

"You don't have to raise your hand, Kathleen," Julia said.

"I know…but…Anne said that *he* gave me the file."

"He who?"

Kathy pointed heavenward.

"Oh, please," Walter said, pushing away from the table. "This has got to stop."

Natalie perked up. "Why?" she asked. "Why does it have to stop?"

"Because it's out of the ordinary, that's why."

"You want to stop it because it's *extra*ordinary?" She stood and walked around the table. "I know I've called this place creepy. And I suppose it is in some ways. But it's also good."

"Creepy is a good description," Walter said.

Natalie shook her head. "It's wrong."

"So what would you call it, Natalie?" Del asked. "Bizarre? strange? weird?"

"I call it awesome," she replied firmly.

"Or astonishing," Julia said.

"Or sacred," Kathy said.

The door opened. The mentors filed in, their expressions somber. The others took their seats at the table, while John remained standing.

"We're sorry for the delay and we don't mean to make it appear so serious."

"Mysterious, is more like it," Walter said.

"As you wish," John said. "But the question was disturbing. It goes beyond the guidelines of our mission."

"And your mission is?" Julia asked.

"Please," John said, raising a hand. "If we're going to do this, we need to do it his way."

"There *he* is again," Walter mumbled. He needed a cigarette.

John ignored him. "I am prepared to make a statement that should answer a few of your questions. However, we are concerned about the subsequent questions our answer will create. These new questions cannot be answered. Will not be answered. What I offer you is a partial explanation on the condition that further questions will not be asked. Is that agreeable?"

"Do we have a choice?" Del asked.

"You have the choice to keep things as they are," John replied.

Walter shook his head. "I want to know. Whatever you can tell us, I want to know."

John looked around the room. Heads nodded. "Then it's agreed." He took a drink of water and cleared his throat. The group shoved their plates toward the center, leaning forward in anticipation.

"This is not the only Haven," John said.

"What do you—" Walter began.

Once again, John held up his hand. "The agreement was no questions." He paused until Walter leaned back in his chair. "There are other cities of Haven located in other states and in other countries."

"That's not so unusual," Walter said. "Lots of states have towns with the same name."

John shook his head. "There's more to it than that. Others, like all of you, have been called to these other Havens. And at these Havens are mentors who have been assigned to help those people, just as we have been assigned to help you. It is said, 'Let the wise listen and add to their learning, and let the discerning get guidance.'"

"I hardly consider myself wise," Julia said.

"You show wisdom in knowing it is wisdom you lack," John said, smiling at her. "We understand that you want to know the whys of your being here. Let me assure you, it will be revealed. But true knowledge comes slowly, one piece at a time. Knowledge is 'a precious cornerstone for a sure foundation; the one who trusts will never be dismayed.'"

"But when?"

"In his time."

Walter stood at his place. "I know we agreed not to ask any questions, but I've got to because of all this 'he,' 'him,' and 'his' business. Are you confirming that God is the one who invited us here? That he's running this thing?"

John smiled. "I can assure you, God is running this thing."

"And he invited us here?"

John looked at the other mentors. They nodded. "Yes. God invited you here. You are his chosen ones."

Kathy shook her head. "I don't know what he wants me to do. I'm not even sure what *you* want me to do."

Anne put an arm around her shoulders. "We'll help you figure it out, Kathy. One step at a time."

Natalie raised a hand. "You mean what's happening here is part of a bigger plan?"

"Everything that happens to you, everywhere, is part of God's plan, Natalie," John said.

"Really?"

Louise spoke up. "'He determines the number of the stars and calls them each by name.'"

Natalie sat back in her chair. "That is so cool."

"As for why we don't have family…" John looked at Del, expecting him to be as eager for an answer as the others. Instead he found Del sitting with his hands in his lap, his eyes downcast. "Del?" John asked.

Del jerked his head erect. "What?"

John put a hand on his shoulder. "Are you all right?"

Del straightened in his chair, slowly focusing on the others around the tables. "Sure. I'm fine. You were talking families?"

John hesitated then continued. "The reason we don't have families is they are allowed to join us only when they are necessary for the final result."

"So Chief and little Donnie are necessary?" Julia asked.

"I would certainly hope so," Chief said, ruffling Donnie's hair.

Laughter eased the tension.

"Yes, they are necessary," John said.

"But I'm not." Del bolted from his chair, toppling it. He ran outside.

The others stood, unsure what to do.

"I'll get him," John said. "The rest of you get another helping of dessert. We'll be back."

Seventeen

He who has been stealing must steal no longer, but must work,
doing something useful with his own hands, that he may have
something to share with those in need.
EPHESIANS 4:28

ART GRAHAM PARKED on the side of the Pump 'n' Eat. He kept the motor running so the car was ready. He didn't want anything to interfere with getting out of there as quickly as possible. He'd considered backing the car in but figured that would be too conspicuous.

A lady pumping her gas looked at him. She did more than look, she studied him, then shook her head like she disapproved.

Belatedly, Art realized he'd drawn attention to himself because of the incessant beat of the bass on the radio. He liked his music loud. He wanted to feel it eating away at him from the inside out. It was better than a heartbeat.

He flipped the radio off. She gave him a second look of approval. That *was* it.

"Mind your own business, woman," he said between his teeth.

She went inside, paid, and left. Art looked around the station. There were no other cars except the clerk's battered Pinto parked at the far end. But he couldn't be positive there weren't any pedestrians inside. He couldn't see in due to the dumb posters plastered on the glass: Coke $2.99/12 pack, Candy bars 2/$1. He might do a little "shopping" before he was through.

He waited a few minutes to see if anyone came out; some wayward kid or something. No one. He squirmed, rubbing the gun against his calf. Timing was everything. Absolutely everything.

Art opened the car door and stepped out. He hid the gun beneath a newspaper tucked under his arm. With his other arm, he wiped the sweat off his forehead. The salt stung his eyes.

Do it! Do it now!

He strode toward the front door, hoping he exuded the confidence of Clint Eastwood—so what if his stomach made him feel like a scared kid? When he got inside, he turned right into the candy aisle.

"Afternoon," the clerk said.

Art jerked toward the voice. The *man's* voice.

Where was the girl? The teenager who'd be scared of him and hand over the money while she whimpered, "Don't shoot me. Please, don't shoot."

"Afternoon," Art responded belatedly.

"Can I help you?"

Art took the chance to look at the man. Forty-five, with a gut used to beer, beernuts, and watching—but definitely never playing—sports. He felt a sneer twist his lips. *Do it anyway. He's a tub.*

Art picked up a Snickers and moved to the counter like he was going to pay.

I'll pay all right. I'll pay with this!

He lowered his gun hand, letting the newspaper fall to the floor. He raised the gun and leered at the clerk. "Give me the money," he said. "All of it."

The man raised his arms without Art asking. Art could nearly see the man's heart beating through his too tight shirt, bouncing under the "Bob" embroidered on the pocket. He heard the man's breath come in short gasps. Wheeze in. Wheeze out. If he wasn't careful, old Bob would have a heart attack—

"Calm it down, Bobby boy," Art said. "If you do what I say, I'll leave you alone. Just give me the money."

Bob started to lower his arms, then raised them again. "I've got to put my arms down to open the drawer."

"Just do it!" Art yelled. "I never told you to raise 'em in the first place."

Bob pushed a button and the register drawer popped open.

"Put the bills in a sack."

Bob fumbled beneath the counter and stuffed the money in a brown paper bag. Art grabbed a package of Twinkies. "Put these in there too. You certainly don't need 'em." He swung the gun in the air. "Now get down on the floor, hands behind your head."

Bob trembled as he struggled to the floor, attempting to manage the act of lying down with his hands clasped behind his head.

"Stay there till your heart gets back to beating normal. I don't want you dying on me."

Art was laughing as he ran out of the store.

Bob waited until he heard Art's car pull away. Then he calmly stood up, dusted off the front of his pants, and made a phone call to the bell-tower meeting room.

"Howdy, Chief. Bob here," he said. "He did it. He's all yours."

Bob hung up and had himself a Twinkie.

⌒⌒

When John went after Del, he saw that the church steps were empty. He searched around the side of the building and found Del sitting along the back fence, hunkered down beside the trash. His knees were pulled close to his body, his arms wrapped around his chest.

"Now, this is pleasant," John said.

Del didn't answer.

John groaned as he eased himself to the ground. He let a moment pass. "He forgives you, Del."

Del looked up, his eyes blazing. "I don't want to be forgiven! Doesn't he understand that? I don't want to be chosen to do anything special. I'm a sinner. A woman is dead. I'm not worth his trouble. Have him get somebody else."

"He doesn't want somebody else. He wants you."

"To do what?" Del snapped. "I've done a bravo job messing up my own life, plus a few others. What am I here for? Am I the token bum?"

"He has his purposes."

Del jumped to his feet. "Quit saying that! I *have* no purpose. I am nothing."

"'Blessed are the poor in spirit, for theirs is the kingdom of heaven.'"

"Oh, I'm poor all right." He pulled out his pockets. A few coins fell on the ground. "That's it, John. That's how poor I am."

"He doesn't mean that kind of poor, Del. He means the humble. God can only use a man who thinks he can't be used. He needs an empty vessel, ready to fill."

"Well, he's got it. I'm empty."

"Then let him fill you up."

Del leaned against the fence, letting it guide him to sitting. He left his money where it was. "How, John? How can I help anyone else when I can't even help myself?"

"Don't worry about gifts you don't have, Del. 'There are different kinds of gifts, but the same Spirit. There are different kinds of service, but the same Lord. There are different kinds of working, but the same God works all of them in all men.'"

"See?" Del said. "I never could do that."

"What?"

"Quote the Bible. These great verses come to you at just the right times. What'd you do, memorize the entire book?"

John laughed. "I wish."

"I can't be like you."

"God doesn't want you to be like me. He wants you to be Antonio Michael Delatondo."

"I'm no great catch. He'll want to throw me back."

"He does not give up."

"But I'm stubborn."

John laughed. "He knows."

"I'm not ready for this, John. I don't know if I'll ever be—"

Chief burst around the side of the building, heading toward his cruiser.

"What's up?" John asked, getting to his feet.

"It's started. The Pump 'n' Eat's been robbed."

"Need any help?"

"Just keep everyone out of the way." Chief slammed his door shut. "And pray."

⌒

Back inside the meeting room, Walter headed out the door after Chief. Gabe pulled him back.

"What?" Walter said. "Let's go. There's news being made."

"Let the police do their job, Walter," Gabe said. "Don't be a pushy journalist, complicating the situation."

"But it's news! People have a right to know."

Gabe led Walter back to their table and pushed a half-eaten piece of carrot cake in front of him. "Eat your cake. Relax. As soon as the police have had a chance to talk with Bob at the Pump 'n' Eat, we'll go over and interview him."

Walter pushed the plate away. "I don't want to interview the victim, I want to go after the robber. I want to be where the action is."

"Ambulance chaser."

Walter blinked at the accusation. "I chase the news."

"Meddler."

"Investigative reporter."

"Sensationalist."

"I feed the theater of the news."

"You haven't been listening to me, Walter."

"What?"

"Remember this afternoon? The Honor Roll? Promoting integrity and family values?"

"But this is real life."

"It's evil."

"Ah, come on," Walter said. "Not that good versus evil bunkum. Isn't that a little simplistic, even for a small-town newspaperman like you?"

"Yes, it's simple. A simple, basic truth."

"Fine. Then let's cover the story simply. I'll only write the basic facts."

"About the criminal."

"Sure, about the criminal."

"You'll find out his parents were mean to him and imply the pattern of crime is not really his fault. You'll try to make us feel sorry for him."

"Come on, Gabe. What happened to the man of God showing a little compassion?"

"For the victim, Walter. For the victim."

"What happened to 'love thy neighbor'?"

"The perpetrator will get his share of compassion after he owns up to the responsibility of his actions. It's not always someone else's fault."

"But I'm my mother's boy, Gabe. I'm my father's son. We *are* affected by our parents."

"Yes, we are, and I don't mean to diminish the pain and circumstances some people have lived through. But every door has two sides, every path leads from something and to something. Everyone has choices to rise above or fall below."

"Free will, huh?"

"Exactly," Gabe said, taking a sip of coffee. "'Teach me your way, O LORD; lead me in a straight path because of my oppressors.'"

"What if you are the oppressor?"

"Repent."

Walter rolled his eyes and waggled his hands on either side of his face. "Repent ye sinners! Repe-e-e-ent!"

Walter expected some reaction to his theatrics. A disgusted

shake of the head, a raised eyebrow. He did not expect Gabe's level stare over his coffee cup. Even though he wasn't hungry, Walter pulled his carrot cake close and cut off a corner.

"Listen to your own words, Walter," Gabe said as he watched him finish the last of his cake.

Walter pointed his fork at himself. "Those aren't my words. I don't think about repentance."

"You should."

Walter shoved his plate away, making the fork clatter into the salt shaker. "So *I'm* supposed to repent? I thought we were talking about the guy who robbed the Pump 'n' Eat."

"It is said that 'whoever keeps the whole law and yet stumbles at just one point is guilty of breaking all of it.'"

"Are you saying I'm as bad as that thief out there?"

"All sins keep us from God."

Walter fingered a spoon, turning it over and over on the table. "What do you know about my sins?"

"It's not for me to know, Walter. It's for God to know. And it's for you to confess."

Walter pointed the spoon at Gabe. "If God already knows my sins, he doesn't need me to confess them." He slashed the spoon through the air. "It's done. Over. Nothing I—or even God—can do will change it."

"But God will change *you*. Jesus died taking all your sins upon himself. That's the only way you can be cleansed."

"I don't need to be cleansed or changed." Walter had a sudden thought, and he smirked. "After all, I'm one of the chosen ones. I'm special."

Gabe took a long breath and leaned toward Walter, putting a hand on his arm. "Remember this. I'll give it to you plain—the bottom line. This is a quote from the source, 'If we deliberately keep on sinning after we have received the knowledge of the truth, no sacrifice for sins is left.'"

Walter swallowed. "Is that a threat?"

Gabe patted Walter's arm and stood. "It's a promise." With

that, he rose and walked away, leaving Walter alone with his thoughts.

⌁

"Is there anything we can do to help?" Julia asked Louise as they walked toward Julia's car.

"Nothing. Chief's good at his job." Louise paused. "Though I might run over to the Pump 'n' Eat and talk to Bob. See if he's okay."

"Am I supposed to come with you?"

"Supposed...?"

"You know," Julia said, "am I supposed to come with you because that's part of my training here?"

Louise stopped walking and faced her. "You don't have to do anything, Julia. We're here to guide you, not force you."

"Then if you don't mind, I'm going to call it a night. It's been a long day."

"Indeed it has," Louise said, walking her to the driver's door.

Julia got in her car. "If there's anything I can do to help, you call me. I don't need *that* much beauty sleep."

"Indeed you do not," Louise said, shutting the door. She waved as Julia pulled away, then said quietly, "And you're not going to get it."

⌁

Art had mapped out his getaway before the robbery. He wasn't going to head up the highway toward the interstate. That was too easy; the first place they'd look. Besides, what he'd gain in speed on the interstate, he'd lose in the network of sophisticated highway patrol cars that could radio his position back and forth until his capture was inevitable.

No, he'd take a back retreat, out the west end of Haven. He'd drive through a few small towns and eventually weave his way onto some dirt back road, then steal another car from some unsuspecting farmer.

200

He glanced at the sky and smiled. Darkness was coming. His friend and ally.

He slid through a stop sign on a residential street, not seeing it until it was too late.

"Come on, Art!" he yelled at himself. "Don't get sloppy now. All you need is to get pulled over for a ticket." He shoved the gun under his right thigh; at hand but out of sight. If some cop did stop him, it would be the last stop the guy ever made.

He shook such thoughts away. "Got up off the floor, yet, Bobby boy? Or has some podunk walked in to buy cigarettes and found you lying in the dust like a scared wimp?"

He laughed at the thought and pulled the brown paper sack to his lap. He opened it with one hand and looked inside. Not a great haul, but a couple hundred bucks. He could live a long time on a couple hundred bucks. He ripped open the package of Twinkies with his teeth and shoved the cake in his mouth, oblivious to the crumbs falling on his lap.

He tossed the bag on the seat as he neared the west edge of Haven. The wide expanse of cornfields on the other side of the motel lured him to freedom. Just a few more blocks, a few hundred yards to—

The car sputtered. Jerked. Died.

Art floored the accelerator. Nothing happened. The car rolled to a stop.

"No!" He slammed a fist on the steering wheel, then turned off the engine and tried it again. The engine churned but didn't catch. It wasn't the battery, it must be the—

His gaze flew to the gas gauge. It was on E.

"I put in two dollars' worth this morning, you hog. What'd you do? Suck it dry?"

Art fought the panic threatening to choke him. Bob would be up by now. Bob would be calling the police by now. They'd be looking for a strange car—and here he was, a sitting duck. He had to get out of Haven. He had to…

He looked in his rearview mirror and saw a silver car at the stop sign he'd just slipped through.

I have to get a new car.

He got out of his car, shoved the bag of money in his waistband, then started walking. He held his gun down, just behind his leg. He walked to the middle of the street and waved his other arm furiously, flagging down the silver car.

It stopped. He moved to the driver's side, smiling. The woman rolled down her window.

"Problem?" she asked.

"For you," he said, shoving the gun in her cheek. "Move over."

She pushed the barrel of the gun aside. "I will not. This is my car, a gift from my husband, Edward, and I will not let you take it."

Art wasn't prepared for a no. His gun made people say yes. Always. He glanced around. There was some activity at the motel. A woman and two kids were being let out of a car. The little boy looked his way.

Art ran around the front of the car at the same moment the woman lurched forward. The car bumped into his thighs. He regained his balance and slammed a hand on the hood. He leveled the gun at her. "Don't even think about it!"

She must have realized he was serious, for she froze.

He scrambled to the passenger door just in time to hear the click of the automatic locks. "Open up!" he demanded as he slapped the passenger window. The woman's smug expression fed his anger. Exasperated, he yanked on the handle. To his surprise—and the woman's, from the look on her face—the door opened. He got in.

"Thanks for unlocking the door for me, lady. Now, drive! Get me out of here."

The woman didn't move. "And where would you like to go?"

Art hit her in the face with the back of his left hand. "Just drive!" he shrieked.

She jerked the car forward, and the little boy watched them go.

"Turn left!"

Julia followed the command, glancing at her agitated passenger.

"We've got to go out of town another way," he muttered.

"There was no need to hit," Julia said, rubbing her cheek.

"Then do as I say, lady. I don't want to hurt nobody."

"Just slap, rob, and kidnap them? Is that it?" Julia could almost hear Edward's reprimand: "Don't antagonize the man, Julia! Just do what he says." Too bad she wasn't inclined to heed what was probably very good counsel.

"I do what I need to do," the young man muttered.

"Is that so?"

"That's so." They passed the school, and her passenger pointed left again. "Get back to the highway. We'll head south."

"You robbed the Pump 'n' Eat, didn't you? Chief knows about the robbery. The police have been called," Julia said.

"That's why I have to get out—"

Suddenly Julia's car sputtered. Jerked. Died.

"What in the world?" She pumped the accelerator.

"No!" he yelled. "Not you too?"

Julia steered the car to the curb as it rolled to a stop. She put it in park, then tapped her fingers on the gas gauge. "It says I'm out of gas. That can't be. I know I had at least half a—"

The boy raised his hands to his face, the gun waving dangerously. "I can't believe this. Two cars out of gas. Why can't I get out of this stupid town?"

Julia jerked to attention and stared at the boy sitting next to her. "Maybe…maybe you're not supposed to."

"Huh?"

She flipped a hand at him. "It's a long story, but I think you wandered into the wrong town, Mr. Robber. Haven is special in ways you could not imagine."

"Is that so?"

"That is definitely so," Julia said.

The thief looked around, obviously deciding his next move. His gaze lingered on the school. "Let's go."

"Go?" Julia looked pointedly at the gas gauge.

"Out!" he yelled in frustration.

She didn't move.

"Oh for—!" He shoved his car door open and ran to her side of the car. Jerking her door open, he grabbed her arm and pulled her out.

"Don't get rough with me, son," she said, yanking her arm from his hand. "If you want some help, I'll give it to you, but on one condition."

"*This* is my condition, lady," he said, pointing the gun at her stomach.

She moved the barrel to the side for the second time. She noticed that she stood a good four inches taller than this boy, yet his highly developed muscles easily made up for his small stature. Julia kept her tones calm and even. "That is *not* the condition, and I resent you resorting to such primitive measures. Put that thing away, and I'll help you."

"I don't need anybody's help," the boy said, but he lowered the gun to his side.

Julia sidestepped to her car and leaned against the hood. "Then I'll just wait right here, if you don't mind. You go do your thing and I'll stay here."

The thief stared at her, stunned. He shook his head incredulously, then looked across the street. Julia followed his gaze and saw a dog trotting toward them, wagging its tail. It sat at the boy's feet, peering up at him hopefully.

"You have a friend," Julia said.

He stomped his foot near the dog, sending it away. "Is everybody crazy? Don't you realize I'm a bad man? You're supposed to be scared of me."

Julia crossed her arms. "Oh, really?"

He grabbed her wrist and pulled her away from the car and across the street.

"Where are we going?" she asked, stumbling to keep up with him.

"Somewhere safe where I can think."

Art pitched the rock through the window, feeling a sense of satisfaction as the glass shattered. He scraped the ragged edges of the mullions, clearing the way for his hand. He flipped the clasp and raised the window.

"Ladies first," he told the elegant woman standing next to him.

"*Now* you get manners?" she said, making Art wonder for the millionth time why he couldn't have tried to steal a car from some scared little old lady instead of this calm, cool, totally-in-control woman with an attitude.

But that would have been too easy. And Art knew for a fact life was rarely easy. Without a word, he extended an arm to help her up.

"These are my favorite Liz Claiborne pants, and if I snag or tear them in any way, I'm holding you responsible."

"You can put it on my tab," Art said.

The woman reached through the window and brushed the broken glass off the sill onto the floor. She took Art's hand for balance and swung one leg over the ledge. She bent over, letting her head and shoulders clear beneath the raised window. She was in.

Art followed, then closed the window behind them.

"Now, that was brilliant," the woman remarked, pointing at the closed, glassless window.

"Habit," Art said, feeling the heat rush to his cheeks.

"So you're a good boy, are you? Always cleaning your plate at dinner? Never throwing your gum wrappers on the ground?"

"Don't make fun of me, lady."

"Don't call me lady," she replied. "My name is Julia." She

fixed him with a firm look. "And you are…?"

He clamped his mouth shut. No way he was giving her his name.

With a shrug, she wandered around the schoolroom. The bulletin boards were bare and the desks stacked in a far corner. "As for making fun of you, whyever not?" She picked up a piece of chalk. "I'm quite certain your mother didn't bring you up to be a thief." She began to write on the board in a flowing cursive.

"Hey!" Art said in alarm. "Don't go writing any notes trying to be rescued."

She stopped writing and looked at him. "Oh, please." She went back to her writing: *The quick brown fox jumped over the lazy poodle.* "There," she said, brushing off her hands. "My teachers always said I had the nicest handwriting in the fourth grade. What do you think?"

Art was in the doorway, looking up and down the hall. "I think you're in another zone, lady. You don't even know what's happening to you."

She pointed a finger at him. "That's where you're wrong, young man. Just because I'm not letting you dictate my emotions, doesn't mean I'm in another zone, as you call it. I merely refuse to let you ruin what has been a great day."

He motioned her into the hall, and she surprised him by following. "What's been so great about it?" he asked as they walked to the left, past rows of lockers. Cardboard signs crowned each room: English, Algebra, Biology. Art's thoughts ran rampant as he searched for the best place to hide.

Julia. Her name was Julia. An expensive-sounding name for an expensive-looking woman. He glanced at her. From the looks of her clothes and hair, and from the way she strolled along as though nothing was wrong, he'd be willing to bet she was someone important.

Great. Just great, Art ol' boy. You can't even kidnap right. You had to go and nab someone everyone will be looking for.…

206

She was talking away, using her hands to illustrate her words. "It really is an amazing story," she said as they passed the English room. "It all started a few days ago when I got this invitation from Louise Loy, the mayor of Haven. Actually, I didn't know her at the time, she just popped into my Book Bus and asked me—"

"Go in there," Art said, shoving her toward the library. "I'm beat. I need to sit someplace comfortable."

Julia headed toward the light switch. "Let's turn on some—"

"No!" Art said, blocking her way. "No lights. Do you want the entire town to know where we are?"

Julia put her hands on her hips. "Well, come to think of it—"

"No lights."

Julia looked around the library. "There's a couch. Why don't you lie down awhile? You must be tired after your...activities."

Art pointed at himself with the gun. "Hey, *I'm* the one in charge here, not you."

Julia raised her hands. "I was only trying to help."

Art bypassed the couch and sat on an upholstered chair nearby. "Sit," he commanded, pointing to another chair.

"Don't mind if I do," Julia said. She got comfortable in the chair. "Since we're spending the evening together, I think it would be appropriate if we told each other a little about ourselves."

"You've got to be kidding," Art said, setting the gun on his lap.

"Tell me a fake name—an alias—if you want." She flipped a hand in the air. "Though it really wouldn't matter. I am absolutely terrible with names. And if that wasn't a handicap in politics, I don't know what is."

Art's heart sank. He was right. She was important. "You're a politician."

"*Was* a politician."

"City dogcatcher? Weed controller?" he asked, snickering.

"Actually, I was the governor of Minnesota." She held out her hand for him to shake. "Julia Carson."

Feeling stupid but doing it anyway, Art shook her hand, keeping his other hand on the gun.

"And you are?" she asked again.

He should tell her a lie, give her some bogus name, but his mind—usually so quick with a lie—couldn't think of one. "Art Graham," he said.

She nodded. "I assume Art stands for Arthur?"

"Nobody calls me that 'cept my grandmother."

"Grandmothers do that," Julia said. "And I happen to agree with yours. I find all nicknames and shortened versions of names cheapen the grand intentions of our parents. If we are so lazy that we can't utter an extra syllable or two as a sign of respect, then I think we should clamp our hands over our mouths and utter nothing."

"What?" Art asked, confused.

She shook her head. "I like the name Arthur. That's what I'll call you."

He moved the gun back and forth. "You won't call me nothing, lady."

"Julia. Please call me Julia."

"Ohhhh." Art leaned his head back, completely exasperated. She was unbelievable. "Are you always like this?"

She cocked her head. "Like what?"

"So…pushy."

She held up a finger. "I am not pushy, Arthur. I am merely assertive. Just as you are assertive doing your thief business, although I do think there is a better way to implement your assertiveness than to resort to such a cowardly—"

"I am not a coward!"

"Oh, I believe you," Julia said, fingering the pages of a May issue of *Newsweek* on the table that sat between them. "*You* are not a coward, but you did a cowardly thing."

He snorted. She didn't know what she was talking about.

"Look, lady—Julia—it takes guts to rob a gas station."

"No, it doesn't," Julia refuted, leaning toward him. "I assume you did it because you needed the money. I mean, you're not one of those truly evil people who rob just to rob, are you?"

"No...I mean, of course I needed the money."

"I thought so," Julia said, leaning back in her chair. "You seem like a good boy. I can see it in your eyes."

"I am not a coward."

"We've been through this, Arthur," she said. "You are not a coward, but stealing is a cowardly act. It takes far more courage to admit you need help. To get a job. To earn your money the honorable way."

He wanted to hit her. To shut her up. Instead, he crossed his arms as though they could give him protection from her words. "I've had a job. It didn't last."

"And whose fault was that?"

Art picked up a *National Geographic*. "The boss was a creep. I was late a few times and he got bent out of shape and fired me. I didn't want that lousy old job any—"

"You blew it."

"*I* blew it?" He stared at her, the anger building inside him. "I didn't do *nothing* 'cept be late. A few stinking minutes."

"How many times?"

He felt the heat in his face again. He hated that. "What does that matter?"

"How many times?"

He looked away. "Six. Maybe seven."

"I would've fired you on number two."

"Two?" He faced her, narrowing his eyes. "You'd fire me for being late two times?"

"You follow the rules or you lose."

"That's not fair."

"Ah," Julia said. "There you have one of the basic rules of life. One it's best to learn early."

"What?"

"Life is not fair. No one ever said it was or was supposed to be."

"But that's not—"

She pointed a finger at him, smiling.

He couldn't help it, he had to smile back. "You got me."

"I got you." She licked her finger and made a mark in the air. "That's one for Julia."

Art slumped in the chair until his head found support. He tucked the gun between the cushion and armrest and closed his eyes. "Actually, my dad used to say that same thing. All the time. Used to drive me crazy."

"Sounds like your father knew a lot."

"Ha."

"Why, 'ha'?"

"He knew a lot all right," Art said. "He knew how to send me and my little sister flying across the room with one swing of his arm. Backhand too."

Julia rubbed her cheek. "So that's where you learned it."

"From a master," Art said. He opened one eye and met her gaze. "Sorry about that." And he was surprised to find that he really was. He wished he hadn't hit her.

She nodded.

Art closed his eyes again, sighing. He was so tired…. "My mom was all right. She tried hard. But Dad was a firecracker. You never knew when he was going to go off."

"He still around?"

Art shrugged. "Who knows? Who wants to know?"

"You, maybe?"

Art opened his eyes and stared at the ceiling. The fresh moonlight cast odd shadows across it. He remembered watching similar shadows when he was a kid, thinking they were monsters. But the real monsters in life didn't dance on the ceiling…. "I got a letter from Mom once. Dad was still hanging around back then. But I've never been back to do my own

210

checking. Once I was out, I didn't see no reason to run back to it. I'm not dumb."

"Where's your sister?"

"Maggie's around. We keep in touch. But she's got her own problems. Married twice, maybe three times by now. A few kids. Cute kids."

"Do you have a girlfriend?" Julia asked.

"Did have. Maybe still have." He shrugged, feeling more tired than ever. If he could just get some sleep—

"What's her name?"

He fixed her with a glare. "You're big into names aren't you?"

"It's better than 'hey you.'"

"Her name's Anie."

"Annie?"

"No, A-nie. Short for Adrianne."

"Now there's a graceful name. Adrianne."

Art turned his head, thinking. "Adrianne. That is pretty."

"Is she pretty?"

He smiled. Oh, yes. Anie was pretty. Beautiful. "She has brown eyes as sweet as a vat of chocolate. And when she smiles, I forget everything. I forget how life isn't fair."

"So why aren't you with her now?"

"She kicked me out."

"She got wise to you, did she?"

Art flinched. He wanted to pounce on her words. Maybe yesterday he would have. Maybe five minutes ago he would have. But now…well, he just didn't. "She got wise to me," he agreed.

"Then you need to get wise."

Art swung a hand around the room. "Book learning. Is that what you're pushing?"

"Wisdom comes from many corners."

"My dad always said books were for sissies."

"And you're no sissy."

211

"I'm no sissy."

Julia put her hands on the armrests. "Can I prove you wrong, Arthur?"

He shook his head, stifling the sarcastic laughter bubbling in his throat. "Oh no, the do-gooder's going to save the poor sinner."

"That's not up to me. All I want to do is read to you. You can lie on the couch, and I'll read to you."

Lie on the couch. It sounded so inviting.... "Read from what?"

Julia got out of her chair. "Give me a minute. I'll find something you'll like."

Art put a hand on the gun, reminding her who was in charge. "Don't go trying nothing."

"Don't be silly," she said, moving into the racks. "I wish you'd let me turn on the lights, the moonlight is so limiting."

"No way."

She moved into the fiction stacks. She hummed a tune that sounded oddly familiar. Art concentrated on it, thinking...he was sure he knew it....

The tune conjured up images of cowboy hats and jeans, girls in checkered dresses. Barnyards with fence posts to lean against, and trees painted on backdrops.

"Hey, I know that song," he called out, pleased with himself. "'Surrey with the Fringe on Top,' right?" He sang the next line.

"Bravo, Arthur," Julia said, applauding. She appeared from the stacks. "Your fine voice indicates you'd make the perfect Curly, but your current hairstyle speaks otherwise."

Art ran a hand across his shaved head. "It wasn't always cut this short."

"What a comfort." She started singing the second verse and he joined in. When they were done, she curtsied to him, and he bowed in the moonlight. "That was great," Julia said. "Where did you learn that song?"

He plopped on the couch. "I was in the chorus of *Oklahoma!* in high school."

Julia sat in a chair. "I love that show. I always wanted to play the lead, but my voice tends to croak when it's supposed to croon."

"It's not that bad."

"For a frog."

He saw the book in her hand. "So what are you going to read to me?"

"*A Tale of Two Cities.*"

"Sounds boring."

"Shows how much you know, Mr. Arthur Graham."

"Sounds old too. Isn't that book ancient?"

"If ancient is 130-some years, I suppose you're right."

Art retrieved the gun from the chair and stuck it next to him as he stretched out on the couch. He sighed. The adrenaline rush he always got from a robbery was long gone, the crash stronger than the rush. He raised an arm above his head, resting the back of his hand on his forehead.

Julia opened to the first page and held the book in the moonlight. "'It was the best of times, it was the worst of times, it was the age of wisdom, it was the age of foolishness, it was the epoch of belief, it was the epoch of incredulity, it was the season of Light, it was the season of Darkness, it was the spring of hope, it was the winter of despair, we had everything before us, we had nothing before us, we were all going direct to Heaven, we were all going direct the other way—'"

"That was written 130 years ago?" Art asked.

"Amazing isn't it?"

"It sounds like today."

"You are wise beyond your years, Mr. Graham."

He nodded, pleased at the compliment. "Go on," he said. "Read me some more."

She did.

Eighteen

Whether you turn to the right or to the left, your ears will hear a voice behind you, saying, "This is the way; walk in it."
ISAIAH 30:21

AFTER THEIR TALK behind the church, John drove Del back to the motel. Del was still not convinced he had a purpose in Haven, and his lack of conviction showed in his lack of energy. When he got out of John's truck, his legs floundered under his own weight.

"You going to be all right, Del?" John asked.

Del's nod was a lie.

"Why don't you get some sleep?" John advised. "But take your rest knowing that you are supposed to be here. Even if you can't fathom the reason behind your presence, you can believe God's got everything under control."

Del met John's eyes and took strength from the compassion he saw there. He managed a smile. "I'll be all right. See you in the morning."

John nodded and drove away. Del turned toward his room but jerked to a halt when the door to Walter's room flew open. Walter burst out, slammed the door behind him, and rushed to his van.

Del blinked, trying to focus his thoughts on the moment. "Where are you going in such a hurry?"

"I've got business." Walter got in the van and started the engine.

Del moved toward the van. "You're not going after the robber, are you?"

"None of your—"

"Chief told John the best thing we could do is to stay out of the way."

"He meant amateurs like you, Del. Not professionals like me."

Del put a hand on the door. "He meant everybody."

Walter pushed Del's hand away. "Why can't people leave me alone? Gabe...and now—I don't need a homeless bum telling me my business. Especially not a homeless bum who killed a woman. Especially not a homeless bum wearing a shabby T-shirt and—"

Del took a step back.

Walter shoved the transmission into reverse. "I'm one of the chosen ones, *Mister* Delatondo. You are just a stowaway—in every sense of the word. So don't you dare tell me what to do."

As the van backed out of the parking lot and drove away, Del stood frozen in place, Walter's words falling like weights on his heart, loading it down, smothering it. *He's right. I am a stowaway. In Walter's van. In life. I'm an intruder. An extraneous being who is of no use to any—*

"Hey, Del." The voice came from behind him. He turned slowly, as though the weight of his realization had pinned him down.

Natalie was getting out of her car. She made a face. "What are you doing standing out in the parking lot?"

Del didn't respond. He wasn't sure he could. He could barely breathe.

"You okay?" Natalie asked, coming to stand beside him.

He tried to nod.

"You going to your room?" she asked softly, nodding toward his hand.

He looked down, surprised to find he was holding a key. He frowned. What was the key for?

When Natalie spoke again, her tone was gentle. "Del, why don't you come with me to the church? Fran asked me to meet her there, and we'd love to have your company."

Del found a wayward breath, drew it deep into his lungs, and shook his head. He looked at the key. He wasn't going anywhere until he remembered what the key was for. And yet, when Natalie opened the door to her car, he couldn't help himself. He staggered in and let her take him away.

~~~~~

Walter slammed his car door with a snort.

What a waste of time that was! He'd rushed to the scene only to have Chief turn him away with, "Go back to the motel, Walter. Leave the police work to the police. The news will be there in the morning. The whole news, not just the news you conjure up to make a deadline."

Shaking his head, Walter went to knock on Julia's door to say good-night. No answer. He looked around, curious. Maybe she was taking a walk....

That's when he noticed her car was gone.

Probably still with the mayor, he thought. He turned back to his room and looked past it to Del's room on the end. He remembered their last conversation and felt a stitch in his stomach. *I was awfully hard on him. It wasn't his fault Gabe was hard on me, but I treated him like it was. I probably should apologize.* He hesitated long enough for his conscience to be overruled. *Nah, I'll do it tomorrow.*

He went into his room and emptied his pockets on the dresser. There was a knock on the door.

Good! It's Del come to apologize for butting into my business.

He flung open the door, ready to make amends with Del. He was surprised to see Kathy and her kids.

"Hi, Walter." The kids peered beyond him into the foreign territory of his room. Kathy shifted from foot to foot. "I've come to ask a favor." She avoided his eyes, then suddenly burst out talking all at once. "I want to take a bath, and if I were at home I would think nothing of leaving the kids on their own, but since we're in a strange place...I tried Natalie's room and Julia's, but they're gone. Del too. You're the only one who's here, and I was hoping...it would just be for a half hour. They'd be no trouble. You could watch TV together." She finally

216

met his eyes. "Would that be all right?"

Walter looked at his watch and glanced back at the solitude of his room. "Actually, Gabe gave me an assignment to watch some TV tonight and I—"

Kathy ushered the kids into the room. "That's fine. Don't change your schedule for us. Like I said, I'll be back before you know it." She kissed both children on the head and told them to be good for Mr. Prescott. Then she left.

Walter stared down at the kids. The kids stared up at him.

"Your mother's very good at fast talking," he told them.

Ryan shrugged and climbed onto the ottoman. "That's 'cause she's a mom."

Walter wasn't sure about the correlation but accepted Ryan's expertise. He checked his watch a second time. The sitcoms started in a minute. He pointed at Lisa. "Why don't you get up there with your brother? Like I told your mom, I have to watch some shows for Gabe. So you two be quiet and behave yourselves. Got it?"

Ryan helped Lisa negotiate the ottoman. They sat side by side and nodded seriously. Lisa hugged her Bunny Bob and sucked her thumb; Ryan put his arm around her protectively.

Gee, that wasn't so hard. And Bette says I'm not good with kids.

Walter rearranged the pillows on the bed, making himself a backrest. He took control of the remote and flicked on the television. The opening music for a sitcom filled the room. The main characters came on the screen, their words volleying back and forth over a laugh track. After a few minutes, Walter felt the bed move. He turned his head to the left, and the kids stopped their climb aboard as if his eyes had the capacity to vaporize them. They waited, watching him carefully.

Walter gave a great sigh of concession. "Oh, all right. Come on up."

The kids scrambled across the bed. Ryan tucked next to Walter's right side, and Lisa cuddled up on his left. He raised his eyebrows. "Sure thing. Make yourselves at home." He pointed a finger at each of them. "But be quiet. Understand?"

They nodded, and Lisa put a finger to Bunny Bob's mouth, indicating that he, too, would be as quiet as a stuffed rabbit could be.

They watched the show. They laughed. Walter was feeling quite domestic and was just thinking how Gabe had overreacted to sitcoms not being family fare when it happened.

The characters started talking about their sex lives. In great detail—or at least more detail than a four- and two-year-old should hear.

Walter fidgeted and tried to think of something to say to drown out the television dialogue. "Hey…um…what's your bunny's name?"

Ryan wouldn't be distracted. "What's sex, Mr. Prescott?"

"What 'ex?" Lisa mimicked.

"It…uh…uh…what did you say your bunny's name was?"

"Bob," Ryan said. "What's sex, Mr. Prescott?"

"Sex?"

Ryan pointed to the TV. "They're talking about it on TV. I want to know."

Walter fumbled for the remote and shut the TV off. "There," he said, as though that would end the conversation. "They're not talking anymore. And neither are we." His eyes darted across the room. He spotted a pad of paper and a pen on the bedside table. "Hey, who wants to play tic-tac-toe?"

"I get the Os!" Ryan said.

Walter and Ryan played seventeen games, and Lisa scribbled four pictures before Kathy knocked on the door. Walter had never been so glad to see anyone in his life.

"Were they good?" Kathy asked as the kids ran to her, waving their papers. "Did you get to watch your program?"

"Part of it," Walter said.

"They talked about sex, Mom," Ryan said. He turned to Walter. "Hey, you never answered my question."

Walter shooed them toward the door. "They're all yours, Kathy."

She nodded with apparent understanding. As the kids ran down the walkway toward their room, she turned back to Walter. "You work in television, Walter. Can't you do something about the programming? I really wish there were more shows we could watch with our families."

"I work with the news. Not programming."

"Can't you do both?"

"It's not my job," he answered, wondering if it would be rude to shut the door in Kathy's face.

"Then whose job is it?" It was Kathy who pulled the door closed between them.

Just then, Walter's phone rang. It was Gabe.

"Well? What do you think of the sitcoms now, Walter? Are they still not so bad?"

"I don't want to talk about it," he said, sinking onto the bed.

"Don't hide from it, Walter. The Honor Roll helps promote the good shows that are already on the air, but what we really need is change at the top. We need the people who buy the programming to realize their audience won't take it anymore. We need to hit them in their pocketbooks. Get to the advertisers and they'll get the programmers' attention. Then, and only then, will the people who supply the shows change the content."

"Dream on," Walter said.

"It can happen."

"It's gone too far. The dike is broken. The dirty water is rushing in."

"So we start repairing the dike."

"How?"

"We give our support to the good shows. We patronize the advertisers who support those shows. And we give financial support at a higher level."

"A higher level?"

"We help produce the good shows."

"Who knows anything about producing television shows?"

"Somebody does. We need to find them and help them do their job. Or you could produce your own."

"What happened to *we*? Why did this suddenly evolve into *me*?"

"You're a smart man, Walter. You know the TV industry."

"I know about the news. I don't know a thing about creating an entertainment program."

"'Just as each of us has one body with many members, and these members do not all have the same function, so in Christ we who are many form one body, and each member belongs to all the others. We have different gifts, according to the grace given us.'"

"You're doing it again."

"I won't apologize for quoting the Bible," Gabe said. "It's the best guidebook there is."

"Will it guide me out of this conversation?"

"I'm a very patient man, Walter."

Walter sighed. "I was afraid of that."

Walter hung up the phone, then stretched out on the bed. His muscles molded themselves to the mattress, their fatigue immediate now that they'd been given the chance to rest. He grabbed the remote and flipped on the television, then tossed the remote on the bed. He didn't care what he watched. He just wanted noise. Company.

He let his mind drift as commercials for laundry detergent and cars droned by. The music blended with the words, wrapping him in a cocoon of mundane mediocrity. He closed his eyes, just for a minute…

He snapped awake as the TV blared. He grimaced as words shouted through the room: "Our investigation has uncovered that Senator Pipkin had an affair when he was twenty-two. The senator, who was the instigator of the much heralded child-protection bill, refused to comment. However, we have an exclusive interview with the woman from his past. She is currently unemployed, and there is speculation that her oldest child might have been fathered by—"

Walter fumbled for the remote and pushed the mute button.

Silence.

He turned onto his side, closing his eyes. *Annoying bunch of drivel.*

The TV broke through the quiet. "Stay tuned as a newlywed loses more than his shirt during a night out with the guys."

Walter groaned, groping for the remote. "I put you on mute. Don't you know how to—"

"And watch tomorrow as an unfaithful husband gets what's coming to him when his lover turns homicidal."

The unrelenting words forced Walter completely awake. "What's wrong with this thing? Doesn't it know when to be quiet?" He punched mute again. Nothing happened.

He pressed the power button. The TV stayed on. He pushed it again. And again.

Still on.

"What's going on?"

The television flipped through the channels of its own accord.

"A disgruntled man murdered—"

"…embezzled 2 million—"

"Condom distribution—"

"A bus blew up today in—"

"Angry protesters—"

"Enough!" Walter said. He pointed the remote at the TV, pressing all the buttons. It was out of his control.

"There was a bombing raid today, killing—"

"Tomorrow, watch men who love women who love women."

"—brought a gun to school and started—"

Walter tumbled off the bed and scrambled for the TV's electrical cord. He yanked it from its socket.

"Looting began when two opposing factions—"

"...man accused of beating his four-month-old—"

Walter put his hands to his ears, squeezing his eyes shut. "I don't want to hear any more!"

Sudden silence filled the room. Walter opened his eyes. The television screen was black. The only sound he could hear was his own ragged breathing.

The phone rang. Walter lunged for it, hoping whoever was at the other end could explain what had happened.

"Hi, hon. What're you doing?" Bette asked.

"Bette! You'd never believe…"

"Walter? You sound scared."

"I am…my TV blasted at full volume, then it—"

"Turn it down."

"I *tried*. It didn't help. Then it changed channels on its own. I wasn't touching a thing." Walter picked up the remote and tossed it to the other side of the room where it bounced off the dresser.

"There must be a malfunction."

"I unplugged it, Bette. I unplugged the TV and it stayed on."

"That's not possible."

"Tell that to the television. Maybe I'm going crazy. Nicotine withdrawal. Haven-itis or something."

"Maybe there was a power surge," she said.

God invited you here. You are his chosen ones.

"Walter," Bette said insistently. "Maybe there was a power—"

God, the almighty, the all powerful…

"That's *it.*" Walter leaned back on his pillow, laughing with relief. "It *was* a power surge."

"Now you're laughing?"

"It's okay. Forget everything I said."

"You act half-crazy and I'm supposed to forget about it?"

"I'm in Haven, Bette. That explains everything. I'm in Haven."

"You're not sounding well, Walter. Maybe you *should* watch a little TV. Wind down. Relax."

"There's nothing decent on TV, Bette. Don't you know that?"

"That's my line, Walter."

"So I'm agreeing with you."

"Did that power surge take a detour through your brain?"

Walter laughed.

"I'm glad you think it's funny, Walter. As for me, I'm confused, and I don't have time to—oh, never mind. I have a six-year-old to entertain. I've got to go."

"Where'd you get a six-year-old?"

"Jon-Jon. The neighbor's boy. I'm watching him while they go to a movie."

"He driving you crazy yet?"

"No, Walter. Believe it or not, it is possible to be in the same room with a child and not go crazy."

"Really?"

"I don't feel up to your ego tonight, Walter. I called to tell you good night. I don't need to be teased and confronted with your prejudices—"

"Whoa, hon. I'm just speaking my opinion. I'm a bachelor who's never been around kids." *Until tonight. And it wasn't so bad. Not really.*

Silence greeted this, then, "We could change that."

"You know I'm not the family-man type."

"Only because you won't let yourself be."

She was right. Having a family meant having someone depend on him, but Walter didn't want to be responsible for anyone else. He had enough trouble taking care of himself.

"You still there, Walter?"

"Yeah."

"Love isn't a fixed commodity. There isn't a bottom to the barrel. It doesn't run out."

"Kind of like fruitcake at Christmas, huh?"

"Fruit—? Love's better than that. The more you give, the more you get."

"That's exactly like fruitcake at Christmas."

"You're impossible."

"It's a gift."

There was silence on the line.

"I thought you were trying to be open, Walter. Open about us."

"I've got a lot on my mind, Bette."

"So do I, Walter." She sighed. "I'm tired."

"I told you six-year-olds were a pain."

"I'm not tired because of a six-year-old," Bette said, her voice heavy. "I'm tired because of a forty-six-year-old."

"Me? What did *I* do?"

"Good night, Walter."

She hung up. Walter replaced the receiver. The room was quiet. And empty. "Don't lose her," he told himself.

He looked at the black screen of the television. He suddenly wished it were on so he could drown himself in violence, hate, and apathy.

Anything was better than the truth.

❧

Natalie and Del pulled into the church parking lot. Natalie got out, but Del stayed where he was, looking like an empty shell.

What in the world happened to him? Natalie wondered for the umpteenth time since she'd spotted him standing in the parking lot. "Del?" She reached out to touch his arm. "We're here."

He pulled out of his daze. "Here?"

"At the church."

He nodded and got out of the car, following her up the steps. When they entered the church, they heard an organ playing. They followed the music into the sanctuary.

"That's Fran!" Natalie said. She took a seat in the back pew, waiting until Fran finished.

The song ended and Natalie applauded. Del managed one clap to her two.

Fran stood at the organ. "I didn't know I had a human audience."

"As opposed to alien?" Natalie said.

Fran laughed. "As opposed to heavenly."

"You're very good," Natalie said. "I didn't know you had so many talents, Fran."

"A church is made up of many members with many gifts." Fran motioned them toward the front. "Come sit, you two."

Del shook his head. "I don't belong here."

Natalie moved next to Fran and whispered, "He's been acting depressed. I found him standing in the parking lot of the motel. Just standing there."

Fran nodded, then went to Del's side and took his arm. "Don't listen to Walter, Del. 'Truthful lips endure forever, but a lying tongue lasts only a moment.'"

Del looked up, his face showing the fresh light of hope. "He was lying?"

"You are welcome here, Del."

"How do I know for sure?"

"You will know." Fran walked back to Natalie.

Del hurried after her. "But how will I know?"

Fran touched his arm. "Be patient. All good things happen in God's time."

Del studied Fran's face. He nodded and took a seat next to Natalie. They looked to Fran expectantly, and she moved behind the pulpit to retrieve a brass offering plate.

Del shook his head. "I don't have any money, Fran. I'm sorry I can't give—"

Fran held up a hand, halting his words. "What do you see here?"

"An offering plate," Del said.

"A brass dish," Natalie added.

"Come on, Miss Writer, you can do better than that. Use

your imagination. What do you see?"

Natalie took the plate in her hands, weighing its bulk, feeling the smoothness of its sides. She ran a finger across the fluted ridge that ran the perimeter of the upper lip. She turned it over, plunking a finger against the bottom.

"It's the captain's plate from a Spanish galleon. He eats on it every night, sopping up his stew with a hunk of bread he places on the ledge. This ding in the side is where his galley slave dropped it one night, making the soup spill onto the captain and the dish fall against the edge of the captain's bench. The hapless slave earned thirty lashes for his lack of grace."

Del gawked at her; Fran beamed.

"Well," Natalie said, noticing Del's disbelief. "It could be true."

Fran nodded and put her hand in her skirt pocket. She pulled out a handful of coins, which she dropped onto the plate, making them clatter.

"Now what is it?"

"It's an offering plate," Del said.

Natalie agreed.

Fran dumped the money onto the pew and took the plate behind the organ. When she returned, the dish was full of Oreos.

"You eat Oreos while you play the organ?" Natalie asked.

Fran smiled. "They are a large part of my inspiration." She held out the dish. "What is it now?"

"It's a food dish."

Fran dumped the cookies in Natalie's lap, then rushed to the narthex.

"What is she doing?" Natalie whispered.

"Proving a point," Fran responded, returning to the front. This time she had an African violet sitting in the middle of the dish. "Now what is it?"

"A plant holder," Natalie said.

Fran jerked the plant out of the dish, turned the dish

upside down on the step and set the plant on top. She held out her hands.

"A plant *stand*," Del offered.

Fran removed the plant and flung the plate toward Del like a flying saucer. He jumped up and caught it, then grinned at the two women. "A Frisbee," he said.

Natalie held up her hands. "Okay, we get your point. The brass dish can be many things. So what?"

Fran took the dish from Del and held it in front of them. "As long as the dish is empty, its potential is great. It can be a pirate's platter, an offering plate, a food dish, a plant stand, even a Frisbee. But once it's filled, its purpose is limited. When it's filled with food, we'd never consider using it for money. And when the violet sat inside, you'd never think of using it as a Frisbee."

"Not unless you want a mess."

Fran held the plate to her chest. "I see before me two vessels, ready to fill."

Del perked up. "John called me that. He called me a vessel."

"John is right."

"But what's with the empty business?" Natalie asked. "I'm not empty. I don't *feel* empty."

Fran knelt in front of them and put her hand on Natalie's knee. "You have to be empty of your own purposes and goals. Your own will. Then, and only then, are you an empty vessel that God can fill in whatever way he wants, in whatever way suits his plan."

Natalie wasn't sure she liked what she was hearing. She crossed her arms. "So what I want doesn't matter? If I want to be famous, that doesn't matter? What if I want loads of people to read my stories?"

Fran popped to her feet. "That's fine! That's great. You've discovered a talent God has given you. It would be a sin to let it lie fallow and wasted. He wants you to use it."

Natalie shook her head. *What* was Fran talking about? "But

you just said our will and goals don't matter."

Fran tented her fingers under her lips, nodding. Thinking. "'In his heart a man plans his course, but the LORD determines his steps.'"

Del sprang to his feet. "I get it! I get it!" He turned to Natalie. "You are a vessel of writing. You have to open yourself up and say, 'Here I am, God. Use me. Use my gift however you want. I trust you.'"

Fran put a hand at the back of Del's neck and pulled his head close until their foreheads touched. "Exactly!" she whispered.

Natalie drew her knees to her chin, staring at the carpet in front of her.

Del started to say something, but Fran raised a finger, silencing him.

Natalie looked up. "So I'm supposed to stop sending my novels off to publishers?"

Fran moved between Natalie and Del. "No, no. That's not what he wants—not necessarily."

"Not necessarily?"

"The key is prayer."

Natalie threw her hands in the air. "That leaves *me* out. You might say God and I have never been properly introduced."

Fran sat beside her. "Just because you haven't prayed in the past doesn't mean you can't pray now."

Natalie shook her head, feeling miserable and discouraged. "But I don't know how."

"Sure you do. All you have to do is talk. At least that's how I do it. You just talk," Fran said. "Tell you what. I'll get you started." Fran held her arm out to Del. "Come join us."

He shook his head, standing alone by the pews.

"Why not?"

"You've got your music, Natalie's got her stories. I don't have any talent. My vessel will stay empty."

Fran rose and went to Del's side. "Everyone has a talent,

many talents, gifts from God. Yours are not the same as Natalie's, but that doesn't make them less important to God and his work."

"But her gifts will reach people. Lots of people. I gave it all up because I didn't deserve...How can I do anything to help others when my own life is such a mess?"

Fran put a hand on his shoulder. "'Does not the potter have the right to make out of the same lump of clay some pottery for noble purposes and some for common use?'"

Del deflated. "I must be the common-use kind."

"Let God worry about that," Fran said. "Open yourself to him and stand back. You might be surprised. God said, 'I am going to do something in your days that you would not believe, even if you were told.'" Del shrugged. Fran took his hand, and he reached out to take Natalie's. Fran went on, "There is no need for fancy words when you talk to God. You say what's in your heart."

Natalie shook her head, unable to do it.

Fran squeezed her hand. "Dear Lord," she began, and Natalie closed her eyes. She was pretty sure that was what she was supposed to do. She focused on Fran's words: "We want to help. We want to open our lives to you. Use us and use our talents to do your will. We also ask for the courage to stay out of the way while you do your stuff...."

Natalie opened one eye. "Your stuff?"

Fran smiled. "Your stuff. Amen."

"That wasn't so hard," Natalie said. "Even I could've handled that."

"You might even have thought of a better phrase than 'your stuff,'" Fran said.

"But how do I get inspiration?" Del asked, and Natalie nodded. She'd been wondering that herself.

"You've taken the first step. You've emptied yourself of your own ideas and opened yourself to God's."

"That's it?"

"The proper frame of mind and heart is the conduit for divine inspiration."

"So now what do I do?" Natalie said. "Just sit at my desk and wait?"

"You write. You might even pray. Open yourself to God's possibilities."

Natalie wanted to believe it was that simple. She really did. "But what if nothing happens?"

"It will," Fran said. "If not tonight, then tomorrow or the next day. God does not work on our time schedule, but he does work. And he does appreciate our work." She smiled. "Speaking of our talents and appreciating them, how about going across the street to the café for some apple pie?"

Del grinned, then blushed. "This empty vessel is always ready to be filled with pie." Natalie took his arm as they headed for the door. Del looked as though he was feeling better. She was glad. Leave it to Fran to know what to do—and how to wrap up the lesson. Her mouth started to water. Apple pie. Now *that* was divine inspiration.

The three sat in a corner booth, eating pie. Natalie picked at her crust.

"Something on your mind, Nat?" Fran asked.

Natalie took a deep breath. "Why is Walter so difficult?"

Del spoke up. "He's not—"

"Yes, he is," Natalie said. "One minute he's nice, then he's saying something totally jerky." She looked at Fran. "If he's really been called here by…well, you know, God, why doesn't he change?"

Fran shrugged. "Being called doesn't mean being perfect, Nat. We all wrestle between what we should be and what we always have been."

Natalie sighed. "I just don't see how God could have called someone so…unlikable."

"God calls all kinds of people," Del said.

Fran nodded. "God chooses the weak, the lowly, and the despised. That way no one can boast about his own goodness. It's Jesus, not we ourselves, who gives us righteousness and redemption. So being unlikable doesn't mean we aren't saved."

Del looked at her. "*Is* Walter saved?"

"That's between him and his Savior. But Walter is changing. It just isn't happening as quickly as some of us would like. Not for Walter—"

"Or for the rest of us," Del finished for her.

Natalie nodded. "So we all have our faults—" she speared her pie with a flourish and grinned—"Walter's just happen to be very obvious. Well, all I can say is God save us from grumpy men."

"And from ourselves," Del murmured.

Fran gave him an understanding smile. "Amen to that."

Nineteen

Submit to God and be at peace with him;
in this way prosperity will come to you.
Accept instruction from his mouth and lay his words in your heart.
JOB 22:21

JULIA WATCHED ART GRAHAM SLEEP. She was on chapter 4 of *A Tale of Two Cities* and her voice was giving out. Odd how she could give speeches for endless amounts of time, but reading aloud made her hoarse.

She glanced at the clock hanging over the library's checkout desk. 10:25. Most likely the other guests of Haven were safely tucked in their beds—their custom-decorated, personalized, cozy beds....

The trouble with being an independent spirit was people wouldn't worry if she wasn't at the motel. They'd just figure she was where she wanted to be. Surely Julia Carson wasn't being held hostage in a school just a hop, skip, and a jump away from the safety of her motel room.

Surely she was.

Leave, Julia! Leave! her inner voice prodded.

She shook her head. She couldn't. For some odd reason she felt she was needed here, with this boy, in this school. She sensed an element of danger—there *was* the gun to consider—but somehow, it didn't matter. Somehow, she knew everything would work out all right.

She closed her eyes. "Be with me, God. Show me what to do."

"Oh, that's ripe," Art said, lifting up on his elbows. "Now she's calling her God down on me." He swung his legs to the floor and ran a finger along the scar that bisected his cheek. He pulled the gun from the cushions and set it beside him.

"He's your God too, Arthur."

"Only on every third Thursday, during leap years," he said with a snicker. "And only if we're both really desperate."

Julia set the book aside and crossed her legs. "So you're a foul-weather believer, are you?"

Art slid the back of his hand under his nose. "I suppose you're going to explain that statement whether I want you to or not."

"Absolutely." Julia cleared her throat dramatically, then recited, "A foul-weather believer is someone who uses God when things are going rough but forgets about him when life's running okay." She looked to the ceiling for inspiration. "Kind of like an umbrella."

"God's an umbrella?"

Julia considered this. "Yes," she finally said. "But he can also be a parasol, to be used in sunny times."

"Lady, you live in another world."

She fixed him with a look. "Obviously, a better one than yours."

Art jerked his head. "Who says?"

"Oh, please." Julia stood and smoothed the lines of her pants. "You can't think that robbing gas stations and taking an older—albeit extremely fascinating—woman hostage is the scenario for a wonderful world."

Art picked up a magazine and started flipping pages. "It's the only world I've got. I don't have a choice."

"Bull manure."

"What?"

"You heard me. I said bull manure."

Art burst out laughing. "The lady can't even cuss."

"There you have it wrong, dear boy. This lady can cuss with the best of them. She has even proved it a few times, producing gaggles of gawking mouths. However, most of the time, this *lady* chooses to use other, less offensive epithets to symbolize her disdain."

He applauded. "Nice speech, Governor."

She curtsied. "I do my best."

"So do I." Art tossed the magazine on the table. It skidded across the top and ruffled to the floor.

"I don't believe that, Arthur."

He threw his hands in the air. "Why doesn't anyone ever believe me when I say that?"

"Perhaps because you lie?"

"As if I'm the only one."

"It only takes one."

"My lying—or not lying—does not change the world one stinkin' bit."

"Ah," Julia said, walking behind the chair. "The boy needs to see *It's a Wonderful Life.*"

"The *boy* has *seen It's a Wonderful Life,*" Art retorted. "So what?"

"So tell me the point of the movie."

Art shrugged. "Some angel guy saves Jimmy Stewart from drowning."

Julia squawked like a game show buzzer. "Wrong! Try again."

Art wrinkled his forehead. "The man goes back in time but everything's different, his wife is a librarian, the town is sleazy…" Art's eyes lit up as he remembered details. "And the old guy from the pharmacy is a bum."

"You are nearing the crossroads, Arthur. Very close."

"I'm right. Everything I said was right."

"Yes, it was," Julia said. "But you haven't stated the movie's point. Why it happened."

"So Jimmy Stewart wouldn't kill himself."

"And why didn't he kill himself?"

"Because…"

"He went into the past and saw what things were like when…"

Art clapped his hands together. "When he wasn't there! He

234

saw all the ways his life had touched other people."

Julia clanged the bell on the librarian's desk. "We have a winner."

Art blushed at her praise, then he laughed. "I forgot the question that started all this."

Julia walked toward him, holding out a finger. "You said your lying doesn't change the world—"

"One stinkin' bit," he repeated.

Julia sat in her chair, leaning toward him. "But it does change things. Every person we touch with words or deeds is affected, either for good or for bad."

Art seemed to study the air. His forehead tightened. Then he sprang from his chair, forcing Julia to lean back. "We've got to go. I've changed my mind. We can't stay here."

"Why not?" Julia asked.

Art began to pace, swinging the gun at his side. "Because of what you said. Because what I've done affects people. I robbed the gas station. Bob, the guy I made lie down on the floor, he'll be mad. The police will be mad. They'll have found my car. They'll find *your* car. They'll put two and two—" He broke off, running the barrel of the pistol across his scar. "I can't change it. It's done. I have to move forward."

"Forward in a positive manner, Arthur. That doesn't mean you have to move out of the school."

"*I* don't have to?" Art started to laugh. "It's not just me anymore, Governor. It's *us*. We're in this together."

Julia leaned back in her chair, claiming her spot by setting her arms on the armrests. "I'm not going anywhere."

"Since when are you in charge?"

"Since I'm your elder."

"Bad choice of words, Governor." He grabbed her arm and yanked her to her feet. "It just so happens my elders treated me like…" He looked at her. "What did you call it?"

"Bull manure."

He pulled her into the hall, walking between the lockers

like a man with a purpose. "A perfect description of my parents."

"Now, Arthur," Julia said, wincing as his hand dug into her biceps. "Surely they weren't that—"

He stopped in front of the office, swinging her to face him. His forehead glistened with sweat, his eyes were cold. He pointed a finger at her face. "You don't know!" he hissed. "You don't know anything about me."

A wave of fear swelled in Julia's midsection. She stopped it before it could go any further. There was something about Arthur's eyes. Something flickered behind the cold curtain he'd pulled closed. What was it? Hope? A plea? Yearning? This macho act was for her benefit—for the world's benefit. This was not Arthur Graham.

"I don't want you to get hurt, Arthur."

He flung her arm away and slammed his hand into a nearby locker. The sound echoed through the empty school. "I'm *already* hurt. Doesn't anybody see that? I'm already hurt."

"I see that."

Art glared at her. "You only say that because I have you hostage. If things were different, you'd only see what everyone else sees."

"And what's that?"

"A no-good, no-account kid destined for trouble. Of no use to anyone. White trash."

"Is that what you want them to see?"

He swung around, turning his back to her. He rubbed his sore hand. "Of course not. But that's where they put me, so that's where I'm doomed to stay."

"Nobody put you anywhere, Arthur," Julia said. "You make your own choices. You have a choice to make right now. You can walk out of here and give yourself up."

Art laughed. "Oh, that's right. I can stroll over to the police station where I can say, 'Hey, there, Mr. Policeman. I'm the one who robbed the gas station, but I'm ever so sorry. Can I go home now?' After they're done laughing, they'll throw me in jail. Some home sweet home."

"So what do you want to do? Keep running, making the same choices, over and over until you're caught?"

"I won't get caught."

"You will get caught. If not for this crime, for the next one. It's inevitable."

He looked up and down the empty hallway. His eyes lingered on the exit. He strode toward the door. "Nothing's inevitable. Isn't that so, Governor?"

He slammed into the pushbar of the door with the full force of his momentum—and ricocheted back when the door didn't budge. He tried it again. No luck. He tried the other side of the double doors.

"These should open," he said. "They may be locked from the outside, but they should open from in here."

"Let me try," Julia said. She pushed on the bar. Nothing happened. Art was right. There wasn't any reason the doors shouldn't open. Unless…Julia repressed a smile. *Interesting tactic, Lord,* she thought. She turned to Art. "We're locked in."

Art bolted down the hallway, calling over his shoulder. "The library has a door. We'll get out there."

Julia jogged behind. She got to the library in time to see him hit the door. Kick it. Swear at it.

"It won't open either?"

Art's eyes blazed. He looked around the library, then out to the hall. He ran past her to the classroom where they'd come through the broken window. Julia hurried to catch up. When she turned the corner into the room, she ran into him. He was stopped dead in the doorway.

"What—?"

Art moved toward the window, his arms in front of him. He touched the glass, running his hands over it like a blind man finding his way. "It's not broken," he said, looking to Julia.

"Maybe it's not the right classroom." The moonlight revealed the desks in the corners, empty bulletin boards, chalkboards.... Her eyes fixed on the chalkboard. Art followed her gaze.

"*The quick brown fox jumped over the lazy poodle.*"

Art grabbed the handles of the window and tugged upwards. It wouldn't budge.

"Open!" he screamed. "Let us out!" He backed away, sweat dripping from his face. He glared at the window, gasping for breath. Then with a primal scream, Art picked up a chair and heaved it toward the glass, raising an arm, expecting to fend off the breaking shards.

The chair bounced off, falling at his feet. The window was intact.

"No!" He picked up the chair and swung it again. Over and over. His breath came in groaning gulps as he tried to break his way out.

Julia moved to put two calming hands on his shoulders.

"Arthur. Art. Stop. We can't leave."

He wheeled, his eyes blazing. "What do you mean we can't leave?"

She took the chair from him and set it on the floor. She helped him sit down.

"Do you know what town this is?"

He wasn't listening. He stared at the window.

"Arthur," Julia said, turning his chin so that he faced her. "Do you know what town this is?"

He blinked twice. "Haven?" His voice was insecure, like a child answering a teacher's question.

"That's right." Julia wiped a bead of perspiration from his forehead. "This is a special town. You didn't know it when you drove in, but you picked the wrong town to rob."

He shook his head. He didn't understand.

She straightened and took a deep breath. How could she explain the unexplainable? She took his hand and held it. "You'll have to trust me on this one, Arthur. Let's just say that in Haven, more than anywhere else in this world, things happen

238

for a reason. And for whatever reason, we're supposed to stay in this school."

"Stay?"

"Yes, son." She helped him stand. "Let's go back to the library where you can lie down. I'll read to you. We were in chapter 4 of *A Tale of Two Cities*. Do you remember that, Arthur? What was happening where we left off?"

Art stumbled, and Julia steadied him. "Mr. Lorry stopped at an inn and asked for a barber. Isn't that right?" he asked weakly.

"Very good, Arthur," Julia said, patting his arm.

~

Del waved good-bye to Natalie as he opened the door to his motel room. He flipped on the light and fell into the chair by the table. A marigold drooped from the vase. He stuck it deeper in the water.

His eyes sought the crucifix hanging above the bed. "I still don't understand why I'm here, Lord. It seems so plain in other people. Natalie's writing, Kathy's painting..." He ran a finger along the edge of the table. "But what about me, Lord? What about me?"

Del took off his shoes and set them neatly by the bed. He folded his T-shirt as if it were a shirt made of the finest linen. It was all he had.

"I wish I had a change of clothes," he said, moving to place the shirt in the dresser. "The others look so nice. Walter's right. I'm just a bum, dressed in shabby—"

Inside the top drawer were two shirts and a pair of pajamas.

"Pajamas!" he yelled, pulling them out. He held them at arm's length. Pajamas were a luxury he'd long done without.

He opened the second drawer: underwear, toiletries. In the third were two pairs of pants.

"You think of everything, don't you, Lord?"

He laid the pajamas ceremonially on the bed and went to indulge in a steamy shower.

The silk of the pajama fabric felt foreign and a bit decadent as he slipped them on. He looked in the mirror, pulling his long hair into its ponytail. He wasn't such a bad-looking fellow when he got cleaned up. He moved to the bed and folded the quilt at its foot. He pulled back the covers, and his eyes brushed over the invitation to Haven, which he'd set on the nightstand.

"I wish you were mine."

He picked it up, regretting the tea stains from Walter's trash. He opened the card, wanting to read the verse again…and froze. He read it again. And then again, hardly able to believe what he was seeing:

Antonio Michael Delatondo is invited to Haven, Nebraska.
Please arrive August 1.
"If you have faith as small as a mustard seed,
you can say to this mountain,
'Move from here to there' and it will move.
Nothing will be impossible for you."

Del ran his fingers over the name as if it were something he could feel. He pulled the invitation to his chest and closed his eyes, reciting from memory what had previously been wishful thinking: "Antonio Michael Delatondo is invited to Haven, Nebraska."

Joy filled him. Joy such as he hadn't known in a very long time. "I belong here. *I* belong here." He looked toward the door. "I should tell Walter. Show him I *am* one of the chosen ones."

He took two steps before he stopped himself. This wasn't between him and Walter. This was between him and—

He took the invitation and placed it on the nightstand in its spot of honor. It had belonged there before when it was just a borrowed invitation. But now, the place of honor was all the more meaningful.

Del knelt by the bed, leaning his elbows on the mattress. His bowed head fell into his hands as he thanked his host.

Although she was exhausted, Kathy couldn't get to sleep. She listened to the rhythmic breathing of her children and tried to mimic them. But instead her breathing followed the flow of her thoughts, stopping and starting in an uneven progression.

She was not alone in bed. Guilt lay beside her. Guilt for coming to Haven against Lenny's wishes. Guilt for taking the chicken's way out and leaving him a message on his voice mail. Guilt for having such a good time without him. Guilt for not missing him.

She looked at the clock on the bedside table. 12:30. If she didn't get some sleep, she'd be a wreck tomor—

There was a tap on the door.

Kathy lifted her head. Had she really heard it? Another tap.

Who'd be visiting in the middle of the night?

She got out of bed, pulling her robe around her, and went to peer out the peephole. Her heart skipped a beat, and she opened the door.

"Lenny."

He rushed inside without saying a word. His eyes swept the room, searching.

Kathy turned on the bedside lamp. She tied her robe around her waist and ran a hand through her tousled hair. "What are you doing here?" she asked.

Lenny strode to the children's beds as if logging in the fact they were there. He came back to her. She held a chair for him, but he pushed it away.

"I don't want a stupid chair," he hissed. "I've been sitting long enough. Eleven hours long."

Kathy busied herself straightening the table. Lisa's coloring books, Ryan's puzzle. Lenny snatched a teddy bear off the seat of a chair.

"Where'd they get *this*?"

"It came with the room," Kathy said, saving the bear from

Lenny's harsh hands. She set it next to the dresser.

Lenny paced up and back. He flicked a hand at the fancy comforter on her wicker bed. "Some room. How much is it setting us back?"

"Nothing," Kathy said. "We get to stay for free."

Lenny's eyebrows threatened to obliterate the bridge of his nose. "Nothing's free."

"This is." She forced herself to sit at the table. She'd done nothing wrong. *Except coming to Haven against Lenny's wishes. Except taking the chicken's way out and leaving him a message on his voice mail. Except having such a good time without him. Except not missing—*

He whipped out a chair and sat across the table from her. He took an orange from the fruit bowl and turned it over in his hands. "Why did you disobey me?"

Kathy sucked in her breath, then forced her chin to be steady. "I am not a dog, Lenny. I don't jump at your commands."

"I'm your husband. I told you not to come here."

Kathy shook her head. He would never understand.

"I'm waiting."

"Too many things happened that told me I had to come."

"More Highway Havens?"

"In a way." She groped for her reasons, then she remembered the paintings. "Sandra Perkins sold four of my paintings."

"You're kidding."

She ignored the cut. "She sold them to a man from New York. That's how we got the money to come here. And with the room being free, and the meals too, I'm not cutting into our money much, Lenny. Just the fare for the bus tickets."

"You took our kids on a bus?"

"How did you think we got here?"

"Don't get cocky with me."

Kathy drew a deep breath. She reached her hand across the

242

table and placed it on top of his. She was relieved when he didn't slap it away.

"I'm sorry, Lenny. I had to come. I'm glad I did." Her face brightened. "This town is amazing, the people are amazing. I've been paired with a wonderful lady named Anne who is a high school counselor. Yesterday I was in her office when this file appeared—it was my file, Lenny, my file from high school. It was there for me to see, and I looked at it and saw the original letter that I sent to Mrs. Robb about getting preg—"

"I don't want to hear about your great time." Lenny pulled his hand out from under hers. "I've had an awful time, driving, worrying, practicing what I was going to say when I found you."

Kathy sat back, bracing herself. "So? What's your speech?"

Lenny looked away. "I'm tired. I don't want to get into it."

Kathy relaxed. "Get your bag and come to bed. We can talk about it in the morning."

Lenny stood and opened the door to get his stuff. He hesitated, pointing a finger at her. "We *will* talk about it, Kath. Tomorrow."

She nodded. Tomorrow.

Twenty

Then the angel who talked with me returned and wakened me, as a man is wakened from his sleep. He asked me, "What do you see?"

ZECHARIAH 4:1

"Del?"

Del opened his eyes, his face buried in his pillow.

A knock sounded on the door. "Del?"

He raised up on his forearms and glanced at the clock. Five o'clock.

The knock was soft but persistent.

"Del, it's me, John."

Del stumbled to the door and opened it. John gave him a once-over. "Nice pajamas."

Del leaned his head on the edge of the door. "Sorry, I don't accept compliments until dawn."

John flipped on the light and brushed past him into the room. "Ah, dawn. That's exactly why I'm here."

Del closed the door and leaned against it. "I hope you're going to explain yourself, because I'm not up to guessing games."

John opened the dresser drawers and pulled out a shirt and pants.

"We going somewhere?" Del asked, taking them from him.

"Let's go ask the sunrise."

"Go what?"

"Ask the sunrise."

Del set the clothes on the bed and crawled across the covers, looking for the opening. "The sunrise and I meet as seldom as possible. And two days ago in St. Louis was it. I was on the 5:20 bus to get to Walter's. I've done my stint."

He stuck a foot under the covers. John whipped the covers

244

away. Del rolled onto his side and drew his knees to his chest, wrapping his arms around himself. "I don't need covers. I'm used to sleeping without them."

John pushed down on the mattress, making it roll. "Wake up, Del! Wake up to your destiny."

Del groaned with the rocking movement. "John…" His voice hinted of brewing thunderclouds. *"Your* destiny is going to be irrevocably linked with my destiny if you…don't. Stop. Bouncing. This. *Bed!"* He lunged toward John.

With a quick sidestep, John eluded him. He grinned at Del. "Well, at least he's up."

Del took two staggering steps. "He is up. He is not willing. And at the moment the only thing he is able to do is detest John."

"You have such a way with words."

Del pulled the pajama top over his head without unbuttoning it. "Keep it up, and I'll show you my way with my fists."

"Now, now," John said, pulling the covers back where they belonged. "What's a few hours of sleep in exchange for a sunrise?"

Del pulled on his pants. "Is this a trick question?" He zipped his zipper then stopped. "Am I allowed to use the facilities?"

"If you're quick about it. The sunrise waits for no man."

Del walked to the bathroom. "And here I thought you people of Haven had everything under control." He shut the door.

"If you only knew," John said to the empty room.

Del was impressed. John had come prepared: two cups of coffee and a sack of donuts sat on the seat between them. Del chose a donut with orange sprinkles. "At least I won't be meeting my destiny on an empty stomach."

"Fortunately—or unfortunately," John said, driving north out of town, "destiny doesn't give a flying fig."

"Flying figs are tasty," Del said. "If you can catch them."

John rolled his eyes. He pointed ahead to the dark band of trees set against the night sky. "That's the river."

"We're going up the river? Is a paddle involved?"

"*To* the river," John explained. "And no paddle. We're going to the field near the river."

"To a field? My destiny is in a field?"

"You're taking this too literally," John said. "Quit trying to explain it."

Del drank the last of his coffee. He thought of the invitation. He *was* chosen. There *was* a purpose for him here. He tucked his cockiness away. "You're right. Too much has happened in the last few days that can't be explained. I'll keep quiet."

"Now *that's* a refreshing idea," John said. He turned right onto a dirt road, slowing to negotiate the ruts. He drove a half mile and pulled onto a fallow field. He shut off the engine and the headlights. The sudden silence and dark fell on them like a theater's curtain. It took Del's senses a moment to catch up.

"It's dark out here," he said.

"A profound statement." John fumbled behind the seat.

"So what now?"

"Now, we walk."

John pulled a blanket out from under the seat and got out of the truck. Del followed. Their feet sank into the soil of the unused field; chaff from past crops stippled the ground.

"I can't see," Del complained as he walked after John.

"You don't have to see."

"Then why are we here?"

John didn't answer. He kept walking until they were a hundred yards into the field. He stopped. "This should do it."

Del turned in a circle. "Ah yes. This looks glorious. I can honestly say you are a man outstanding in his field." He spread his arms to indicate the flat openness of it all. "Why do we need to be in the middle of nowhere? Are we waiting for a spaceship to land?"

John spread the blanket on the ground and sat on it. "Of a sort."

Del stood at the edge of the blanket. "You've got to be kidding. We *are* waiting for a spaceship to land?"

John patted the blanket. "Sit down, you fool. Quit spouting off like a fear-crazed nitwit. Where's your trust? Where's your faith?"

Del sat on the blanket. "Is that what this is about? Faith?"

"'We live by faith, not by sight.'"

"Good thing, considering I can't see a thing."

John sighed. "See with your heart, Del. Not your eyes. See the ways of the Lord, not the ways of the world."

Del picked up a stick and scribbled in the dirt. "I haven't been a part of this world for a long time."

"That's not true. You allow this world to rule you."

"I do not. I've given up everything. No home, no career, no family."

"The martyr, Delatondo."

Anger swept over Del and he jumped to his feet. "I don't have to take this. I've given up everything, *everything* because…because…"

"Because of your guilt."

Del stuffed his hands in his pockets. "I have reason to feel guilty."

"Yes, you do."

He stared at John, nonplussed. Then he shook his head. These people were unbelievable. "I won't ask how you know about it."

"That's just as well."

"But you see, that's why I gave up everything. To make amends."

"That's not the way to make amends, and you know it. You have to ask."

Del faced the eastern sky, which showed the faintest glow of light. "I can't do that."

"You can."

"I can't."

A bird flew between them, pecked at the dirt, then flew away. John pointed after the bird. "God provides for the smallest birds and animals. They never waste a moment in worry. If he cares so well for those who cannot ask, why not for man who is so much more important to him? Worry will not add one moment to your life."

"Who says I'm worrying?"

"You worry about all the things you've given up."

"I want to be like other men."

"But you aren't like other men."

Del faced him. "I'm not sure I like the sound of this."

"Just because true wisdom is not always welcomed, doesn't make it any less true."

"A quotable quote from John Crawford? *Reader's Digest* is waiting."

John shrugged. "You've given up the material possessions of the world, Del. And that's good. They're of no importance."

"But highly preferable to nothing."

John waved this away. "Unfortunately, you haven't replaced the material with the spiritual. That's the next step."

Del pulled at the fabric of his new pants. "So these are spiritual pants and a spiritual shirt. And I'm sleeping in a spiritual bed?"

"You're being sarcastic."

"Really?"

John looked at him, his eyes full of patience. Del wondered if the man ever got frustrated. If he ever felt hopeless, irredeemable...

"You've given up what most men cannot." John's words drew Del out of his gloom. "You have nothing. You are empty, an empty—"

"'Vessel, ready to fill,'" Del quoted in a singsong voice. "You guys are a broken record."

"As many times as it takes," John said.

"Takes to do what?"

"To fill you up."

Del laughed. "Those donuts did the trick quite nicely. I won't need any more filling for at least another—" A dirt clod smacked into Del's chest. "Hey! What's that for?"

"That's for being such a blind idiot. Don't you see what I'm offering you? What Jesus is offering you?" John struggled to his feet.

Del opened his arms. "A field of dreams?"

John put his hand at the back of Del's neck and turned him toward the east with a less than gentle tug. Okay, so maybe John did get a bit frustrated at times....

The horizon was a rosy shade of pink with color radiating upwards, touching the night. "*That* is what I'm offering you, Del." He pointed to the light. "What do you see?"

Del's eyes wandered over the horizon. The far-off trees that dotted the flat plain were no match for the clouds towering above them. As he watched, the crescent of the sun peeked above the earth, illuminating the sky, its prisms adding reds and oranges to the higher purples and blues beyond.

"What do you *see?*" John whispered again. Del didn't respond. Instead, he felt himself relaxing. John removed his hand from the back of his neck. "Look closely, Del. Can man do that? Man tries to understand it. Man tries to dissect it. But man cannot create it. Why, Del? Why?"

"Because it comes from God," he said as the sunrise took the sky captive.

"It's a gift from him." John reached down and took a handful of soil. "This is a gift from him." He pointed to the river, then a flock of birds rising above it. "That is a gift from him." A farmhouse. "And that." The truck. "And that." And finally Del. "And that."

"Me."

"You, in your entirety, are a gift from God. He made you, you belong to him."

"I'm not worth—"

249

"How dare you!" John snapped. "How dare you downplay your importance to him! Such false modesty degrades the very majesty of his creation!"

Del's head swam with a desperate confusion. "But I betrayed him. I don't have anything left to give—"

John swept his hand toward the sunrise. "What does the sunrise have to give, except itself? What do the trees have to give except themselves? What do you have to give except—"

"Myself."

John raised his face to the sky, his hands outstretched. "Yes!"

Del ran a hand through his hair. "Me."

John pointed to the sunrise, the sun full in the sky, the red and pink surrendering to the day's blue. "You just watched God come up in the sunrise. God filled the sky with his power. Let him fill *you*, Antonio. Let him fill you!"

Del wanted to do it, wanted to let go, to lift his arms and rejoice the way John was doing. He felt a tear slide down his cheek. He wanted to, but…

"I can't!" he cried. He spun around and ran through the field, away from God's sunrise, back toward Haven.

Twenty-one

See to it, then, that the light within you is not darkness.
LUKE 11:35

"JULIA?" Walter knocked on the door to Julia's room for the second time. "Julia, it's me, Walter."

He put his ear to the door. Not a sound. He glanced at the parking space in front of her room. Her car was gone.

The door to the next room opened.. Natalie stepped out, stretching. The melody of "Thunder Rolls" came with her.

"Hey, Natalie," Walter called. "Have you seen Julia?"

She looked toward Julia's parking place. "Not since last night. Maybe she went to breakfast early." Then she frowned. "Hey, whose car is that?" She pointed at a car that Walter didn't recognize.

The door to Kathy's room opened and, to Walter's astonishment, a man in bare feet stepped out. "What's going on out here? Can't a man get a little quiet?"

"Who are you?" Walter asked, wondering if he should be alarmed.

The man went to his car and unlocked the trunk. He pulled out a pair of shoes and slammed the lid closed. "Who wants to know?"

"Where's Kathy? Is she okay?" Walter took a step toward Kathy's room. "I'm the one who drove her here. She's my responsibility and if anything happens to her—"

The intruder took a step toward Walter. "I thought she took a bus here."

Walter blinked. "Well…she did, but I picked her up in Grand Island and—"

"Who asked you to do that?"

"Why, she—" Walter looked to Natalie.

"My wife never told me about no man picking her—"

Walter took a step back. "Your wife?"

Kathy came out of the room, a brush in her hand. "What's going on out...oh, morning, Walter. Morning, Natalie. This is my husband, Lenny. He showed up...he came in last night."

"Obviously just in time," Lenny said.

Walter stepped forward again. He didn't like the man's tone of voice. "Hey, don't imply things that aren't true, buddy. I hardly know Kathy. I just met her and the kids yesterday."

Lenny pointed a finger at Walter. "But you've known her long enough to drive her from Grand Island to—" He turned to Kathy. "Where were the kids when all this was happening?"

The brush stopped in midair. "In the backseat. Lenny, there's no reason for you to be jealous of Walter."

"I'll be the one who determines whether there's a reason to be—"

Ryan came out the door and tugged on Kathy's dress. "Can we go see Donnie now, Mommy?"

"Who's Donnie?" Lenny snapped. "Is he another man you've—"

Husband or not, enough was enough. Walter was about to shut the man's mouth when Kathy put her hands in the air. "Stop it!" She took a deep breath. Lenny started to speak, but at the look on Kathy's face, he fell quiet.

Kathy held her hand out to the man beside her. "Walter, Natalie, this is my husband, Lenny Kraus. Lenny, these are my *friends*. We all arrived yesterday. We all received an invitation to Haven. *That* is our common bond. This is Natalie from Estes Park, and you've already met Walter from St. Louis. Del and Julia are obviously still asleep, though how they could ever sleep with the ruckus you're causing I'll never know."

Ryan clung to Kathy's leg. She cupped his head under her hand. "And Donnie is a friend of Ryan's." She fixed her husband with a glare. "A *six-year-old* friend of Ryan's."

"Oh," Lenny said.

"Oh," Kathy echoed.

Walter suddenly remembered his original objective. "Kathy, have you seen Julia? She's not in her room. Her car's missing."

They all looked at the empty parking space. "Maybe she's at breakfast?"

"What kind of car was it?" Lenny asked.

"A silver Intrepid," Walter said.

Lenny pinched his lower lip, shaking his head. "It wasn't here when I drove in last night."

"When was that?"

"Twelve-thirty, quarter to one."

Natalie ran a hand through her hair. "There's not much to do in Haven that late."

"Maybe Del knows," Walter said. He walked to the room and knocked. He called Del's name. Nothing.

"That's strange," Kathy said. "Both Del and Julia gone."

"Del doesn't have a car," Natalie said. "I drove him back here last night around ten thirty. I saw him go into his room."

"Maybe they're together," Lenny said.

Walter shook his head, "I don't think Julia would willingly have much to do with Del."

"What's wrong with him?" Lenny asked.

"Nothing's wrong with—" Kathy began.

"He's homeless," Walter broke in. "He stowed away in my van, for cryin' out loud." Walter knew he should keep his mouth shut, but he was sick and tired of it. Of seeing a guy who'd been scrounging around in trash cans being treated like he was special, like he was worth something...like he was worth as much as Walter was. At least he was making some kind of contribution to the world. He had a reason for existing. And Del? The man was a waste of space. Why couldn't anyone else see that? "He doesn't belong here. He's not one of us."

"That's not true," Natalie said, stepping forward. "When Del was with us last night, Fran told him he was welcome."

"She was just being polite," Walter said.

"No, she wasn't."

"Yes, she was. There's no way a nobody like Del belongs in Haven."

"How do you know?" Natalie asked.

He brushed her question away. "It's common sense. What could God do with a man like that?"

"What could...God?" Lenny asked. "What's this about God?"

Kathy put a quieting hand on his arm. "Later, Lenny."

"Mama," Lisa said, tugging on her other leg. "Donnie!"

"See, Mommy?" Ryan said. "Lisa wants to play with Donnie, too."

"Kath, answer my question," Lenny said, pulling his arm away. "What's this about God?"

Kathy raised a hand in the air. "One thing at a time. First, let's find Julia and Del." She turned toward their room, motioning everyone inside. "Since we have the biggest room, come on in and we'll call around to Louise and John. We can also call Fran and see if they're at the Fillerup. Let's not get panicky until we have reason to."

Everyone followed Kathy into her room. She opened the curtains, letting in daylight. She pulled the covers up on the bed before she sat on its edge near the phone. She picked up the receiver, then stopped. "Does anyone know the phone numbers of these people?"

Most shook their heads. Natalie said, "I have Fran's. I'll go get it." She ran out the door, leaving it open to the morning air.

Kathy dialed directory assistance and got the phone numbers of the rest of the mentors.

She called Louise first, but she had no idea where either Julia or Del were. Kathy dialed another number, then hung up. "No answer at John's. I'll try Anne's number."

Anne said she hadn't seen either of them but would be right over. She'd call Chief who was already at work.

"Donnie!" Lisa said.

"Soon, sweetcakes. Donnie will be here soon."

Kathy called the last number and talked with Gabe, but her crestfallen expression told Walter her hope was failing. She hung up. "All Gabe had to offer was his concern." Worry was evident in her voice. "Now what?"

Natalie returned from her room, munching a soda cracker. "I called Fran. Neither Julia or Del have been in for breakfast. Speaking of which, I really need to get something in my stomach. Mornings aren't good for me."

Walter looked at her. "Why not?"

Natalie and Kathy exchanged a look. "Because I'm pregnant," Natalie said.

Walter tried to keep his expression noncommittal, but he felt his eyebrows raise. "You married?"

"No."

"Going to be?"

Natalie looked away. "We don't know."

Walter shook his head. This made even less sense than Del. "And God chose you? I'll never understand that. Why would he choose...well, you know."

Natalie strode up to him, her chin jutting forward. "How dare you!"

Walter took a startled step back. Clearly he'd blown it. "Well, I—"

"You are the most egotistical, judgmental, narrow-minded, arrogant prig I've ever met! Is your life so *perfect,* Mr. Prescott, that you can judge us all so freely?"

Walter took a seat at the table and pretended to interest himself in Ryan's Bugs Bunny puzzle. "I've had my—" he broke off. Darned if he was going to offer true confessions to a group of strangers. "I'm not perfect," he said.

"So he admits it," Natalie said, raising her hands to the ceiling. "Then why are you so quick to condemn me for my mistake?"

"I don't condemn you. Forget I said anything."

"I can't forget it," Natalie said. "Not when you act as though I'm not worthy of being here because I'm unmarried and pregnant."

Walter raised his eyes, then looked away. "It's not right."

Natalie slapped her hands on the table. "You insolent, nefarious, conceit—"

Walter raised a hand, stopping her. "I can tell you're a writer, Miss Pasternak."

"Don't change the subject," Natalie said, her nostrils flaring.

"I don't pretend to be above sin," Walter said, holding a puzzle piece, hunting for its place. "But I am wise enough to recognize it in others."

Natalie stepped forward. "You b—"

Kathy grabbed her arm. "Don't say it, Natalie." She pulled her away. "He's not worth it."

"Fortunately, God doesn't agree with you," Walter said.

Kathy took a step toward Walter. "May I remind you, Mr. Prescott, that the mother of the Savior was an unwed, pregnant teen? And that the mother of Solomon, who was considered the wisest man who ever lived, was an adulteress? And that the Bible lists Bathsheba, the adulteress, and Rahab, a prostitute, in the lineage of Christ?"

"See?" Natalie said. "I'm not so bad. I'm here and you're here. We're *all* here for the same purpose."

"Of which you have no idea."

"And you do?"

She had him there. But he wasn't going to concede a thing. "I've figured out more than most people."

Natalie grabbed the puzzle piece away from him and placed it in Bugs' ear. "Clean your own houses before you attempt to clean mine."

Lenny clapped. "Nice going, little lady."

Of all the nerve! "You stay out of it," Walter snapped. "You have no right—"

"I have every right," Lenny said. "It's my family who's a part of this…whatever it is. They've come here, and now I've come to take them home."

"Home?" Kathy asked. "We're not going home."

"Oh, yes you are."

Walter stood, shoving his chair backwards. He caught it before it toppled over. "Oh, no she's not. She's one of *us.*"

"No, she isn't," Lenny said. "She's one of mine."

"Yours?" Kathy said. "I'm not your possession, Lenny."

"You're my wife."

"But I'm not your possess—"

"Howdy, folks." Everyone turned to find Chief standing in the doorway. "Is there trouble in paradise?"

Suddenly ashamed of how he'd been acting, Walter looked away, noticing as he did so that Kathy and Lenny were doing the same. Apparently they weren't feeling very proud of themselves, either.

"I'm glad you're here," Natalie said. "Julia's missing. Del too."

"I know," Chief said, taking off his sunglasses. "I just found Julia's car near the edge of town. It was abandoned. Her purse was on the floor of the front seat."

"Her purse?" Natalie said. "She wouldn't leave her purse."

"No, she wouldn't," Chief said. "Not if she's anything like my wife. Anne takes that thing with her into the shower."

"I do not," Anne said, following Donnie into the room. "I leave it on the counter." As if to prove her point, she stuffed her keys in the purse hanging off her shoulder. "Did I hear you found Julia's car abandoned?"

"Not far from here," Chief said, brushing the top of his son's head as Donnie ran off to play with Ryan. "But that's not all. I found a car matching Bob's description of the robbery vehicle on the west side of town. Also abandoned."

"The robber's still in town?" Walter asked.

"Could be. Unless he stole another car. It wouldn't be that

hard to do. The people of Haven are pretty trusting."

"Not anymore," Natalie said.

Chief shrugged. "Crime tends to do that; brings out the worst in everyone. Anger, fear, suspicion."

"Mommy?" Ryan said, standing at her elbow.

"Not now, sweetie," she said. "Go play."

"But, Mommy. I saw a man take the Julie-lady."

They all spun to stare at the little boy. Kathy knelt and took his arms. "Julia?"

"Yeah," Ryan said, raising his shoulders against the pressure of her hands. "Last night when we got back to the motel, I saw her silver car up there," he pointed east. "A man ran up to her window and yelled at her. Then she talked back. Then he ran around the front of the car and got in. They drove away real fast."

"In which direction?" Chief asked.

"That way," Ryan said, pointing behind him. South.

"The man acted mad?" Chief asked.

Ryan nodded. "He put a gun to her face."

"A gun?" Kathy yelped. "Why didn't you say something last night?"

He shrugged. "I thought it was like on TV. Just pretend."

"You let him watch crime shows?" Anne asked.

"I...no," Kathy stammered. "I don't *let* him, but sometimes he does. I can't watch him twenty-four hours a day, and Lenny's hardly ever—"

"Don't blame me," Lenny said. "You're the mother."

"And you're the father. It's your responsibility—"

"Stop it, you two," Chief said, raising a hand. "You can discuss the merits and maladies of your parenting skills later. Right now we need to find Julia."

"And Del," Natalie said. "What about Del? He's missing, too."

Chief put a hand on Ryan's shoulder. "You didn't see Del, did you, Ryan?"

Ryan shook his head vigorously.

Chief spoke to Kathy. "When you called around asking about Julia, did you ask about Del too?"

"I did," Kathy said. "But no one's seen him. I got a hold of everyone except John."

"John's his mentor," Natalie said. "Maybe they're together."

"Maybe," Chief said, scratching his head with the earpiece of his sunglasses. "But with Julia disappearing and a robber in our midst, we can't take anything for—"

"What's going on?"

Everyone turned toward the voice. It was Del.

"What's up?" he asked.

They rushed toward him. "Where have you been?" Walter demanded, torn between relief and anger. "We checked your room and you were gone."

"Julia's missing and we thought you were—" Natalie began, but Del cut her off.

"Julia's missing?" he asked.

They explained the situation to him.

"I helped," Ryan said, proudly wanting to preserve his center stage.

Kathy gently pushed him toward the toys. "Go play with your sister and Donnie, sweetie. You've been a big help, but now it's time to let the adults—"

"I can't, Mommy," Ryan said, squirming under her touch.

She pointed a finger at his nose. "Yes, you can, young man. We have a serious situation here and you need to let us concentrate on finding—"

He shook his head. "I don't mean that, Mommy," he said. "I mean I can't play with Lisa."

"Why not?"

"Because she's not here."

Kathy's head sprang to attention. She scanned the room. Lisa's rumpled bed. The Barbie house. The cars. The dolls. She lifted the dust ruffle and looked under the bed.

"Where is she?" she asked, her voice taking on an urgent tone.

"I dunno," Ryan said.

She looked to Donnie. Donnie shrugged. "She wasn't here when I got here."

Walter had had just about enough. First Julia, then Del, now the little girl. This was getting ridic—his thoughts came to a halt when he saw the look on Kathy's face. He followed her gaze toward the open door. The door leading to the parking lot, the street—

"The street!" she screamed, as though she'd been reading his mind.

She pushed through the crowd of people.

"Kath?" Lenny asked, running after her. "Kathy!"

Anne looked to Walter. "What happened?"

"Lisa's gone."

"Gone?" Anne nearly screamed. "What are you doing just standing there?" She turned to the group, barking commands. "Lisa's gone! Everybody outside! Find her!"

"Her parents are already look—" Walter began, but Anne's glare closed his mouth on the words.

"I believe I said everybody?" she remarked pointedly.

With a shake of his head, Walter moved for the door, wondering why he seemed to be the only one who hadn't gotten up on the wrong side of the bed that morning.

⌒

Julia moved. She groaned. Her back was stiff. Her neck ached.

Why am I so sore?

She opened her eyes. Sunlight poured through the windows of the library, revealing it to be a friendly room with bright posters on the walls and mobiles hanging from the ceiling.

She sat up, the small of her back screaming as she shoved it against the cushion. She placed her feet flat on the floor and used her arms on the armrests in an attempt to push herself to standing.

"Uhhh," she said.

"What?" Art whipped his head toward the sound, his eyes wide.

"Morning, Arthur," Julia said, taking a few steps. She forced her back to straighten, then arched it. "I am not as young as I was yesterday."

Art sat on the couch, rubbing his face. "I should've let you have the couch. Where I sleep doesn't matter much to me."

"It doesn't matter much to me either," Julia said. "As long as it involves a mattress, a pillow, and a horizontal position."

"It's morning," Art said, noticing the sunlight.

"A new day."

"I'm thrilled."

"Such optimism," Julia said, reaching her arms toward the ceiling. "So what's on the agenda for today? Embezzlement, blackmail, or espionage?"

"Escape."

"We haven't gotten very far in that regard," Julia said. "Seems we're exactly where we started."

"Not by choice," Art said. "If you remember, the building wouldn't let us leave?"

"Yes, I do recall having a problem with various means of egress."

"The doors and windows wouldn't work."

"That too," she said.

"You have any ideas?"

Julia studied the ceiling. "Breakfast would be good."

"Yeah," Art laughed. "You think the Fillerup delivers?"

She fluttered her hands near her face, trying to wake up. "Very doubtful, my boy. Oof. I need coffee." She headed toward the hall.

"Where are you going?"

"There's got to be a teacher's lounge around here. A coffeepot. Maybe some vending machines."

Art stuffed the gun in his waistband, grabbed the sack of money, and ran after her. "I've got money."

"A Three Musketeers for breakfast," Julia said, wallowing in the milk chocolate. "I should try this more often."

Art grinned at her. She was still as elegant as ever, but somehow she seemed more approachable, more like a…friend. Pushing the odd feeling away, he shoved half a Mars bar in his mouth. "I eat a lot of candy bars." He pinched a piece of chocolate that had fallen on his jeans and transferred it to his tongue. "That and chips."

"You need a good, home-cooked meal. Everyone can benefit from home cooking."

Art stared past Julia's shoulder, nearly forgotten memories suddenly drifting through his mind…. "Mom used to make dinners—real dinners. Fried chicken and corn on the cob." He could almost taste it, and he smiled. "I love corn on the cob."

"Slathered in butter," Julia said.

"Mmm."

Art pulled another dollar from the crumpled sack. "You want another candy bar?" he asked. He felt generous. No, he felt good. Almost happy. "More coffee?"

"I'm fine," she said, waving his money away. "Though I need to use the rest room."

"Me too," Art said. "Let's go—" he looked at her, suddenly wary—"but don't try any—" He closed his mouth when she glared at him. What was it about her that could make him feel like a little boy?

"That's enough of that, Arthur. I'm with you till the end of this, and I resent you implying that I'm stringing you along, befriending you, reading to you as a ploy to run away. I hope you realize I could have escaped anytime during the night when you were busy snoring."

He felt the heat creep into his cheeks. "I don't snore."

"You snore like a freight train."

He shrugged. "Sorry."

She shrugged. "I'm used to it. Edward rumbles the china with every breath."

As they left the lounge, she touched his arm. He looked down at her hand, where it rested gently on his sleeve, then up at her. "You do trust me, don't you, Arthur?"

He looked at her brown eyes. They were like Adrianne's, or his grandma's. His grandma would never approve of him stealing and kidnapping...

"I trust you," he said, turning toward the rest rooms. "But don't be long."

Julia turned into the women's. "Just long enough to get beautiful."

He turned into the men's room and called after her. "That won't take long at all."

"Flatterer," she called back.

Art walked into the hallway. He heard Julia singing "Oh, What a Beautiful Morning" from the women's rest room. The echo of the room did not help her voice.

He wandered down the hall, glancing in the classrooms as he passed. The school was a generic school like those he used to go to. Vinyl tile floors with flecks of white and gray. A metal desk for the teacher, an empty paper tray, a wastebasket, and a stapler sitting on top for the summer. A pull-down screen that would cover the center of the chalkboard up front. Side-arm desks with a place to shove books under the seats.

Art felt a surge of anticipation at the sight of the rooms, the signs with their subject names perched proudly above the doors. He'd always liked school, liked the routine of it, the sameness of it, the security of it. He was good at math and history—he'd listen to Civil War stories from now until forever—but liking school and doing good in school were two different things. He'd tried—for a while. But never, in all his years of schooling, did his parents ask to see his schoolwork. He'd come home, waving a test or a paper he'd written only to have his mother say, "Not now, Artie, I'm too tired." Or his dad say, "Don't bother me." Once in sixth grade, his father had torn up a history final because Art had mentioned it covered the Vietnam War.

"That war didn't happen," his father had said. "Erase it from your mind. That's what I try to do." Then he'd taken the test, ripped it into three long pieces, and handed them to Art. "Take this in the bathroom and flush it. That's where 'Nam belongs."

Art had stopped trying after that.

He looked down the hall as Julia raised her voice to start the third verse of the song. The words rang out, bold and joyful. Art continued walking. He was nearing the end of the hall. There was the music room on the right and the art room on the left. He stuck his head in the music room. The conductor's music stand stood in front of the tiered rows of seats.

A light flashed to his left and behind. Art jerked his head back into the hall. His eyes were drawn to the cardboard sign above the door across from the music room. But it wasn't cardboard anymore. It glowed in bright red neon: ART.

He took a tentative step toward it. He heard the hum of the neon as it ran through the tubes. ART. And what was that other sound, a higher singsongy sound?

I'm seeing and hearing things.

Art checked the sign above the music room and took a quick glance down the hall at the other rooms. Cardboard signs, stenciled in black ink. Handmade. Nothing fancy. None of them in neon, except...

ART, the sign glared.

He suddenly took a step back, reclaiming the spot where he'd first seen the sign.

"That's me."

As if to confirm his thinking, the sign pulsed to a brighter red.

Art looked down the hall, wishing Julia would come out of the rest room. She'd tell him he was just seeing things. She wouldn't let no fool sign get the best of them. She'd tell that sign to behave itself, and it wouldn't dare do different.

The chorus of "Oklahoma!" rang out. She was loudly, clearly having a great time.

Isn't she ever coming out of there?

He opened his mouth to call to her, but closed it. He was in charge here. He couldn't go screaming after some woman just because a sign appeared to be glowing at him. *Appeared.* That was the key word. Maybe it wasn't really happening.

Art closed his eyes tight. He counted to three and opened them again.

ART.

He tossed his sack of money at it. Bills scattered to the floor. The sign pulsed brighter, taunting him.

"What do you want with me?"

The sign went to black, then turned back on as if starting a new sentence. ART.

He craned his neck past the sign, peering into the room. "Do you want me to go in there?"

ART.

He ran a hand down his chest, wiping his sweaty palm. He felt the gun stuck in his waistband and pulled it out. Holding it in front of him, he flexed his knees, ready for flight, then walked toward the doorway.

Going through the door, he braced himself, almost fearing the sign overhead would send deadly bolts through his body like an electric wire. He went through unscathed. He snapped his head toward the singsong sound he'd heard before.

"…down came rain, wash spider out."

He lowered his gun.

At first he thought the music was coming from a painting on an easel. It was a portrait of a child sleeping, and somehow, the voice seemed perfectly suited to the painting. Moving a step further, he saw beyond the painting to a model's platform. The same little girl was lying on the platform, using a paint-brush to paint invisible pictures in the air.

He watched her in silence, mesmerized by her actions, her complete concentration. *Snap out of it!* he finally told himself. Where did this kid come from?

He glanced around, but there was no one else there. No one but him and the little girl.

"Hi."

He looked over to find her smiling at him. He couldn't hold back the answering smile. He moved closer. "Who are you?" he asked.

She rolled over on her stomach and brushed the carpet. "Lisa," she said. "Who you?"

"Nobody," he answered almost automatically, then felt a pang of regret at the small frown on her face. "I'm Art."

She came to him and slipped her hand into his. He stared down at her, wondering at the trust in her big, sweet eyes... and asking himself yet again what he'd gotten himself into by pulling into this crazy town.

Twenty-two

If a man owns a hundred sheep, and one of them wanders away,
will he not leave the ninety-nine on the hills and go
to look for the one that wandered off?
MATTHEW 18:12

KATHY'S ROOM was turned into the base of operations. Within minutes of discovering Lisa was missing, Fran and Louise arrived bearing breakfast rolls and pots of coffee. Anne took Ryan and Donnie to her house, and Gabe called around town, asking citizens to be on the lookout for Lisa and Julia—and, while they were at it, for the robber of the Pump 'n' Eat.

Kathy sat at the foot of Lisa's bed, rocking back and forth, clutching her daughter's stuffed rabbit. Natalie sat with an awkward arm around her.

"They'll find her," Natalie said, keeping one eye on the open door where people came and went in a sea of busyness. "She can't have gone far."

"Not by herself," Kathy said. "But what if someone took her? What if that criminal who's still on the loose took her?"

Natalie shook her head, hoping it wasn't so. "The timing's against it, Kathy. He would have had to drive by just as Lisa was walking outside the motel. He would have had to scoop her up on a whim. I don't think—"

"Scoop her up," Kathy repeated. Her voice turned into a moan. "No-o-o-o-o."

Natalie closed her eyes, regretting her careless words. "I'm sorry. I'm not very good at this."

Kathy wiped her eyes with a tissue. "You can't know how it feels to have a child in danger." Suddenly she looked at Natalie's abdomen. "Or maybe you can."

Their eyes met, and volumes were silently spoken. They

each looked away, the question unresolved.

Walter burst into the room. "Look what I found!" He held up a red canvas shoe with rubber toes. Kathy shot across the room.

"It's Lisa's!" she cried. Her eyes widened and she stared down at the shoe. "It's Lisa's!" she said again, her voice choked with horror.

Fran and Natalie helped the sobbing woman to a chair. Gabe moved to Walter. "Did you show this to Chief?"

Walter nodded. "He told me to come back and get more of you. I found the shoe in the field behind the motel. We're supposed to cover the entire area, heading up toward the school."

Kathy raised her head, her tears suddenly stopped. "She's been at the school before. We were up there with Anne."

"Let's go," Gabe said. "Louise, you stay by the phone in case someone calls back."

Louise nodded and the rest of them funneled out the door, running to the back of the motel. The grass between the motel and the school grounds was overgrown, thigh-high on an adult, head-high for a two-year-old. Walter, Chief, Lenny, Del, and Bob from the Pump 'n' Eat were already halfway to the school, walking twenty feet apart, their heads turning right, then left, then right again as they searched.

"Where'd you find the shoe?" Natalie asked Walter.

"Over here." Walter ran to the spot. The others followed him as if hopeful a trail of rubber-toed sneakers would magically lead the way to Lisa.

Kathy knelt at the spot, touching the grass where her child might have sat. Natalie could imagine Lisa talking to herself as she tried to retie her shoe, crossing the white laces, bending them in a feeble attempt to mimic what the adults around her did many times a day.

"Where are you, sweetcakes?" Kathy asked the depression in the grass.

Natalie wanted to comfort the woman but wasn't sure what

to say. Some writer you are, she told herself. But maybe this was one of those situations where words weren't really necessary. She touched Kathy's shoulder.

"We need to spread out, Kathy," Fran said. "Staying in one spot won't accomplish anything."

Kathy nodded, but Natalie saw she was having trouble tearing her eyes away from where the shoe had been found. Kathy shouldn't be by herself. "I'll stay with Kathy," Natalie said to Fran. "You look that way, and we'll head over here."

Fran nodded, then moved to the left, walking toward the school, sweeping her eyes and the tops of her hands over the tall weeds.

"Come on, Kathy," Natalie said, pulling her up and turning her in the right direction. "Look for Lisa."

Kathy nodded but didn't move. She gazed at the school, then back to the motel. She tried to take a deep breath, but the effort ended in a sob. She covered her face with her hands. "What if she's…"

Natalie encased her in a hug. "She'll be all right, Kathy. I know she will. Bad things won't happen to her. We're in Haven, remember?"

Kathy shook her head violently. "That doesn't matter. Bad things happen everywhere. You can't escape them. Julia's gone. Lisa's gone. Lenny's here." Realizing what she'd just said, she looked at Natalie, her eyes wide and startled. "I didn't mean that."

"Yes, you did," Natalie said gently.

Kathy hesitated. "Yes, I did." She hugged herself as if a wave of cold had broken through the August heat. "I'm not a good wife."

"I'm sure that's not true," Natalie said.

Kathy nodded vehemently. "It is true. It must be true. Otherwise, Lenny wouldn't be having affairs. Otherwise, he'd be home with us. He'd be proud of me. My painting. My mothering."

Natalie didn't know how to respond. "I'm sure he is proud of you. You've got a lot to offer. You're good with people. You're eager to help." She paused. "You've helped me."

"You?"

Natalie kicked at a clump of weeds. "Maybe. I mean, I haven't decided yet for sure. But maybe there's a way out of my predicament."

"You're going to keep the baby?"

Natalie looked to the sky and sighed from deep inside. "I don't know about *keep,* but there is a chance I'll *have* the baby."

Kathy flung her arms around Natalie. "Oh, Nat, I'm so happy for you. You've made the right decision, I know you—"

Natalie pulled away and held up a hand. "I haven't made a decision—yet. You've got me thinking, that's all."

Kathy nodded quickly, and Natalie grinned. Apparently a partial victory was better than none. "Our children will be all right," Kathy said, taking a step toward the school. "Both of them."

Natalie could only nod and follow Kathy into the grass.

⌐⌐⌐

"Arthur?" Julia called from the hallway. "Where'd you go? My singing wasn't that bad, was it? I think you'll agree the wait was worth it. Although I didn't have my purse for some heavy-duty repair work, I am definitely close to my old, beautiful self."

"In here," Art answered from the art room.

"What are you doing in—" Julia came in the room and stopped short at the sight of Art and Lisa, sitting on the raised platform, two papers on the floor, a box of watercolors between them.

"We're painting," Art said, sitting up straight. "This is Lisa, and we're painting pictures of cats and dogs."

"Doggy!" Lisa said, holding her picture up for Julia to see.

"That's very nice, hon. Arthur, this is Kathy's child. They're staying at the motel in the room next to mine. How'd she get here?"

Art shrugged. "I dunno. I heard her singing and—" He fell silent for a moment, then pointed with his brush. "Would you go back outside and tell me what you see above the door to this room?"

"Out in the hall?"

"Right."

She backtracked and looked above the door. "There's a sign that says ART."

"What kind of sign?"

Julia wrinkled her forehead and looked again. "White cardboard. Poster board. The letters are stenciled with black marker. All capitals." She came back in the room. "Why the big interest in the—"

Art pushed past her to see for himself. "It's gone," he said, pointing to the sign.

"No, it's not," Julia said, joining him in the hall. "It's right there. A sign just like the ones above the other classrooms."

Art shook his head. "It was different. While you were in the rest room, I came down the hall and this sign—or another sign above this door—started glowing in red neon. It said ART."

"That's what room it is. But red neon?"

"Red neon," he repeated firmly, reaching a hand above the door to touch the white cardboard. "And it blinked on and off, like it was calling to me. You know…my name. Art."

Julia put a hand to his forehead. "A personal message for Art in the art room? Is that it?"

He pushed her hand away and went back in the room. "I saw it."

Julia considered this a minute and remembered…the phantom semi horn that had saved her life, the lightning striking the tree to show Edward the way, a crossword clue, a place for growth of the spirit.

Haven.

"I believe you," she said quietly.

He turned to her. "You do?"

271

She nodded. "God leads us to do what needs to be done. He needed you to find Lisa."

"You're telling me God made the Art sign glow?"

"Why not? Would you rather believe some dark force is calling you?"

"No," Art said, looking to Lisa who was oblivious to their discussion as she swathed red paint across a paper. "But God doesn't usually bother with me."

"How do you know?"

He gave her a look. "If you recall, I haven't been very good."

"Neither have I."

He waved her away. "Oh, please," he said, walking to join Lisa. "What great sin have you committed? You forget to say 'pretty please'?"

"Don't think you have a monopoly on sin, Arthur Graham. I've done my share of lying, cheating, and deceiving."

"Sounds juicy. Out with it."

"I confess only to my maker. And you ain't him."

Art added a green ball of yarn to his painting of a black cat. "No problem. But I've found it's best to keep *my* doings to myself. I keep God out of it."

"You're a fool."

Art's eyes flashed. "I am not."

"You are." Julia moved to get a better look at Kathy's painting of Lisa. "You think God can't see you because you don't want him to?" She put a hand over her eyes, mimicking a child. "You can't see me, Daddy."

"Don't treat me like a kid."

She dropped her hand and thought a moment, wanting him to understand. "I'm not making fun, Arthur. But you're not being honest with yourself if you think God doesn't see you."

He shrugged. "So he sees me? Big deal. It's my business, not his. Or yours."

Julia thought of a witty comeback but held it in. He was right. Butting into other people's spiritual lives was not her style. How many times had Benjamin told her to keep her beliefs to herself? And now she was spouting off to a virtual stranger—her kidnapper, no less! Who was she to give advice about God?

"Sorry," she said. "You're right. I usually don't talk about God things. I think about them a lot, but I don't talk about them."

"Why not?"

Julia bit her lower lip and shrugged. "When you're in politics, you learn to keep your opinions to yourself."

Art snickered. "I don't think so. Politicians are full of opinions, how they'll fix this and change that."

Julia nodded. "True," she said. "And I was allowed to talk about the issues, but I was discouraged from talking about items that were...sensitive."

"Scared to lose a vote here and there?"

"Votes," Julia said. "That's the name of the game."

"You're a coward."

"I am not—"

"Okay, then what you *did* was cowardly." He tapped a finger on his cheek. "Now where have I heard that before?"

"So you *were* listening."

"Did you give me any choice? You talk enough for both of us. I can't see you keeping your mouth shut about anything. That's why it surprises me you let people tell you what you can and can't talk about."

Julia considered this. "It *is* surprising, isn't it?"

"Seems to me voters would like a person who says what she thinks, even if they don't agree with everything she says."

"Maybe they would..."

"I'd vote for you." Art dipped his brush in a jar of water.

"You would?"

"Sure. If I ever voted."

"Why don't you vote?"

He shrugged. "What's the use? I've never seen or heard of

no politician who gives a rip about me and what I need."

"And what's that?"

"Hope."

Julia hesitated. "You want me to speak my opinions, Arthur?"

"Right now?"

"Even if you don't agree with them?"

He shrugged. "Go for it."

Julia sat at the edge of the platform and ran a hand across Lisa's back. The little girl kept painting.

"Your best source of hope is God."

Art frowned. "I told you, God and me don't get along."

Julia shook her head. "If that's the case, you'd better get out your asbestos galoshes, Arthur. It's mighty hot…" She pointed down.

Art threw his brush across the room. "I am *not* going to hell! I haven't killed nobody." He glared at her. "Yet."

"You've got it wrong, son. There are murderers in heaven and people in hell whose worst offense is getting a parking ticket."

"That doesn't make sense."

Julia rose and held out an arm, coaxing him toward the window. "Leave Lisa to her painting. Come sit with me."

Art took a step toward her, then stopped. "I think I've changed my mind about you speaking your mind. I don't want a lecture. I don't need nobody telling me what a bad person I am."

"I won't mention your name once."

"Promise?"

She crossed her heart. "Stick a needle—"

"You left out the 'hope to die' part," he said, joining her as she set two chairs near the window.

"Nobody hopes to die, Arthur," she said, taking a seat. "But it will happen. It's inevitable."

"I don't think about that."

"But a little thinking will save you an eternity putting out some mighty hot fires."

"I'm not going to hell."

"So you believe in Jesus?"

"Sure," he said. "I know who he is. I'm not dumb."

"And you know he died on the cross?"

"Sure."

"And rose again three days later."

Art hesitated. "I never got that part. It was kinda spooky."

"Nothing spooky about it, Arthur." Julia studied the boy before her thoughtfully. *I don't believe I'm doing this, God, but I am. So help me say this right. Give me the right words so Art can understand.* She sighed deeply. "You think I'm a good woman?"

"You were governor, weren't you?"

Julia laughed. "Believe me, one plus one doesn't always equal two."

Art smiled. "I get your meaning. But, yeah, I think you're a good woman." He closed one eye. "Are you?"

"I try to be. But try as I might I still do bad things."

"Yeah. You mentioned something about lying and deceiving. What's that about?"

Julia stared past him. "When I was running for governor, I told some lies to get elected. Bent a few rules to get some campaign pledges."

"Everybody's doing it."

"*I* wasn't. But I did it anyway. It was easier to go along with my adviser's suggestions than fight them."

Art propped a foot on his knee. "I know what you mean."

Julia continued. "And when my daughter was growing up, I wasn't very patient with her." She shrugged, looking at her lap. "I yelled. A lot. Once, I even slapped Bonnie so hard I left a handprint on her face."

"My dad did worse than that."

"Hopefully he feels bad about it."

"I doubt it."

"Well, the truth is that everyone's done things that are wrong. And every day, when the sun comes up, try as we might, we mess up again."

"We're human," Art said.

She pointed at him. "Indeed, we are. And that's the key, Arthur. You've just clinched it. We're human, and no deed can earn us a way into heaven. Or hell."

Lisa came over to Art and showed him her picture. He nodded and she climbed onto his lap. "Then if nobody can *do* anything to get to heaven, how do we get there?"

"Only one way."

"How?"

"Jesus."

"We're supposed to chant his name or something?"

"A little more than that," Julia said, leaning toward him. She noticed Lisa was missing a shoe. "Where's your shoe, honey?"

Lisa pointed outside. Julia nodded. "We really should get her back to the motel. Kathy will be worried—"

"You were saying stuff about Jesus?" Art said.

Julia felt a stitch in her stomach. It wasn't just *her* spouting her beliefs anymore, Arthur was *asking*. The stakes had risen. She closed her eyes. *Help me say the right thing*, she prayed again.

"Earlier, you said we were human," Julia said.

"We make mistakes."

She nodded. "And God realizes that being human, and trying as we might, we can't be as perfect as we need to be to deserve a place like heaven. That's why he sent his Son to earth, to live like us, to be one of us. And then, hard as it was for him, he let men kill his Son. Yet God was still in control. It was part of his plan. He let Jesus take the punishment all of us deserve: death. All the sins of the world died with him. Those before, those happening right then, and every sin ever after. Jesus took the rap for all of us. So we don't have to."

"He was punished for things he didn't do?"

276

Julia felt her throat tighten. She nodded. Her words came out in a whisper. "That's how much he loves us."

"But his coming back to life…that didn't really happen. That was just, you know, symbolical, right?"

Julia cleared her throat, her voice strong again. "It happened. He lived again. People touched him. He ate and drank and taught his disciples for forty days until he rose up to heaven to be with his Father. But it was also symbolic. His resurrection represents us, when we are renewed, without sin. Forgiven. If we acknowledge what Jesus did for us personally, and appreciate it and tell God we're sorry for the sins we keep doing, he'll make us new again, just like he did for Jesus."

"He'll make us new in heaven?"

"Yes, Arthur," she said, touching his knee.

"So what do we—what do I have to do?"

"You have to tell Jesus thank you and tell him you'll accept his gift of forgive—"

"There he is!" came a yell from outside.

Julia whirled toward the window. *No, oh, no! Not now!*

A man was standing outside the window, pointing at them. Julia heard Walter's voice yelling out, "He's got Lisa! And Julia!"

Art shot to his feet, spilling Lisa on the floor. She started crying.

"Come on!" Art yelled, grabbing Julia's arm. "And bring the kid."

"Arthur, you don't have to do this anymore," Julia said, picking up Lisa. "I'll tell them we're all right and we can leave—"

He cut her off by yanking her into the hallway, away from the windows. "Where's your Jesus now, Gov?" he asked. "So much for forgiving my sins. He's forcing me into new ones."

"He's not forcing you into anything," Julia said, trying to calm a wailing Lisa. "He—"

Art pulled her to a stop in the hall and retrieved the gun from his belt. He brought his face to an inch from hers with the gun not far behind. His eyes were full of tears. And fear.

"It's too late! Don't you understand? It's too late for me!" He pulled them down the hall and shoved them into the women's rest room. "Stay in there," he said. "And shut her up!"

"But Arthur—"

He pointed a finger at her. "You had your chance, Gov. But it looks like God wasn't listening. He has other plans for me, and I'm not buying into them. We're going to do things my way. Do you get it, lady? My way!"

He spun and left them alone.

Twenty-three

KATHY RAN TOWARD LENNY as he stood with the men at the front of the school. He held out his arms to her, but she skimmed past him.

"You found her?" she gasped, scanning the school.

"Inside."

"Then go get her!" She lunged toward the entrance, but Lenny and Del grabbed her, holding her back.

"Stop, Kathy! You can't barge in there! She's not alone."

She stopped struggling. "What do you mean she's not—"

"The guy who robbed me is in there," Bob said. "He's got her. I saw them through the window."

Walter stepped forward. "He's got Julia, too."

Kathy closed her eyes. Her legs threatened to give out. Then her eyes snapped open and her muscles tensed. "Get her! Now."

Chief joined the group. "It's not that easy, ma'am. Bob says the guy's got a gun. Your son even said so. We can't go busting in there and scare him into using it."

"I don't care about *him* being scared," Kathy said, glaring at the school as if it were the one who'd taken Lisa. "My child is scared, and I intend to get her out."

Lenny came up behind her and pulled her close. "They'll get her, Kath. Don't worry, they'll get—"

She tore herself out of his grip and swung around to face him, her fists clenched. "Since when do you care about the kids? Or *me*, for that matter? You're rarely around, and when you are—"

"That's not fair!" He glanced at the others, checking their reaction to his humiliation.

A cold rage filled Kathy. Even now he couldn't concentrate just on her.

He went on, defensive. "I've got a job that takes me out of town."

"Does your *job* take you into the arms of other women?"

Those who were pretending not to hear the argument couldn't help but react to this newest bit of information. They turned their bodies away, but Kathy was sure they were still listening.

Lenny grabbed her upper arm and pulled her a few steps away. "Now is not the time, Kath. We'll talk about it—"

"Later?" she snapped. "Later may never come, Lenny. Not if something happens to—"

Chief moved toward them, his arms outstretched. "The first thing we have to do is get back, folks. I can't do my job with all of you standing out here in the open. Move over to the side of the building, there, by the gym. You need to stay away from the windows." He looked to Bob and Del. "Come on, fellas, help me get folks where it's safe."

Kathy complied, but she couldn't help wondering if she'd ever feel safe again.

~~~

As Del and Bob eased the group around the side of the building, Walter leaned toward Chief.

"Why'd you have *him* help you?" He flipped a hand at Del.

Chief did a double take at Del. "Why shouldn't I?"

"Because he's not one of us. He's a stowaway. He's a killer."

Del must have heard Walter's words, for he started to turn. Natalie put her hand on his arm.

"Don't listen to him, Del," Walter heard her say. "You belong here like the rest of us."

Del nodded but kept his eyes on Walter, piercing him with a look. Walter turned away. If they wanted to gang up on him, so be it.

"You want to make yourself useful, Mr. Prescott?" Chief asked.

Walter shook his head. "Forget it. I know what I'm supposed to do. I'm here to cover the story. I'm the news."

"You are, are you?" Chief asked. He waved Gabe over. "Since Walter here is too busy 'being the news,' would you run down to the cruiser for me? I need my cell phone. Then swing by my house and get the keys to the school from Anne. Fast."

Natalie stepped forward. "I'll get the cruiser, Chief. I can run faster than Gabe can—no offense, Mr. Thompson. Then I'll drop the phone off, pick Gabe up, and he can show me the way to your house."

"Do it," Chief said, tossing her the keys. Natalie ran toward the motel.

Walter reached into his pocket and retrieved a notepad and pen.

Chief's eyes warned him.

"What?" Walter asked, shrugging. He concentrated on jotting down notes.

"There is a right way and a wrong way," Chief said.

"Can I quote you?"

Chief pointed a finger at Walter and held it there a moment before walking to the others. He held up a hand, stopping their questions. "We don't know where we stand at the moment, which is to our disadvantage. As soon as Natalie gets back with a phone, I'll give Art a call."

Walter's head jerked. He walked closer, his pen poised above paper. "Are you saying the kidnapper's name is Art?"

Chief put a hand to his mouth, stifling a cough. "You misunderstood. I said, 'I'll give *him* a call.'"

"No, you didn't," Kathy said, stepping forward. "You said

281

Art. How did you know his name, Chief?"

"You know this guy?" Lenny asked, stepping even with his wife.

Just then Natalie pulled in front of the school in the cruiser. Walter watched with interest as a relieved look crossed Chief's face. *Questions too close for comfort, were they?* he thought as Chief jogged to the vehicle and got the phone. Gabe went to get in the passenger's side, and he and Natalie took off.

"What's the plan?" Del asked.

Chief took the phone and dialed the school's number. "The plan is to talk to the guy. Find out what he wants."

"I bet he wants money," Del said.

"That's a sure thing," Walter said, moving to join them.

"Mr. Prescott," Chief pinned him with a hard look. "Why don't you be responsible for keeping everyone back. Can you do—"

Before Walter could respond to this obvious attempt to keep him at a distance, Chief broke off, focusing on the phone. Someone must have picked up.

"Hello?" Chief said. "Art? Is that you?"

~~~

Art held the phone away from his ear, staring at it.

How does he know my name?

Julia appeared in the doorway of the school office. She balanced Lisa on her hip, letting the little girl play with her necklace.

"What's wrong, Arthur?"

He blinked at the sound of Julia's voice. "I told you to stay in the rest room. Get back there!"

Julia straightened her shoulders. "We will not."

He pointed the gun at her. "This says you will."

Julia raised a hand, covering Lisa's view of the weapon. She spoke softly. "Put that thing away, Arthur. You didn't need it before and you don't need it now."

He looked at the gun as if seeing it for the first time. "You know, this is the only thing I *can* depend on. The only thing in this entire world."

"That's not true. You can depend on me. You can depend on God."

He leaned his head back and laughed, trying to ignore how ragged the sound was. "Is God watching me now, Gov? Is God loving me now?"

"He loves you, yes. But he despises what you're doing."

"What does it matter?" laughed Art. "Jesus died for me. All my sins are forgiven. It doesn't matter what I do."

"Yes, it does."

He pointed the gun at her. "You said it didn't matter. God would forgive everything."

"He will. If you ask."

Disgusted, he turned away. There was always a catch. "Maybe I don't want to be forgiven. Maybe I like what I'm doing."

"I don't believe that."

She was so arrogant! She thought she knew him so well, but no one did. No one but himself. He was the only one who knew how really hopeless it all was. "Believe it," he said, a hard note in his voice.

He realized he was still holding the phone, that the person on the other end of the line had heard everything they'd just said. He put the phone to his ear. "Did you hear that?" he yelled into the receiver. "I *like* what I'm doing. I like robbing, I like kidnapping, and…and you don't want to know what else I like."

"Let Julia and the child go, Art," the man on the other end said.

He shook his head. "And have you grab me as soon as I do? I don't think so."

A woman's voice came on the line. "You give my daughter back, you creep! If you've hurt her in any way I'll—"

Art moved the receiver away from his ear, swallowing the sudden lump in his throat.

"Art?" It was the man again. "Art, are you there?"

He put the receiver back to his ear.

"Sorry. That was the little girl's mother. You know how crazy parents can get when one of their children is hurting."

Lisa's not hurting. I'd never hurt a little girl.

"I wouldn't know about concerned parents," Art said. He raised his gun hand to his eyes, covering them so Julia wouldn't see that he was about to cry like some little kid. How did he get into this mess? All he'd wanted was a few dollars. But then he met Julia and found himself liking her. And she liked him. He knew it. He'd found a bit of hope back in the art room. Hope that he could start over, that he wouldn't be stuck in this endless cycle forever. But now…now they thought he'd hurt a little girl. Now they expected the worst from him. What choice did he have but to give it to them?

Julia set Lisa on a chair by the door and held out her hand for the phone. "Let me talk."

Art pulled the receiver to his chest. "This doesn't involve you."

Julia planted her hands on her hips. Her expression was incredulous. "Excuse me?"

He shook his head, trying to clear a way through his thoughts. "I can handle this."

"*We* can handle this better."

"If you want to help you can stay away from me," he said, shooing her back to the doorway with his gun. "I don't need you."

"Yes, you do."

He squeezed his eyes shut, forcing back the tears. "I do not! I don't need anybody." He heard the sound of muffled voices and put the receiver back to his ear. "I want a car brought out front—filled with gas. I want a thousand…no, make that two thousand dollars sitting on the front seat."

"When do we get Julia and Lisa?"

"I'll come out with both of them. You can have the kid then. The governor's coming with me till I get out of town. I'll let her off after I'm sure no one's following me. Get it?"

"Are they okay?" the man asked. "They're not hurt or anything?"

What kind of guy do you think I am? "They're fine," Art said, but added for effect, "for the moment."

"Let me talk to Julia. Make sure she's—"

"You think I'm lying?"

"No, no," the man said. "Take it easy, son. What can it hurt to let me talk to her? Just a few words."

Art wiped the sweat off his face with his arm. He was hungry. He was tired. He was hot. He wanted to be left alone. He wouldn't bother anyone again if only they would leave him alone. Let him go.

"Just a few words," the man said again.

"All right," Art said since the guy wasn't going to let up. "But make it short." He handed the phone to Julia. "Short," he repeated to her.

She nodded and took it. "This is Julia." She listened for a moment, then, "Hi, Chief. I'm fine. And Lisa's fine too. Arthur never intended for things to get this far. He's a good kid. Actually, I've enjoyed getting to know him."

Nice try, Gov. Art held out his hand for the receiver.

Julia met his eyes, and her expression made his throat choke up again.

"I've got to go," she said quickly. "Like I said, he's a good kid, Chief. Don't hurt—"

Art grabbed the receiver away from her. "Got that, Chief? I'm a good kid. Don't hurt me." He laughed. "Don't you believe it, mister. You don't know the things I've done, the things I *could* do. So how about it? You agree to my conditions?"

"We need some time to arrange things," Chief said.

"How long?"

"A half hour?"

Art looked at the clock above the principal's office. "Thirty minutes. Not thirty-one."

"You got it."

They hung up.

Julia opened her mouth to speak but Art pointed a finger at her. "I don't want to hear it. I don't want to hear any more about me being such a good kid...or God, or heaven, or hell. The ball is rolling and none of those things make a difference."

Julia shook her head. "I pray you're wrong."

Art just turned away. "Pray all you want. It won't change a thing."

Art sat and leaned his head against the wall, closing his eyes. Maybe he should give himself up. If they shot him, so be it. If they threw him in jail...he'd done the detention route before. But now he was older. The stakes were higher. He'd be tried as an adult.

He opened his eyes, reassuring himself that he wasn't in that awful place. Not yet. He relaxed. For the moment.

If only Anie hadn't walked out on him. She was a good influence—though not good enough considering he'd kept living a step away from trouble. Besides, it was her fault he stole the car. She broke up with him. He figured if she was leaving, so was he. He wasn't going to stick around and be humiliated...to sit in the dark apartment alone, to hear the pounding of the neighbor's stereo as it matched the pounding of his loneliness. No hope. No reason to live.

He felt a tiny hand on his knee. He cracked an eye to see Lisa standing beside him. She held up a picture she'd drawn with some markers Julia had found in an office drawer.

"Doggy," she said.

"You like to draw doggies, don't you, kid?"

"Ruf, ruf."

Art laughed. "That's pretty good. How's a kitty go?"

"Meeeew," she squeaked.

He looked to the ceiling, trying to remember the game he'd played with his little sister eons ago.

"How's a cow go?"

Lisa raised her shoulders until they touched the bottom of her curls.

"Moooooo," Art said, in a rich cow baritone.

Lisa giggled.

"How about a—"

"Giraffe," Julia said.

"They don't make any noise," Art said. Then he reconsidered. "Do they?"

"I have no idea," Julia said. "I was hoping you'd know."

"Raf, raf, raf," Lisa said, climbing back on her chair by the door.

"Sounds good to me," Art said. He glanced at the clock. Ten minutes to go.

Julia followed his eyes. "You nervous?"

The pat answer threatened, but he held it in. He was too weary to play the macho game.

"I'm big-time scared."

Julia rolled a chair beside him and sat down. "Then stop the whole thing. Send me outside. I'll go to Chief and tell him you're ready to give yourself up."

"And then I'm supposed to surrender in front of all those people? Just walk out with my hands in the air like a loser?"

"A live loser."

"That's not living," Art said.

"Who cares if everyone sees you surrender? Is pride so important?"

Art shrugged. "I don't have much else."

"What happened to hope?"

"Easy come, easy go."

"So it's gone?"

Art waved a hand across the air.

287

Julia stood and grabbed his arm, trying to pull him to standing. He resisted.

"What are you doing?" he yelled.

"If you're out of hope, then you might as well march outside with your gun blazing and let Chief put a bullet in you."

He shook her hands away. "Stop it!"

She brushed her hands on her pants. "Why? You've given up. Why not end it? I've got things to do. Lisa wants her mom. You're wasting our time if you're doing all this for nothing, if you have no hope that something good will come out of it."

He snickered. What world did this woman live in? "Good? That's ripe."

She stared at him as though amazed by his words. "You don't do things to have good results?"

"Of course I—"

"But you just said you'd given up hope. When there is no hope there is no goodness. And with no goodness, there is no hope. They go together."

Art stood abruptly and moved to the edge of the window, hugging the wall so he wouldn't be seen from outside. She was going to drive him crazy. All this talk about hope and goodness. It didn't mean a thing. He peered outside. His getaway car wasn't there yet. He turned back to Julia. "You're talking in circles, Gov. Highbrow circles that don't mean diddly-squat."

"It's perfectly logical," Julia said. "You just won't let yourself understand."

"I have better things to do than listen to your high-and-mighty theories."

"Better things?" Julia laughed. "Like what?"

He pointed to a dead cricket in the corner. "Actually, I'd rather eat bugs than listen to your bull."

"I scare you that much?"

He gave her a hard look. "You don't scare me a bit."

She grinned. "Yes, I do."

He felt his anger rise and, with difficulty, beat it down. "You think you're hot stuff, don't you, Gov?"

"As a matter of fact—"

He took a step toward her. "You probably had a nice mommy and daddy who hung on your every word. You had piano lessons, dance lessons, and a stocking with your name on it hanging above the fireplace every Christmas."

"I did."

He pointed a finger at her. When it trembled, he curled it into his fist. "That's where you and I differ. You had it all. I had nothing. Therefore…" He held out his hands to take in their present position.

"So you rob and steal because you didn't get Lincoln logs for Christmas?"

"What are Lincoln—"

"Sorry, wrong decade." She shook her head. "You didn't get Legos so you're robbing gas stations? Is that what you're trying to tell me?"

He paced the perimeter of the room, avoiding the prospect of looking at her eye to eye. "There's more to it than that. I told you, my dad liked to beat us up."

Julia softened her tone and reached out as though she would touch his arm, but he walked out of her reach. She dropped her hand. "I understand that, Arthur. And I'm truly sorry such a thing has to happen to any child in this universe. But you can't change your parents or the past. You can only change yourself."

"I can't change nothing. I just want to be left alone."

"This is not the way to do it. Stealing and making people hate you insures their attention. Their negative attention."

"I'm used to being hated."

"Once again, it's someone else's fault."

"It's not mine."

Julia shook her head. "Adrianne loved you."

"Adrianne left me."

"So get her back."

He snapped his fingers. "Just like that?"

"It's not going to be that easy," Julia said.

"Oh, really."

"But holding hostages in Haven, Nebraska is not going to do it, either."

"This wasn't my choice."

Julia's mouth hung open. "Excuse me?"

Art fidgeted. "Well...not really."

This time it was she who gave him a hard look. "Who took whose car?"

He waved a hand in the air. "All I wanted was your car. Not you. But you wouldn't give it up."

"I was hoping you would walk away—or preferably run. I didn't think you'd kidnap me."

Art sank into the chair and rubbed his hands across his face. "I took you, but I didn't take her." He pointed to Lisa. "I don't know how she got in, but I'm being blamed for taking her. I didn't do that."

"You didn't bring her here, but you *are* keeping her here. Let her go."

Art looked up and laughed. "Who knows if this school will even let us leave? The doors and windows wouldn't cooperate before."

Julia pointed to Lisa. "She got *in*, didn't she?"

Art considered that. It was true. "Then we should be able to get out." The clock showed twenty-nine minutes had passed. They heard a car drive up, and Art went to check the window. He turned back to Julia. "It's time."

She put a hand on his forearm. "There's still time to stop it, Arthur. There's still time for hope."

He looked in her eyes a moment, then turned away. He stuffed the sack of money under his shirt, picked up Lisa, and pulled the gun from his waistband.

If only he could believe her. If only she was right. But he knew better. Life had taught him not to believe in such things.

It had taught him one hard, stinkin' truth....

"Hope is dead, Governor."

~~

Chief picked up the phone and dialed the school. It rang once.

"Yeah?" The word was harsh, impatient.

"We've got it," Chief said. "The car. The money. Bring them out." He heard Art's heavy breathing.

"Make sure everyone's backed away," Art said, his voice cracking. "I don't want anybody within fifty feet. Got that?"

"Got it. Just remember, you promised to let Lisa go."

"I remember," snapped Art. "I don't break my promises."

"We know."

"What?"

"We...we trust you."

A pause. Then, "Get everyone back and I'll come out."

Chief hung up and ran to the others.

"He's coming out but he wants everyone back. Actually, I'd like all you folks to return to the motel where its safe and I'll—"

"I'm not leaving," Kathy said.

"He has a gun, Kathy," Chief said. "I don't think he'll use it, but if he's spooked...I don't want any of you getting hurt."

Kathy crossed her arms. "I'm not leaving."

"We aren't either," Del said. Chief looked at him, then at the others, seeing the same mixture of fear and resolve on every face.

Chief ran a hand over his chin. "You folks are the most stubborn—"

"We're staying," Del said. "For Lisa. And Julia. We want them to see we're behind them. They must be terrified. We have to show them we care."

Walter shouldered his way to the front of the group. "I need to stay in order to take pictures. I only wish I had a cameraman here. This is hot stuff."

Chief sighed, shaking his head. "Your compassion is touching, Walter."

Walter's expression showed that he realized his *faux pas*. "Hey, I like Julia and the kid as well as the rest of you, and I don't want them to get hurt, but this is news, people. This is news." He pointed to Gabe. "He's here. He's a newspaperman."

"But he's not waving a camera in my face," Kathy said, her voice shaking. "He isn't acting like the news of *what's* happening is more important than the *people* it's happening to." Lenny put an arm around her shoulders, nodding his agreement.

Del spoke softly. "You keep saying you're chosen, Walter. Is this what God chose you for? To cover the news of Haven?"

At first he didn't respond, then he said, "Whatever's supposed to happen is supposed to happen to me, not you." He poked a finger in Del's chest, then walked to the edge of the group, fiddling with his camera. The others let him go.

"All right, folks," Chief said. "Nothing's going to happen until you move back. That little girl is waiting to see her mama. So let's do it."

The group moved as a single unit along the wall of the gymnasium. Kathy, Lenny, Del, and Walter up front; the rest behind. As soon as they were settled, Chief used the phone.

"They're out of the way, Art. Come on out."

Chief hunkered behind the patrol car. He held his gun over the top of the hood.

~

Walter stared at the door of the school, filled with frustration.

I have to get closer!

"I can't see," Kathy whispered from her place against the wall. "How can this be happening when I can't see!"

The desperation in her voice stirred Walter's heart, but he pushed the reaction aside. No time for sloppy sentimentality now. He scanned the area, then made a dash for a bush thirty feet from the school.

"Walter?" Del called from where he was standing with the others. "What are you doing?"

Walter knelt behind the bush, putting a finger to his lips. He held his camera ready.

The sound of a pushbar on the school door clanged. Walter clicked his camera, cursing the twigs of the bush that got in the way of a great shot. He saw a kid with a shaved head emerge from the building, holding Julia in front of him. Lisa was in Julia's arms. In the kid's other hand was a gun. It wavered from the police car past Walter's hiding place, to the edge of the building where the rest of the people were gathered.

Walter felt his pulse jump and his heart race. This was going to be dicey. Oh, why didn't he have a camera crew on hand?

⁓

Art took short steps, keeping his back to the school, glancing to his right, in case other police officers appeared from the back of the school. No one was there.

"Let the little girl go, Art," a man in uniform called from behind the police cruiser. Chief. It had to be.

"Mama!" Lisa yelled, and Art followed her gaze to a woman standing near the building. Lisa squirmed in Julia's hands, giving Julia no choice but to let her down. Before Art could react, Lisa ran toward her mother. The woman raced to meet the little girl, and some guy followed right behind her.

Art's eyes grew wide as he watched his planned scenario being taken away from him. He yanked Julia close, wrapping an arm around her waist.

"Arthur, let me go!"

Suddenly someone popped up from behind the bush and something flashed in the sunlight. Art swung toward the sudden movement. He raised the gun and aimed.

"No, no," Chief muttered to himself, steadying his gun on Art. But he didn't have a clear shot.

He watched as Art trained his gun on Walter. Just then, Del bolted. He dove between Walter and the gun.

A shot sounded.

The bullet found flesh.

Del fell to the ground; Walter stood above him.

Chief raised his gun again to shoot at Art, but Julia prevented a clear shot—until she rammed an elbow into Art's ribs, making him loosen his grip. She shoved outwards, stumbling away.

Closing one eye, Chief took aim.

Julia spun around just in time to see Art freeze, his attention drawn in too many directions. The police. The photographer. The downed man. The little girl. And…

"Julia!" he screamed.

She saw him reach for her like a drowning boy, begging to be rescued. She made a decision and took a single step toward him.

A shot split the air.

"Arthur!" Her own scream echoed in her ears as she watched him crumple to the ground. He dropped the gun, a red stain growing on his shoulder. She ran to him and knelt beside him, cradling him in her arms.

"I didn't mean it!" he cried, grimacing with pain. "I'm so sorry. I didn't mean it!"

She shushed him and stroked his cheek, running a finger over the scar. His blue eyes were the eyes of an innocent. All pretension was gone. His past was gone. "I forgive you, Arthur," she said. "And God forgives you, too."

"He'd do that…for me?"

The brightness in his eyes was interrupted as he winced in pain.

Julia raised her face to the chaos swirling around them. She saw Lisa safe in her mother's arms...Walter cradling Del's head, much as she held Arthur's...Chief on the phone, calling for help. The sounds faded, became mute. There was only her and Arthur. Alone with their God.

"God will do that for you, Arthur. Jesus is your Savior."

Art smiled, the pain gone from his face for a moment. "He's mine," he said.

Then he passed out.

Julia kissed the tips of her fingers and placed them on Art's forehead. "And you are his."

Twenty-four

Greater love has no one than this,
that he lay down his life for his friends.
JOHN 15:13

"KNOCK, KNOCK," Walter said, as he rapped his knuckles on the open door of Gabe's office.

Gabe looked up from his work, then down again. Clearly he wasn't thrilled to see Walter. His words were further proof. "The great reporter lives."

"Thanks to Del."

"Thanks to God."

"Him too." Walter hesitated. "May I come in?"

"That depends."

"On what?"

"On the openness of your mind."

"Are you implying it isn't open?"

Gabe shrugged and got up to stir the crockpot of chili. "Oyster?" he asked.

"Sure." Walter took a seat in front of Gabe's desk and waited for his bowl. "When did you have time to make this?"

"There's always time for chili."

"Put it to music and you've got yourself a jingle."

Gabe sat at his place, took a spoonful of chili, and blew on it.

"What were you working on?" Walter asked, taking his own bite. "An article about the shooting?"

Gabe raised an eyebrow. "An article about the saving."

"Oh," Walter said, looking down at his bowl. "As soon as I'm through here I'm going to see Del. To thank him."

"He's a noble man. Not many would risk their lives for another. Especially…"

Walter pointed a spoon at his own chest. "Especially me? Is that what you were going to say?"

Gabe shrugged. "You haven't been very nice to him."

"Hey, he's the one who stowed away in my van. I brought him here, put him up in a motel room along the way, paid for things."

"You're keeping score?"

"Yeah——" Walter broke off, feeling the heat fill his face. Why was everyone always turning things around on him? "I mean no, of course not. But don't act like I've been a total scumbag. I've been nice to Del."

"As nice as you could have been?"

Walter looked at the ceiling. "I didn't put him up at the Ritz or buy him a bottle of Dom Perignon with his dinner, if that's what you mean."

Gabe added more crackers. "Those are material things, Walter. A dinner is consumed. A night in a motel is over and gone."

"So what do you expect me to do? Adopt the guy?"

"He is your brother."

"Oh, please. He's a bum. He lives on the streets, eats out of garbage cans——"

"'Whatever you did for one of the least of these brothers of mine, you did for me.'"

Walter stirred his chili but didn't spoon any up. He wasn't hungry anymore.

"What's the matter?" Gabe asked. "Guilt and chili don't go together?"

Walter scowled. "Nothing goes with your chili."

"I'm wounded."

Walter flipped a dismissive hand at Gabe, and silence settled in between them. Walter squirmed in his chair, his thoughts were as hot as the chili. He kept his eyes downcast, looking anywhere but across the desk at Gabe. Finally, he couldn't take it anymore. He had to ask.

"Why'd he do it? Why'd Del fling himself in front of that bullet?"

Gabe shrugged. "It was the right thing to do."

"But most people wouldn't do it. I wouldn't."

"Not doing the right thing is the wrong thing."

Walter stood, setting his bowl on the desk with a clatter. He walked to the window, drawing in steadying breaths. "Why is it so hard?"

"Doing the right thing?"

"Yes." He looked back at Gabe. "Most of us can stay away from doing wrong, but few of us take the challenge of doing right."

"You are a wise man, Walter Prescott. 'When pride comes, then comes disgrace, but with humility comes wisdom.'"

Walter looked out the window. "I don't feel wise."

"The true mark of humility."

He snorted. "Feeling dumb?"

"Knowing how little we know."

Walter walked back to his chair, rubbing his chin, longing to understand. "You've told us we are chosen. It bothered me when I first heard it. It bothers me now. Look how I've handled this whole thing. I let it go to my head and thought I was God's gift to the world." He scuffed his shoe against a dustball on the floor. "I'm afraid the world deserves a refund."

"God sees your potential, Walter. Quit fighting it."

Frustration filled him. "How am I fighting it?"

"By trying to control things. Give it up, Walter. Give your life to Jesus Christ. He'll handle everything. He'll make you more than you ever dreamed. He'll give you a good life here and an everlasting life in heaven."

"I'm not into that kind of stuff."

Gabe shoved his chair back and stood. Walter watched him, wide-eyed. The man was clearly irritated. Gabe balanced himself against the edge of the desk, breathing in and out, calming himself. With a deep sigh, he walked to Walter, facing him. "I understand how hard it is for you to acknowledge that you can't do it alone. But once you take that step and give your life to Jesus, you will be free—truly free. Your worries will belong to God. Your fears will belong to God."

"You make it sound so easy." Walter cringed at the sarcasm in his own voice.

"No! It is not easy. You will have struggles and crises. You will experience sadness and strife."

"Then why—"

Gabe held up a hand. "By giving your life—every part of your life—to God, you will not be alone through any of it. He will listen to your concerns and lead you through. He is your father. He is your comforter. He is your God. There is nothing you can't do with God by your side."

"But *what* does he want me to do? I still don't get it."

Gabe backtracked to his desk, shuffled through the mess, and found a blank piece of paper and a pen. He brought it to Walter. "Write the story about Del, about Art, about Julia and Lisa."

"For your paper?"

Gabe shook his head. "Write it for you."

He stared at the paper in his hand. "Like a reporter?"

"Like you."

Walter shook his head, so frustrated he could scream. "You're confusing me."

Gabe grabbed his arm and pulled him out of his chair, leading him into the main room and settling him at a desk. He planted both hands on the desk, then lowered his face to meet Walter's gaze. "Write the truth, Walter. Write the truth through God's eyes."

Walter held up a hand. "That's impossi—"

Gabe pointed to the paper. "Write."

Walter chewed the end of the pen. He looked out the window of the newspaper office onto the streets of Haven. He looked down at the blank page in front of him. Zero energy expended equaled zero energy created. Why was he having such a hard time writing a simple story? Back in his reporting days, he'd whip up a piece with deadlines sitting on his shoulders. No problem. Just do it.

Just do it.

Big problem.

Big problem solved. Lisa was back with her family.

Lisa. Walter wrote down the name. What had happened this morning involved so many people. Everyone had contributed, wanting to help. Except him. He hadn't wanted to help, he'd wanted to take...take away the private moments so the entire world could eavesdrop and spy on something that was none of their business. Legalized Peeping Toms. See it! Be it! The need to know overshadowed common sense.

Kidnapper Wounded in Shootout at School. That would've been the headlines he'd tout for the news at KZTV. They'd find the dope on Art's background, his rap sheet, his economic and social past. Walter would order an interview with Art's mother, or maybe with his last employer. Or a neighbor. He'd search out a scapegoat—would it be an abusive childhood, the welfare system, or the weather? It had to be someone's fault. Pick a blame, any blame.

He felt a rumbling in his chest. A string of coughs erupted from deep within. The effort made him straighten. He felt his face redden and sweat pop onto his brow. *Stupid cigarettes! If it weren't for them I wouldn't have this thing growing inside me. I should sue the cigarette manufacturers. The tobacco growers. Teddy Mason, the kid who gave me my first cigarette back in eighth—*

Pick a blame, any blame.

The coughing stopped as suddenly as it began.

"Now they've got me doing it." His hand slapped against his lips as soon as the words escaped. *Does it ever end? Now I'm blaming others for making me blame others.*

He spread his hands flat on either side of the paper, took a

300

cleansing breath, and was genuinely surprised when it didn't disintegrate into a fit of coughing. He looked around the office to make sure no one was watching him. Then he closed his eyes, bowed his head, and prayed.

"Help me, God."

The bells began to ring in the bell tower.

Walter barely noticed. He was too busy writing.

Walter sat next to Del's bed. He adjusted the quilt around him. Del stirred, and Walter took his hands away.

Del opened his eyes as if they were weighted. It took two attempts before he succeeded.

"Walter." His voice cracked.

"Yeah, Del. It's me."

Del looked around the room without moving his head. "Where am I?"

"You're back at the motel. You were shot. The bullet grazed your side. The paramedics said a few inches to the left and who knows...?"

Del squirmed a bit, testing out the movement of his torso. He quickly found his limit. "Oh-h-h-h," he groaned.

"That's the place." Walter got out of his chair to get a glass of ice water, needing to do something, anything, to be useful.

Del shook his head. Walter set the glass on the maple nightstand.

Del closed his eyes, then forced them open. "Julia...Lisa?"

"They're fine," Walter said. "Chief shot the creep who took them. Too bad it was only in the shoulder. He's in a hospital in Kearney. Going to be fine. Until I get a hold of him, that is."

With difficulty, Del shook his head against the pillow. "No."

Walter stared at him in disbelief. "Why not? He robbed the gas station, he took Julia and Lisa. He shot you."

Del moved his tongue across his lips. "Maybe I will... water."

Walter helped him take a sip. Del settled back, holding his

side. "The boy was scared."

"Who cares?" Walter said with quick anger. "Julia was scared, Lisa was scared. Shoot, even *I* was scared."

"You spooked him."

Walter jumped up. This was too much. "Me? You're saying this is my fault?"

Del shook his head. "I'm saying you made things worse."

"I was taking a few pictures. I was no threat to him. Most criminals love the attention. They thrive on it."

"If that's so," Del said, moving up on his pillow, "why would you give them what they want by taking pictures?"

Walter stared at Del, stunned. "I...it's news."

"So what?"

"It's my job."

Del shrugged.

Walter felt his heart start to race. "Some job? Is that what you're implying? Some job?"

Del shrugged again.

Walter thought about showing Del the article he'd just written at Gabe's. It was good—the best he'd ever written, the kind of writing that would prove he was—or could be—a good reporter. But he didn't show it to Del. Why should he? Why should he try to prove anything to a bum?

He moved to the foot of the bed. "At least I *have* a job. At least I'm not a homeless mooch, a burden to society, a nobody who nobody cares—"

Del grabbed his side and moaned. Quick regret washed over Walter, and he stopped his tirade and went back to the bedside. "Hey, I'm sorry. I didn't mean..." He slumped into the chair and ran a hand over his face. "I need a cigarette."

Del smiled. "Same old Walter."

Walter's chin jerked up. He felt as though he'd been smacked with a baseball bat. *Same old Walter.* The words rang inside of him, repeating over and over. *Same old Walter. Same old Walter...*

Suddenly a terrible clarity filled Walter's mind. He shook his head, incredulous at his own thoughts. But he couldn't deny the truth.

"You've just pegged it," he said slowly, looking at Del. "I'm the same old Walter. Egotistical, brash, bossy. Selfish, opportunistic—" he broke off, giving Del a sideways look. "You can stop me any time, you know."

Del shook his head, smiling. "You're doing fine."

Walter laughed. "I have a confession to make to you, Del."

"What's that?"

"You know this *chosen* business I keep ragging you about?"

"I believe I've heard it once or twice."

"It's all a bunch of bunk. I've been acting like a big shot. Like somebody who's important. But that's not what I feel."

"No?"

Walter swallowed, uncomfortable. But he'd gone this far, he might as well get it all out. "What I really feel is *I* don't belong here."

"Why not?"

He laughed harshly. "The idea that I, Walter Prescott, would be chosen by God to do something good in this world is laughable. Just ask anyone who knows me."

"Ha, ha."

"See?" Walter said. "I've been giving you a hard time about not getting an invitation when all along I've seen that you're more deserving than I am. I've been thinking God made a mistake. Maybe Gabe got the address wrong. Maybe he was supposed to deliver it to you when you were hanging around outside my apartment."

"I think God knows what he's doing," Del said.

Walter shook his head, taking the glass of water off the table so he had something to hold. He ran a finger over the condensation, wiping it on his pants. When he finally looked up, he found himself fighting tears. "You saved my life, Del. You jumped in front of me and took the bullet. You could've been killed."

"But I wasn't."

He nodded. "Remember in front of the school, when I told you whatever is supposed to happen is supposed to happen to me, not you?"

"You were wrong."

"No," Walter said. "I think I was right. You were the one who was shot, but something happened to me, too. I think you were shot for a reason."

"If you think of one, let me know."

At the wry humor in Del's voice, Walter gave a small smile. He shook his head. "If I'd been shot, I'd still be the same old Walter we were talking about. I'd still think I was hot stuff—that I was more important than I really am. I'd be a martyred big shot. I could've played that up for days and days."

"Hmm." Del raised his eyebrows. "Maybe I should try that."

Walter laughed. "It's not your style." He looked to the ceiling. "I'm just glad you weren't killed. Your pain is hard enough to face, much less your death."

Del put a hand on Walter's arm. "I'll be fine."

"That's what they say."

"Will you be fine?"

Walter's eyes filled. He waited to speak until his throat loosened enough to let the words out. "What happened today has changed things. I've always felt I was in control. But in an instant, I saw it was a lie. A total lie. The only thing I'm in control of is messing up my life—and everybody else's." He sighed. "I'm a coward, Del. About today, yesterday, and especially tomorrow." He began to cough and took a drink of the water.

"We all have things we'd like to change," Del said, looking away.

Walter knew Del was thinking about the woman he felt he'd killed. The sadness on Del's face was almost a tangible thing. Suddenly, Walter had an idea. He grabbed Del's arm. "Hey! Don't you see, Del? It's even now. Your past. Your present. Today you wiped the slate clean." He shook Del's arm.

"You made it even by saving my life."

Del hesitated. "I don't think it works that way."

"Why not?" Walter stood and paced at the foot of the bed. "Maybe that's why all this happened. Maybe some good came from me being a coward. Because I was a stubborn pain-in-the-rear who wouldn't stay where I was supposed to, I gave you the chance to save me."

Del laughed. "Thanks for nothing."

Walter swatted the quilt. "You'll see, Del. You'll see it's true. Everything's even-up now. You're forgiven."

Walter was sure he was right. It only made sense. And yet, even as he said it, he felt a tug of uncertainty…as though something was trying to reach him. But he pushed the feeling away. He had to be right. *Something* good had to come out of this rotten situation. God had called him here, right? So what better reason could there be than to help restore Del and set his record straight?

Del, however, didn't seem to be buying it. "We can't buy forgiveness, Walter. God doesn't have a tally in heaven where he keeps track of our good deeds and our bad ones, checking them off like an accountant's balance sheet of liabilities and assets."

Walter made a face. "Are you sure? It sounds kinda neat."

Del slipped deeper under the covers, shoving the pillow against his ear. "I'm sure."

Walter stared past the bed, thinking hard. "There's got to be something we can do to make up for the bad stuff."

Del opened one eye. "Not a thing."

"What?"

"We can't earn forgiveness. Christ gives it. As a gift."

"For nothing?"

Del sighed. "All we have to do is ask."

"And we're forgiven? Just like that?"

"Just like that."

Walter shook his head. There had to be a catch. "It's too

easy. Being forgiven should take work. Hard work."

Del ran a hand over his eyes as if it were hard for him to talk about it. Walter frowned. Was that a tear Del just wiped away? "Del? Are you okay?"

Del sniffed. It *was* a tear! "You're right about one thing, Walter," he said. "Being forgiven should take work, hard work. I'd sure feel better about my past if God held a grudge and made me suffer for it."

"But you've suffered. You've been homeless."

"*I* did that. I chose to suffer because God wouldn't *make* me suffer."

"Huh?"

Del wiped his eyes and his nose with the sheet. He took a deep breath. "Jesus suffered for us. He took the punishment we all deserve. He died for us—was nailed to a cross for us and died in the most excruciating way for a man to die. Do you get that, Walter?" The fire in Del's eyes made Walter uncomfortable. "God loved us rotten, stupid, ignorant, worthless men so much that he allowed his Son to die for us. Jesus got what *we* deserve."

"That doesn't sound very fair."

"It *wasn't* fair." Del closed his eyes. Walter didn't like how pale he looked. "Not for Jesus anyway. He suffered the raw end of the deal. We're the ones who benefit."

Walter plunked into the chair. "Wow."

Del smiled, though his eyes remained closed. "Yeah. Wow."

Walter sat a moment, mulling it over. *If Jesus did the hard part…if he's already died for our sins…if we can be forgiven just by being sorry and asking…then,* "Why don't you ask, Del?"

"What?"

"Why don't you ask God to forgive you for…for that woman's death?"

Del put a hand in front of his face, palm out, as if fending off Walter's question. "I'm tired, Walter. You'd better go."

Walter felt a lump in his throat. This was a heavy-duty conversation and he wasn't sure exactly how to handle it. He got up from the chair and moved to the door. He paused, his hand on the knob. "If everything you say is true…you're wrong not to ask, Del." In a burst of impulse he added, "I'll pray for you."

He left, totally shocked at the words that had come out of his mouth. *His* mouth. Then, shocking himself even more, he went back to his room, closed the door, and did what he said he'd do.

Walter prayed to this Jesus who had died for him. He prayed for Del and for himself.

~

Art felt someone take his hand. He felt it being sandwiched between theirs, making him feel safe. Warm.

"Mama?"

"Arthur?"

He opened his eyes. Julia. "Gov. You're here."

"I'm here."

His eyes wanted to close, but he forced them open, looking around the room. "Where's here?"

"You're in a hospital in Kearney. It's a town near Haven. You were shot in the shoulder, remember?"

His shoulder throbbed. He remembered. It was over. He was alive. He was safe.

He was doomed.

He pulled his hand away and shook his head. "I'm not going. I'm *not* going."

"Not going where, Arthur?"

Was she completely dense? "To jail! I'm not going."

The way she looked away told him he'd blown it. Big time. Robbery, car theft, kidnapping, shooting…not exactly things the law would overlook.

"I'll speak up for you, Arthur. I'll do what I can."

He thought of something. "You're a governor! Can't you pardon me or something?"

"I was a governor. But even if I could, I wouldn't abuse my power by pardoning you."

Art looked away. It figured. That's the way it was with do-gooders. They talked big, but when it came down to doing something that could really help, they fell through.

"I didn't mean it," he said, putting on his best I'm-sorry face.

She gave him one of her looks. "You may feel bad for what you did now, but you meant it at the time."

He tightened his jaw. *Just like I thought. They fall through.* "What happened to your forgiving God? He'd want you to pardon me. *He'd* pardon me."

"Yes. And he will. That doesn't change."

Art raised his good arm in the air and dropped it. "But what good does it do if it won't keep me out of jail?"

"God loves us enough to give us consequences."

"Some love."

Julia looked out the window a moment, then back at him. "There was once a man who God loved very much. His name was David. He was even called a man after God's own heart. But as much as God loved David, when David did wrong, God let him suffer the consequences. And do you know what David did?"

Art snorted. "I know what I'd do."

"But do you know what David did?"

"Something stupid, I bet."

"He praised God."

"Like I said. Stupid."

"It wasn't stupid, Arthur. David realized he'd done wrong. He also realized that God used that wrong to teach him something. If there were no consequences, there would have been no lesson."

Was she for real? "I can handle no lessons."

"You don't mean that."

He laughed. "Wanna bet?"

"You've got to think past today, Arthur. Think about tomorrow."

"I am thinking about tomorrow. Today I'm free, tomorrow I'll be in jail."

"I mean the forever type of tomorrow."

There she went again, talking about that Jesus stuff. Forgiveness. Eternal life. As if he'd want to live forever. Art shook his head. "I don't feel up to thinking that far ahead. I'll think about it…"

"Tomorrow?" Julia wasn't smiling.

"Yeah, tomorrow." Art squirmed in the bed, making himself wince.

Julia hung her head, and a pang shot through him. He didn't want to hurt her. If only she'd—

"What can I do to change your mind?" she asked.

"You can call up your God and have him zap me out of here. Turn back the clock or something. Arrange for some heavenly magic."

Julia opened her mouth, closed it, then spoke in a rush. "Why should he?" She crossed her arms in front of her chest. "Why should God do anything to help you out of the mess *you've* made?"

Art felt sudden fear. "But you said—"

"I said God would forgive all your sins, but there's one condition. You have to believe in his Son, Jesus—believe in what he did for you. You have to ask for forgiveness." She glared at him.

He hated that glare. Almost as much as he craved her approval. He closed his eyes, wishing he had what she had. Wishing he understood this God that made her so confident, so right.

"You are sorry, aren't you, Arthur?"

"Well, yeah…I'm sorry I'm shot, I'm sorry I got caught, I'm sorry I don't have the money anymore, I'm sorry—"

Julia stood and headed for the door.

No! She couldn't leave him! "Julia! Don't go!"

She swung around, her eyes blazing. He wanted to crawl into a corner.

"Why should I sit here and listen to you feel sorry for your-self? What about me? What about Lisa? What about Bob and all the countless others you've hurt? God doesn't want a cocky little—" She stopped and took a deep breath. "God wants a humble man who knows he's as flawed and weak as *every* human being. God wants you to need him, to look to him for every breath, every thought, every beat of your arrogant heart."

Don't hate me. Don't be mad at me. Help me. You're my only friend in the world. "My heart is not arrogant."

"Obstinate."

He hesitated. "I don't even know what that means, but I'm not that either."

Julia smiled. "We really have to work on your vocabulary, Arthur." She returned to her seat by the bed. "If your heart is not arrogant or stubborn, then what is it?"

Art fingered the edge of the sheet, wishing he was a kid again so he could give in to the tears pushing at his eyes. "How about desperate?"

Julia considered the word a moment. "That's not bad. Desperate we can work with."

The soft words and the warmth in her eyes enveloped him. "We can?" He barely got the words out, his throat was so tight.

"If you're willing."

Art felt a shiver pass through him. Willing? Oh, yeah, he was willing. He wanted it more than he'd ever wanted any-thing. "Help me, Julia. Help me do it right."

She took his hand and squeezed it. He held on to her, afraid to let go.

"God's been waiting for this, Arthur. For you."

He nodded. He didn't know why, but he knew it was true. Following her lead, he bowed his head, and they talked to God. Together.

Miles away, the bells of Haven rang for the second time.

Twenty-five

Blessed is the man who perseveres under trial,
because when he has stood the test, he will receive the crown of life
that God has promised to those who love him.

JAMES 1:12

NATALIE CURLED UP in her beanbag chair and looked at the swath of sunlight that fell across her legs. The light reminded her of the moonlight that had shone on her legs—and Sam's—as they'd sat on the boulder back in Estes, talking about coming to Haven. Talking about God.

"Sam." Natalie put a hand on her abdomen. Sam didn't even know about the baby. What would he say? What would he want her to do?

"Marry me," Natalie said. She shook her head and pushed herself to standing. "That's not what he'd say. I'm just feeling gushy after all that's happened." She moved to the sink and looked at her reflection, remembering how Julia and Lisa had been saved from the robber...how Del had saved Walter.... "Maybe I want someone to save me." She studied the frown line between her eyes. "Fat chance." She bent over to splash water on her face. She grabbed the towel, noticing as she did so that she'd splattered water on the Bible. It was still sitting on the counter from the day before.

She picked it up and wiped it dry.

Then she remembered. Yesterday, there had been two Bibles. She never had figured that out, how one Bible on the bedside table had suddenly turned into two Bibles, one at the counter and one—

She looked over to the bedside table. The Bible wasn't there.

She ran over to the table, tossing the first Bible on the bed.

She yanked open the drawer, then looked under the bed. Nothing. It was gone. She remembered lying on the bed, her back to the Bibles, uncertain—no, afraid—of the power they contained. She stared at the Bible on the bed, wondering.

Could she tap into that power?

She sank onto the bed and ran a hand through her hair. "Okay. Now I really need saving. I'm losing my mind." She laughed as she realized she was talking to herself. "I'm even talking to—"

Her hand fell on the Bible beside her. It lay open.

Save yourself. Save your child. Read it.

Natalie looked around the room, unsure if the voice had come from inside her head or…

She picked up the Bible and looked at the heading at the top of the opened page. Ecc…Eccle—siastes. She frowned. What did that mean? A few lines on the right-hand page were highlighted in yellow. Apparently someone had read this Bible before her.

Natalie read the lines out loud. "'As you do not know the path of the wind, or how the body is formed in a mother's womb, so you cannot understand the work of God, the Maker of all things.'"

Natalie felt a flutter in her abdomen and sucked in her breath. No, it couldn't be. It was too soon. The baby couldn't move yet.

Her eyes fell back on the verse, "…you cannot understand the work of God…"

You're right. I don't understand.

"The Maker of all things."

The Maker of my baby.

Natalie lifted the Bible and clutched it to her chest. *God made my baby. I didn't make it. Sam didn't make it. God made it. The baby belongs to him.*

Maybe she could be saved after all. Maybe her baby could be saved.

She remembered Fran's words about prayer. "Just talk, Nat. Say what's in your heart."

Natalie closed her eyes and gave it a try.

And the bells rang out in jubilation.

~~~

Kathy sat on the rocker in her room. Lisa's head was snuggled under her cheek, their arms were interwoven. They rocked to the common rhythm of mother and child.

Lenny sat on the bed, flipping channels. He kept glancing at the two of them, his face twitching. He shut off the TV.

"Can't you let her down?" he said. "You've been holding her since we got back. She's fine. There's not a scratch on her."

"Not on the outside," Kathy said. She continued to rock.

Ryan came over to Lenny and ran a Hot Wheels car up his father's leg. Lenny brushed the car away. "Don't give me any of that emotional psychobabble. She's a kid. She'll get over it if you don't baby her."

"There's nothing wrong with babying a baby," Kathy said, keeping her voice conversational. If Lisa weren't cuddled in her arms, her words would be rising along with her temper. She nodded toward Ryan, who had moved his car to the checkered roadway of Kathy's comforter. "Someone else could do with a little babying."

Lenny cocked a thumb at Ryan. "He's a boy."

"Boys need hugs too."

"Not my son."

Kathy rolled her eyes. "Sometimes I'm glad you're gone so much."

"Yeah?" Lenny stomped across the room. "Well, that's just fine. Why don't I just make it all the time?" He grabbed his keys from the dresser and pointed them at her. "Whatever I've done, or will do, you forced me to do, Kath."

She'd gone too far. She knew it. She didn't want him to leave. Just the fact he'd come to Haven was a miracle. She didn't want him leaving without something good coming from his being there. She stood and carried Lisa over to the bed. She laid her down, and though Lisa wasn't asleep, she instinctively remained in position, curling her Bunny Bob under her arm.

Kathy moved to the door, signaling Lenny to follow her outside. She closed the door behind them, creating a barrier between their anger and their children.

"What do you want?" Lenny said, heading toward his car. "I've got things to do."

"In Haven?"

"What I need can be found anywhere."

Kathy felt jealousy and anger yank at her stomach. Her marriage was a thin thread, threatening to break. One wrong word—one wrong action—and she and Lenny would hurl in opposite directions.

She moved between him and the driver's door. "I need you, Lenny. We need you."

He shoved his hands in his pockets. "What for? My paycheck?"

"More. Much more than that. We're a team, Lenny. You and me. We have been since high school. We're meant to be together."

"We were forced to be together."

She swallowed back her tears. "Are—are you saying you wouldn't have married me if I hadn't been pregnant?"

He didn't answer, but scraped his toe back and forth in the gravel.

"Do you love me?" Her voice betrayed her loss of energy.

He looked up from his wandering foot. He met her gaze, then looked away. "Sure, Kath. I love you."

"But…"

He walked to the back of the car. He wrote her name in the dust on the trunk. "But I feel trapped. Like there's no tomorrow. Only a past that can't be changed and a today that's the same as yesterday."

Kathy felt her anger rise and forced it under control. "I feel trapped too."

He looked up, surprised. "How? You don't work. You get to stay at home all day long and do…whatever it is you do."

Her thin thread of control snapped. She stormed toward him, wiping her hand across the dusty name he'd written. "Whatever it is I do?" she yelled. "I take care of our children. I teach them, hold them, feed them, play with them. I'm there from the first moment they wake up to the last moment before they fall asleep. I'm aware of every breath they take during the night. They are a part of my life that doesn't go away. *You* go away, Lenny. *You're* the one who isn't there."

"I have to work," he said, walking to the other side of the car. "You want me to stay home with the kids and you work?" He laughed derisively. "You work, now there's a good one. What can you do?"

Kathy nearly said "nothing" but she didn't.

"I paint."

"Oh, yeah, I forgot," he said. He bowed. "The great artist."

They saw a door open two doors down. They waited for someone to emerge but no one did. They lowered their voices.

"I sold four of my paintings," Kathy said. "Why won't you acknowledge that?"

"A fluke."

"How many will it take to make you believe my painting is real? A talent, not a hobby?"

"That's not the point," he said. "I've seen your stuff. Pictures of kids. Who'd want that on their walls? People want scenes of mountains, sunsets, that sort of—"

"Dogs playing poker?"

He jabbed a finger toward her. "You putting me down?"

"You're putting *me* down."

"I'm telling you the truth."

"You're telling me your opinion."

"What else is there?"

"There's *my* opinion."

"And mine," came a voice from two doors down. Natalie came out of her room.

"This is family business," Lenny said coldly. "We don't need outsiders butting in where they're not wanted."

Kathy took a step toward Natalie and held out her hand, inviting her closer. "*I* want her opinion."

"Only because she's on your side," Lenny said. "I bet if I had Walter out here or one of the other men, they'd be on my side."

"I don't think so," Natalie said. "They aren't nearly the petty chauvinist you are."

Lenny took a step toward her, and Kathy stepped between them. "Leave her be, Lenny. She's my friend."

"And I'm your husband."

Kathy realized he was right. *I know, Lord, I know. My main responsibility is to my family...my husband. But how can I be on his side when he's so illogical and closed minded?*

Natalie stepped around Kathy and walked toward the car. She put her hands in her pockets, strolling casually. "I have no fight to pick with you, Lenny. I don't know you enough to like or dislike you. But from what I've heard—and I couldn't help but hear, the way you were yelling—you've underestimated your wife's contributions to the world."

"If you're talking about those dumb paintings—"

Natalie held up a hand. "I've never even seen her 'dumb paintings.' But what I have seen is a lady who has a lot to give in other ways."

Lenny eyed Kathy suspiciously, as if she were hiding something from him, but she didn't know what Natalie meant, either. She turned a curious look at the young woman, who continued. "Your wife has the power to change lives, Lenny. She has the power to make a difference."

"Oh, right." Lenny gave a snort. "She can make a huge dif—"

Kathy ignored him. Sheer joy was bubbling up inside of

her. If Natalie meant what she thought she did…she moved toward Natalie, taking her arm. "Have you made a decision?"

Natalie nodded.

"You're having the baby?"

She nodded again.

Kathy flung her arms around the girl, rocking her back and forth in a bear hug. "I am so happy for you!" She pushed Natalie to arm's length. "I knew you'd do the right thing. I *knew* it."

"Excuse me?" Lenny said, waving a hand to get their attention. "You two want to let me know what's going on?"

Kathy put her arm around Natalie's shoulders and walked her toward Lenny. "Natalie is pregnant and she's decided to have the baby."

Lenny stared at them a moment, then he walked around the car, opened the door, and got in. He started the engine, revving it, then called to Natalie through the window. "Bad decision, little lady. Bad decision."

~

Julia knocked on the door to Del's room. "Antonio? It's me, Julia."

He called out for her to come in, and she walked inside. He was sitting in bed with pillows propped behind him, a book in his lap.

"What are you reading?" She took the seat next to the bed.

He lifted the book toward him, revealing the title.

"Have you always been a Bible reader?"

"I knew this book well once. I've chosen to ignore it for many—too many—years."

Julia noticed the lack of inflection in his voice. "Are you feeling all right?"

He touched the bandage at his side. "Sore. And stupid."

"Why stupid?"

"Who'd have thought? I mean, I'm probably the least likely to be heroic."

"Heroes don't plan their heroism. It's an instinctive reaction that comes from the heart."

"And bypasses the brain."

She laughed. "Seems to me the brain should be bypassed more often."

Del ran a hand over the opened page. "It does complicate things."

"What 'things' are we talking about?"

"I'm not much of a philosopher. I was once but...now I lean toward reality. Surviving. And there are things in my past that are so real I can't..." He closed the Bible and held it close. "If only my heart could take over. My heart would let it go, but my mind holds on to it as if the reality, the permanence of it, is a noose around my neck, just waiting for the moment when I walk off the edge of the platform."

"What would your heart do?"

Del looked to the ceiling and smiled, giving Julia the distinct impression he'd thought about this often. "My heart would acknowledge the sorrow, the pain, the guilt...but it would let me go. It would understand that I'm sorry. It would let me ask for forgiveness."

"You have a good heart."

He smiled again.

She arched her spine, envying Del his soft bed. She could really use a good night's sleep....

"I've been to the hospital," she said. "With Arthur. The boy who shot you."

"How's he doing?"

Julia laughed at his concern. "You have a *very* good heart, Antonio. Not many people would forgive so quickly."

"I can't judge him. I don't even know—"

"But you can judge yourself, eh? And rather harshly at that."

"I know me."

"It's the past, Antonio. God will forgive you. All you have to do is ask."

Del gave her a teasing look. "What's this, Governor Carson? Is this religion I hear coming from your lips? How politically incorrect of you."

"I know." Julia shook her head. "My staff would cower in the corner if they heard me talking this way. It was not allowed."

"But now it is?"

"I'm not running for office."

"Yet."

Julia squinted an eye at him. "You haven't been talking to a pushy politico named Benjamin, have you?"

"He wants you to run?"

"For Congress."

Del took a few moments to picture Julia in Washington, D.C. "Can you imagine the heads you'd turn if you spoke your mind? If you talked to the public like you're talking to me right now?"

"I don't think heads would turn. They would most likely roll."

"Chicken."

"Call me fried, baked, or broasted."

"You could do it, Julia. You could make a difference out there."

"So could you."

Del looked away. "I still don't know why I'm here in Haven. John talked to me, told me I'm supposed to give of myself. But that's a generality. How? Where? Those are the specifics he won't—or maybe can't—explain."

"Because he doesn't know."

"Only God knows," Del said. "I've heard it. But I'm no good at dissecting God's intentions." He brushed a hand across the face of the Bible. "I don't know him well enough. I thought I did, oh, how I thought I did—"

"Tell me about the woman, Del."

He hesitated. "She haunts me." His fingers traced the lettering on the cover of the Bible. "I was an arrogant fool who thought I sat at God's right hand. I thought I was better than those I'd been asked to serve."

"Serve?"

"I was a priest."

Julia felt her jaw drop. "A homeless priest?"

Del laughed. "I was a priest first. I chose homelessness as a result of my actions. It was my penance."

"But why? How?"

Del closed his eyes and sighed. "I judged others when I had no right to judge."

"But wasn't that part of your job as a priest? To judge the sins of others and get them on the right track?"

"No. I had the responsibility of guiding, but never judging." He turned the pages of the Bible, hunting for a verse. "Here it is: Romans 14:10. 'Why do you judge your brother? Or why do you look down on your brother? For we will all stand before God's judgment seat.'"

"So what happened with the woman?"

Del leaned his head against the pillow and once more closed his eyes. "Her name was Mellie." He opened his eyes long enough to laugh. "She was pretty and knew it. Advertised it in ways that were…indiscreet. Low-cut blouses, high-cut skirts. Skin. Lots of skin. For sale."

"A prostitute?"

"A wife and mother."

"Hardly the June Cleaver type."

"I certainly never saw her wearing pearls and an apron." Del shook his head, thinking back. "Still, she had something in her. We all have it I guess. A need to be loved and appreciated. Unfortunately, she ignored her potential and zeroed in on her physical attributes."

"So she *was* a prostitute?"

"Off and on. We were working on getting her away from that life when she was killed. At least, that's what *I* was working on."

"And Mellie?"

Del raked his hands over his face as if he could rub the memories away. "She became a hooker right out of high school. Got in with the wrong crowd. No future, that sort of thing. Hooking meant fast money. Then she met Al. A customer at first, he fell in love with her and offered to take her away from the life. She took him up on it, and they got married and had two kids. They were doing okay. Al worked the night shift at a factory. Mellie stayed home with the kids. But soon after the birth of their second child the rumors started. I heard Mellie was sneaking out at night and was back in the life. On the side.

"One night, I went downtown to see for myself. There she was, half-dressed, strutting her stuff. I pulled her into the car and gave her what-for. I mean, how could she do that? She had a good life going, a house, kids, and a husband who loved her.

"'You don't understand, Father,' she said. 'Things aren't what you think. I don't have a choice.'

"She had a black eye. 'Your pimp give you that?' I asked her. She laughed, then started sobbing until I thought she'd die of it. I pulled over and let her cry it out. I didn't have a clue what to do. I patted her hand and told her she needed to stop prostituting herself. Like Jesus told the adulterous woman, 'Go now and leave your life of sin.' It was all very awkward. I'd always had the wall of the confessional between me and the person confessing. Up until that point I'd never realized what a safety net that wall was, keeping me emotionally distant from the humanity of people, keeping my strength at arm's length from their frailty."

"So how did she die?" Julia asked.

Del sighed deeply, putting a hand on his wound as the movement made it ache. "Mellie and the kids started coming to church regularly. Never saw much of Al. I thought things were going all right for her until one day she knocked on the door to my office and staggered in with another black eye, her wrists black and blue."

Del stopped talking, his eyebrows knitting together as he fought for control. Julia took his hand.

"What happened?"

He drew a deep breath and stared straight ahead. "I was an egotistical, arrogant, judgmental—"

"Del…"

"I didn't let her talk. I jumped on her, accusing her of going back to prostitution. 'Is this the kind of life you want for yourself and your children?' I asked her. 'Getting beat up by your pimp, demeaning yourself, shaming yourself before God and man?'"

"Tough words," Julia said.

Del sniffed. "Oh yeah. I was full of self-righteous indignation. She was a sinner and I was a lofty priest. I told her she needed to confess her sins before God and then march right back to her husband and be a good and humble wife. She needed to remember her marriage vows to love, honor, and obey."

"So did she?"

Del shook his head. "I should have known something was off-kilter when she just sat there and didn't respond. Her face went blank. Resigned. As if all her choices in life had been snatched from her. When I was done with my ranting, she stood and walked to the door of my office like a zombie. At the last moment she turned and said, 'Pray for me, Father.'"

Del hid his face in his hands. His shoulders shook.

Julia leaned close, putting an arm around him. "Antonio, it's all right. It's all—"

He pushed her attentions away, his face flaring. "It was not all right!" he snapped. "Next morning her body was found. She'd been beaten to death."

Julia sank into her chair. "Her pimp killed her?"

Del met her eyes. "Her husband killed her."

Julia swallowed. "For going back to prostitution?"

"For *refusing* to go back to prostitution," Del said. "Her hus-

322

band had become her pimp. He was the one who had forced her back into the life—for the money."

"He was the one who'd been hitting her?"

"Hard and often," Del said. "And I was the one who sent her back into his arms because I was too arrogant to listen to what she had to say. She couldn't win. 'Stop sinning by prostituting yourself!' I told her. 'Be a good wife and obey your husband.' I was quick enough to condemn her with my own self-righteousness. After all," Del said, his voice turning sarcastic, "I was a priest, a man of God." He laughed. "A representative of God's love and compassion, healing wounds, bringing people closer to the Father's awesome power."

"You made a mistake," Julia said.

"A costly mistake."

"That's why you left the priesthood?"

"I had no right to stay. A woman had lost her life because of me. A man was in jail because of me. Two innocent children were without their parents because of me. I deserved to have what they had. Nothing."

"God must think differently, Del. After all, you're here. In Haven."

He shrugged and attempted a smile. "And in your beautiful company."

"You betcha," she said.

Del squeezed her hand. His face relaxed. "So how do we do it, Julia? How do we know which path to follow? Which thought and plan is God's, and which is our own?"

Julia rose from her chair and walked the length of the room, her hand at her mouth. "That's a good question, and one I've been considering." She stopped at the foot of his bed. "On the drive to the hospital and back I had time to think about all that happened the last twenty-four hours. I was kidnapped. Can you believe that? I was kidnapped!"

"You must have been scared."

She raised a finger and resumed her walk. "That's the odd

part. I wasn't scared. Arthur had a gun and a past that told me he was capable of using it, and yet I never considered—maybe I never allowed myself to consider—that he would actually hurt me. Only on the way back from Kearney did it hit me— the danger I'd been in. I had to pull to the side of the road, I was shaking so hard. Why didn't I feel that way when it was happening?"

"What kind of man is he?"

"For one thing he's not a man. He's a kid. Maybe that's the reason I wasn't scared. I saw a person who was on the wrong path, yet a person who had potential. His fate wasn't set in stone. He could be helped. He could be liked. Loved."

"Walter wondered why you ran to Art when he was shot. He wondered why you helped a criminal."

"I wasn't helping a criminal. I was helping Arthur."

"Not everyone would make the distinction," Del said.

"You see? That's how I know God was running the show. He didn't give me the normal reactions to the situation. He led me in a different direction. He took away my fear and gave me compassion. And he gave me the words to talk to Arthur about him." She looked at the floor, embarrassed, yet filled with a sense of great joy. "At the hospital, Arthur accepted Christ as his Savior."

"Oh, Julia…"

She nodded, smiling. "It wasn't me talking…I mean it *was* me but they weren't my words. I think that's why I'm here in Haven. To help Arthur." She sat beside him. "And maybe you're here to save Walter. And yourself."

"Myself?"

"Ask for forgiveness, Antonio. Cleanse yourself of the guilt. Free yourself."

"Just like that?"

"It's not 'just like that,'" Julia said, her voice rising like a mother chastising her son. "How long has it been since Mellie's death?"

"Three years."

"Long enough," Julia said. She reached across the quilt and took his hands. "I'm here to pray for you, Antonio. Pray with you, if you want me to. But you are going to do it. Rid your heart of the past so you're free to start a new future."

"I don't know—"

"Don't talk back to your elder, Antonio," she said. "Didn't your mama bring you up to respect your elders?"

"Yes, but—"

"Then do as I say. I know what's best for you."

"What's best for me is..." he pulled her hand to his lips and kissed it. "Is to do as you say."

"Good boy."

For the second time in a day, Julia brought a repentant soul to God. And the bells rang.

~

"Two more."

"He is pleased."

Twenty-six

Unless the LORD builds the house, its builders labor in vain. Unless the LORD watches over the city, the watchmen stand guard in vain.
PSALM 127:1

KATHY SAW JULIA coming out of Del's room.

"How is he?" she asked.

"He's great, marvelous, sensational," Julia said, feeling a bit of those feelings herself.

"Wow. Where can I get some of that?"

Julia laughed and pointed a finger skyward. She was on a roll.

"He's happy because of God?"

"And God's happy because of him."

Kathy leaned against Julia's car, a sad look on her face. "I don't think God's very happy with me."

"Why not?"

"Lenny's mad. He drove off."

"Is that your fault?"

Kathy shrugged. "It takes two to argue."

"I thought it took two to tango."

"That too."

At the bleak expression on Kathy's face, Julia put an arm around her shoulders. "Why don't you come in my room and we can talk—"

"I can't. I was on my way to the school to get something. Natalie's looking after the kids." She hesitated, then met Julia's eyes. "I heard you were at the hospital, looking after that fiend who took Lisa."

"He did not take Lisa. Lisa found her way into the school all by herself. He kept her there, but he did not take her."

Kathy shook her head. "I find it hard to believe that a two-

326

year-old could—or would—walk across an open field toward a strange building and go inside. How did she open the door?"

"I don't know. We found her playing in the art room. Singing actually. She and Arthur painted some pictures."

Kathy's look was filled with disbelief. "He painted with her?"

"He was very gentle. Lisa liked him, and he liked her. I liked him."

"Even though he kidnapped you?"

Julia shook her head. She didn't feel up to defending Arthur again. "I'm just glad everything turned out all right."

Kathy closed her eyes and put a hand to her face. "I must be crazy, getting after you, the person who kept Lisa safe." She opened her eyes and held out her hand. "Thank you, Julia. Who knows what would have happened if Lisa had been alone with that man."

"Nothing would have happened, Kathleen," Julia said, hoping she was right. "Arthur's done some bad things, but he's not a bad person."

"They go together," Kathy said.

Julia shook her head. "Haven't you ever done something bad?"

Kathy looked away. "Sure, but—"

"Should I assume you're a bad person?"

Kathy nodded, conceding the point. "As a parent I'm supposed to tell the child the action was bad, not the child. I love you but I don't like what you did."

"Exactly."

"That doesn't make it easy."

"Going against human nature rarely is."

Kathy paused a moment, thinking. "Would you like to come with me to the school? I was going there to get something for you anyway."

"Something for me?"

"Come along and you'll see."

327

"How can I resist?" Julia looked down at her clothes. "Do I have time to change clothes? These are beginning to have a life of their own."

Kathy checked her watch. "If you hurry. We have to be at the tower room at five."

"For what?"

Kathy pointed a finger. "That's right, you were gone. A gathering is scheduled for five o'clock in the meeting room. Someone's coming to talk with us."

"Who?"

"I don't know. They didn't say. But Anne was excited about it." She took a quick breath. "And there's more good news! Natalie's having the baby." A moment after she spoke, she clamped her lips shut, then shook her head regretfully. "I'm sorry. I forgot you wanted her to have an—"

"I wanted no such thing," Julia said.

"Yes, you did. At the park. You talked about a woman's right to control her own body, and you mistakenly implied a baby's life doesn't begin at conception."

Julia held up a hand. "I was wrong."

"You were—you admit it?"

"I was spouting other people's opinions, not my own. One of the downsides of being a politician."

"What changed your mind? What made you willing to share *your* opinion?"

Julia pointed skyward again.

Kathy laughed. "He's had a busy day."

"And I have a feeling he's not done with us yet."

Julia pulled in front of the school. It was hard to imagine that only hours earlier two people had been shot a few yards away.

"How are we going to get inside?" she asked Kathy.

"Anne said it would be unlocked for us."

"Good. I'd rather not get in through a broken window like I did yesterday."

328

"You went through a window? Maybe that's how Lisa got in."

Julia got out and shut her door. "I'd say yes if the window hadn't fixed itself."

"Fixed—?"

Julia chuckled as she walked toward the school. "It's better to show than tell."

The front door was unlocked. As they went inside, the stale smell of the closed school brought Julia immediate memories: *A Tale of Two Cities*; candy bars and coffee; Arthur and Lisa lying on their stomachs in the art room, painting dogs and cats.

Kathy was watching her face. "Brings back bad memories?"

Julia blinked, surprised herself at the truth. "Good ones, actually."

"You don't make sense, Julia."

"Never claimed to." Julia turned into the classroom where she and Art had entered the building. "This is it. This is the place where Arthur and I—"

"What's wrong?"

Julia moved to the window—the window that had been broken and then mended, the window that had prevented them from leaving the school.

It was broken. Shards of glass scattered the floor.

"This is wrong." Julia looked around, struggling to make sense of it all.

"I'll say," Kathy said. "It really bugs me when vandals break—"

"No. You don't understand. Arthur broke this window so we could get in, but when we tried to leave, it was whole." She noticed a chair lying on the floor and went to it. "He even took this chair and banged it into the windows, trying to get out. But the glass wouldn't break."

Kathy wrapped her arms around herself. "He must have broken it."

Julia knelt next to the broken glass on the carpet. She picked up a large, jagged piece and used it as a pointer. "The broken glass is on the *inside*. Meaning the window was broken from the outside. This window is the way it was when we first entered."

"Maybe you went back to the wrong room when you were trying to get out?" Kathy suggested.

Julia ran to the chalkboard, pointing to her writing. "This is the place. I wrote this."

Kathy moved toward the door. "I don't like it here. What you're saying is impossible."

"But it happened."

Kathy swallowed slowly, then asked, "Does this type of thing happen all the time, Julia? In the outside world, I mean. Does it happen, and we're just too blind to see it?"

"It's never happened to me before," Julia said.

"Me neither."

Kathy looked around the classroom as if there were eyes looking down at her. "It's this place...Haven. It's...different."

Julia studied her friend's face. "Different better, or different worse?"

Kathy shook her head. "It's like everything has a purpose, nothing is put before us or done by chance. It's all planned out."

"Like we have no choice?"

"Not exactly," Kathy said. "It's like we have the same choices we've always had but things are clearer. The path is clearer."

"Our destiny awaits?"

Kathy laughed. "Before coming to Haven I never thought I had a destiny. Destinies were for world leaders, scientists, and great teachers. Not for housewives who live in Eureka Springs, Arkansas...who've always lived in Eureka Springs, and probably will always live in Eureka Springs."

"But now you feel different?"

"I don't claim to be as important as the rest of you, but—"

Julia started to protest, but Kathy held up a hand, stopping her.

Kathy went on. "But I get the feeling it doesn't matter. Somehow, as small as I am in the scope of things, I matter. I can make a difference."

"What more can we ask for?" Julia said.

"We can ask not to waste any more time pretending it isn't so."

Pleased at Kathy's words and insights, Julia patted her on the back. "I'm impressed. The shy mama with her eyes focused on potty training and Cheerios turns into the dedicated mother with her eyes focused on the plight of the world."

"Don't assign me the world," Kathy said wryly.

Julia laughed. Fair enough. "We'll start you small. How about the western hemisphere?"

"Smaller."

"North America?"

"Smaller."

She gave Kathy another chiding look. "You're limiting yourself, Kathleen."

"I'd settle for Eureka Springs. Or to go smaller yet, I'd settle for making a difference in my own family."

"A fire starts with a spark."

"And you need dry wood to get it blazing."

Julia hesitated. "What's that supposed to mean?"

Kathy let out a laugh. "I have no idea! I'm glad Natalie's the writer. I'll stick to painting. Speaking of which…" She crooked her finger toward the hall. "That's why I came here. To get a painting I made of—"

"Lisa!" Julia said, remembering the beautiful painting. "I saw it. It's wonderful. You have talent, Kathleen. You don't just capture a moment on paper, you capture an emotion."

"It's not hard considering my subject matter," she said, heading for the art room. "Kids speak to me, even before they can speak."

Julia followed her into the room. They stopped ten feet from the painting. Lisa slept on a bed of green. Her thumb gave her security; the draped cloth, the scene's warmth, and the blush of her cheeks spoke of her innocence.

"You never signed it," Julia said. "You really must."

Kathy nodded and found a pen on the counter. She knelt down to claim the painting as her own. She unclipped the paper from the easel and handed it to Julia.

"This is for you. For taking care of Lisa when I couldn't."

Touched, Julia held the painting at arm's length, appreciating it with the new eyes of ownership. "I will treasure this, Kathleen. Somehow it represents my whole experience in this place. The innocence and security Lisa has…and that Arthur lost." Her eyes grew misty. "Once it's lost, can we ever get it back?"

It was Kathy's turn to put a comforting hand on Julia's shoulders. "Only God knows that."

Julia stretched out on her bed, uncaring of the wrinkles it might create in her clothes. Such things didn't matter. Talking to Edward mattered.

She pulled the phone off the nightstand and dialed, wedging it between the pillow and her ear. It rang once. Twice.

"Be there, Edward," she whispered.

"Hello?"

The dam broke. Julia couldn't answer. All she could do was sob.

"Julia," Edward said softly. "Julia."

He had a talent for that—for knowing when her sobs stemmed out of immediate need and when they were a healing of something past. Their thirty years of marriage had molded their emotions into a whole, like two hands intertwined, becoming stronger together than apart.

"Edward," she said.

"I love you, Julia."

His words dried her tears, giving her the strength to tell him her story.

Twenty-seven

For many are invited, but few are chosen.
MATTHEW 22:14

WALTER HELD THE PAGE to his chest protectively. It was the best thing he had ever written. He picked up the phone in the newspaper office and dialed Bette's number. He was sure Gabe wouldn't mind the long-distance charge.

"Hello?"

"Bette!" he said as soon as he heard her voice.

"Walter? What's wrong?"

He laughed. "Nothing. Absolutely, positively, never again, nothing."

"You take a cheerful pill, Walter? This isn't like you."

"Don't dissect it, Bette. I want to enjoy it. I'm afraid it will wear off."

"So you have taken something?"

"No, no. I've done something."

"Nothing foolish, I hope."

"Me? Foolish?"

"Something frivolous?"

"I am never frivolous."

"Then tell me," she said. "Why are you soaring?"

"I've written a news story."

There was a pause on the line. "The news is your business, Walter. I don't underst—"

"I've written a news story that is fair, positive, and enlightening."

"Who says?"

"Where's your confidence in me, Bette?" He saw his reflection in the window and smiled at it. *I even* look *happy.*

"I've read what you've written, Walter. I've listened to the stories you condone. I know what angle you're after."

"The newsbreaking, juicy tabloid tidbits of sensationalism?"

"Uh, yeah. That about does it."

"No more," Walter said, sweeping a hand across the air as if writing a banner. "There's another way."

"I know," Bette said, cautiously. "I mean I've always suspected you could present the news in a better—"

"Better?" Walter said. "This is *great*. It will revolutionize the news industry. It will make people grab their kids and sit them down by their side as they watch the evening news together. It will give them hope amid the specks of evil trying to worm their way into this world."

"Specks of evil?" Bette asked. "There are more than specks of evil out there."

"Not as much as you think, Bette. And that's our fault. The media's fault. We pounced on the negative because we thought it was best for our ratings. But in doing that, we've given people the idea that evil reigns. That evil is in control. That there is no hope for good people, and the good *in* people, to triumph."

"Oh, Walter." There was a catch in Bette's voice. "That sounds...what made you change your mind? I've been trying for months and months—"

"I know," he said softly. "And I apologize for dismissing your concerns. You were right but I wouldn't see it. I don't think I could see it. I wasn't ready."

"But you're ready now?"

"I'm ready now."

"What happened?"

"I was an egotistical, obnoxious moron."

She laughed. "Oh really? Glad I missed it."

He put a hand to his forehead. He'd been so blind for so long. "How have you tolerated me, Bette? How has anyone tolerated me?"

"You were—are—a good TV news producer, Walter. You've worked hard to get where you are."

"I didn't get where I am by being good, but by going along. I did what they expected me to do."

"Isn't that the way it is with any job?" Bette asked.

"That's the *easy* way. But that's not necessarily the best way. Or the right way."

"You've never been too concerned about right before."

"I've never had a gun pointed at me."

"A *gun?* Walter! What happened?"

"I'm fine. There was an...incident. I stood up like I was invincible and stuck a camera in a criminal's face. I scared him. He pointed the gun at me. He pulled the trigger. A friend of mine—a very good friend of mine—" Walter smiled, because it was true—"jumped in front of me and took the bullet for me."

"Is he all right? Are *you* all right?"

"He's fine. And I'm fine. In fact, I think in saving me, he might have saved himself."

"Huh?"

He shook his head, realizing how strange it must sound. "I'll explain it to you later. In person."

"You're coming home soon?"

"There's a final meeting tonight. A send-off. We'll be leaving tomorrow."

"So what was it all about, Walter? The invitation? Haven?"

He hesitated. How could he put all his mingled feelings into words? He'd come to Haven with a chip on his shoulder, ready to show the world what he was made of. He'd come as a hot-shot TV producer who had money, power, and more insight than anyone else. His only weakness had been his fear of dying...his dread of the biopsy and his anger at finding out his own vices had been the cause of a fatal disease.

But now...now he was different. A man with nothing had risked everything he had—his life—to save him. And seeing that, Walter realized sacrifice was something he'd been avoiding. He hadn't taken the job in New York City because he hadn't wanted to sacrifice the easy comfort in St. Louis. He

335

hadn't married Bette because he didn't want to sacrifice the control he had over his single lifestyle. And his disease…he hadn't gone to the doctor sooner because he didn't want to sacrifice the pleasure of cigarettes or the fantasy that he was invincible.

But Del had thrown himself in the path of a bullet to save the selfish being that was Walter Prescott. And in the process, he'd opened Walter's eyes. *God* had opened his eyes.

"Walter?" Bette said, still on the line. "What's it all about?"

Walter nodded at his reflection—both Walters agreed. "It's about a second chance. I'm getting a second chance and I'm not going to blow it."

~

Before Kathy could use the key to her hotel room, Natalie opened the door from the inside. Lisa was by Natalie's side, wearing a lavender ruffled pinafore over a white eyelet dress.

"You'd never believe—" Natalie started.

"Where'd Lisa get the dress?" Kathy cut her off, walking inside.

Ryan ran up to her sporting a navy blazer, gray pants, and a red tie on a white shirt. "Lookie, Mommy! A big-boy suit." He turned in a slow circle while Lisa twirled, making her dress rise.

Kathy knew her mouth was open, but she couldn't shut it. "Where'd they get the clothes?"

"Anne brought them by for the meeting tonight. And that's not all," Natalie said. She moved to the closet and pulled out an ivory voile dress with a gathered skirt and tiny pearl buttons marching up the bodice. "This is for you."

Kathy reached to feel it. "It's beautiful. It looks like a Victorian lawn dress."

"And there are shoes and a shawl to match," Natalie said, retrieving a pair of ivory pumps and an embroidered shawl from the closet. "And a suit for Lenny."

"He hasn't come back?"

Natalie shook her head. "Don't worry. He'll be here."

Kathy held the dress under her chin and looked in the mirror. "It's perfect," she said. Then she turned back to Natalie. "Did you get one too?"

"You bet." Natalie reached past Lenny's suit in the closet. She pulled out a dress of royal blue crepe. Knee-length, it was a simple sheath with short sleeves and a scoop neck. "Blue shoes to match." Natalie held them out. "Blue's my favorite color."

Kathy laughed. "Would you expect them to give you anything less?"

Natalie headed for the door. "It's time to get beautiful for whoever is coming tonight."

Kathy put out a hand, stopping her. She spoke softly so the children wouldn't hear. "Who do you think it is? They're going to a lot of trouble, making sure we have fancy clothes."

"Must be someone important," Natalie said.

"But we've already met the mayor of Haven, and the chief of police. Who else is there?"

"Maybe the queen."

"It's a he," Kathy said. "I heard Anne say it was a he."

"A king then," Natalie said, opening the door. "Maybe we're going to meet the king of Haven." She waved good-bye and went to her room to get dressed.

⁓

Julia heard knocking in her sleep. She struggled to keep it there but it was insistent. The dream wavered, and reality settled around her.

Knock, knock, knock.

She opened her eyes. She didn't remember getting under the covers, but that's where she was. She must have been more tired than she thought.

Knock, knock, knock.

"Who's there?" she asked, her voice cracking. "Who's there?" she asked again.

"It's Louise, Julia. It's almost time for the meeting. I have something for you. A present."

Julia climbed out of bed and attempted to smooth her rumpled clothes. She opened the door to find Mayor Louise Loy holding out an emerald green suit. A chiffon skirt was paired with a fitted brocade jacket complete with rhinestone buttons. "For you," Louise said.

"Is this for the meeting tonight?"

"Yes, it is." Louise handed it over. She added a pair of green, dyed-to-match shoes.

"Who's getting married?"

Louise laughed. "Don't look at me."

"I didn't realize this was such a big production," Julia said.

"We have a guest speaker."

"That's what Kathleen said. Who is it?"

Louise smiled. "A man."

"That narrows it down."

"A good man."

"Even more."

Louise turned to leave. "You'll like him, Julia. Just like he likes all of you."

"So we've met him?" Julia asked.

Louise raised a hand. "Be there at five."

$\sim$

Walter knocked on the door of Del's room. He was told to come in.

"I thought you might need help getting ready," he said. He noticed Del sitting on the edge of the bed trying to tie his shoes without bending over. He hurried to his side. "I guess I was right."

Del sat upright, sighing. His brow was moist with sweat. "It's hard to get dressed when you can't bend."

"I believe it." Walter finished tying the shoes and looked at Del's stricken face. "You don't look so good. Maybe you should stay here tonight. I'm sure everyone would understand."

"No!" Del said adamantly. "I'm going. I didn't come this far to miss the main attraction."

"Which is?"

Del hesitated. "I was hoping you'd know."

Walter adjusted Del's paisley tie. "I don't think anyone knows. It's a big secret." He waved his hands next to Del's face and turned on his melodramatic voice. "Maybe our host is coming to visit."

"That's not funny, Walter," Del said, turning away. "You shouldn't make fun of God."

Walter sighed. Del was right. Why were old habits so hard to change? "I'm sorry. I'm not making fun. Not really." He went to adjust his tie in Del's mirror, then turned to face Del again. "Truth be told, it's got me a little nervous. So much has happened in the thirty-six hours we've been here. I don't know how they can top a robbery, a kidnapping, a missing child, and a gun battle."

"I hope it's not another crisis," Del said, moving to leave, a hand supporting his side. "I'm not up to it."

Walter hurried ahead of him to open the door. "I think you're safe. You've already done your part."

He was wrong.

Twenty-eight

When he thunders, the waters in the heavens roar;
he makes clouds rise from the ends of the earth. He sends lightning
with the rain and brings out the wind from his storehouses.
JEREMIAH 10:13

NATALIE WALKED IN the meeting room of the bell tower, then stopped. She scanned the room in silence, full of questions.

"What happened to the room?" she whispered, not wanting to violate the quiet. The rich tapestries that had covered the stone walls were gone. The plants, which had given the room warmth, were absent. All that remained was a circle of chairs in the middle of the room.

"Eight chairs," Natalie counted aloud. "Not enough for all of us and the mentors." She shivered, suddenly apprehensive. "Fran's not going to be here? She has to be. I need her. I have so much to tell—"

Lisa burst into the room and ran to Natalie, flinging her arms around Natalie's legs.

"Natty!"

"Hi, there, sweet girl. Where's your—"

Kathy came in the room with Ryan and Julia. Their eyes took a quick inventory.

"What happened to the room?" Julia asked.

"This is a new kind of decorating," Kathy said, touching the cold stone of the walls. "Bare bones."

"And where is everyone?" Julia asked.

"Everyone is here now," Walter said, coming up behind them. He swiped an arm through the air, clearing a path for Del. "Make way for the conquering hero."

"Walter, don't make such a big deal—" Del walked in the room and stopped like the others had done. "What happened?"

Ryan tugged at Kathy's dress. "Where's Donnie?"

"He'll be here soon."

"I don't think so, " Natalie said. "There are only eight chairs. For the five of us and your family."

"Speaking of chairs," Del said, holding his side. Walter helped him settle in.

"All dressed up with no place to go," Julia said with a wry smile.

"Why *did* they give us these fancy clothes only to come to a stripped-down room?" Natalie looked at the others, hoping someone could explain, but they all seemed as puzzled as she was. She shook her head. "Not a single person here to impress."

Julia sat on the chair next to Del. "Perhaps our clothes are not meant to impress, but to show respect."

"Or to signify the importance of the occasion?" Kathy said, displaying the embroidered shawl. "Maybe something important is going to happen? The mentors kept saying, 'He's coming.'"

"He is."

They turned toward the voice. John stood in the doorway. Gone were his work clothes and Colorado Rockies baseball cap. In their place he wore a brown caftan with a rope around his waist.

"What's with the monk getup?" Walter asked. "We get all dressed up and you go for drab and comfortable?"

"Appearances are not important," John said.

"Then why did you give us these fancy clothes?" Natalie asked. "Not that I don't love them, but I don't underst—"

"It was a way to convey to you the significance of the evening."

"Where are our mentors?" Walter asked. "I was hoping to see Gabe. I have something to show him."

"The mentors' missions are complete."

"Complete?" Kathy said, wrapping the shawl close. "You mean I won't see Anne again?"

341

"And *you're* here," Walter said. "You're Del's mentor. That's not fair."

"I came with a message."

"Then give it," Walter said.

John waved a hand toward the chairs. "Please be seated."

Seven of the chairs were filled. One remained empty. Kathy looked at it, clearly nervous. "Lenny's not here. He had some business to attend—"

"I'm here." Lenny lurched into the room, casting a malevolent look back at Chief, who was spurring him on. "I don't want to be here, but I'm here. He even made me stop at the room and put on this monkey suit."

Chief shrugged. "Sorry for the delay, folks, but one of the lambs was lost. 'Rejoice with me; I have found my lost sheep.'"

"I'm not a lost sheep," Lenny said.

Chief chuckled. "Not anymore." He stepped out of the room, closing the door between them.

"Come join us, Lenny," John said, indicating the one remaining chair.

Lenny strode across the room, his eyes avoiding all others', especially—Natalie thought—those of his wife.

John clasped his hands and went to stand in the middle of the chairs. "The circle is now complete."

Walter crossed his arms. "I don't get this. Everybody talked like this great speaker would be here tonight and it's just you? You've been here all the time."

"I am not your speaker, Walter. And yes, he has been here all the time."

Julia shook her head. "I've been here too long. I'm beginning to understand the cryptic way you talk."

John smiled. "You've made progress, Julia." He turned in the circle in order to look at each of them. "You've all made progress in your short time here. But now it's time to make your decisions."

"Our decisions?" Kathy asked. "What kind of decisions?"

John didn't answer. He moved out of the circle and headed toward the door.

Lenny stood. "Hey! Answer my wife," he demanded, pointing a finger at John.

John paused at the door and turned toward them, his smile patient. "She already has the answer. You all do."

He left and closed the door, leaving them to their assignment.

"I vote we leave," Natalie said, raising her hand. "I knew this was too good to be true. It's been nice, but it's getting creepy again."

"Don't use that word," Kathy said. "What happened to awesome?"

"That was before we were left in a cold, stone room to fend for ourselves." She looked around. "I'd hoped there'd be dinner. I'm hungry."

"You'll live," Julia said. "They've provided for us up to now, I'm sure they'll provide for us tonight, too."

"Cackers," Lisa said.

"Macaroni and cheese," Ryan added.

Kathy shushed them. "We need to do what John said. Make a decision."

"But what decision?" Walter asked. "I wish these people would be more specific. I'm used to facts and figures, not this philosophical mumbo jumbo that makes my head ache."

"That makes your mind work," Julia said.

Walter met her eyes. "Touché."

"I say we get out of this place," Lenny said. "Go home where we belong. Leave these weirdos to themselves."

"They're not weirdos," Kathy said.

"They're not normal people."

Kathy cocked her head. "Maybe not normal in the way that means ordinary. They are definitely not ordinary."

Natalie stood up. "I think they're fabulous. I wish everyone in the world were like the people here in Haven. They care. They listen. They're willing to help us—"

"Help us complicate a perfectly good life," Lenny said.

"Our life was hardly perfect," Kathy said.

"That's for me to determine, not—"

"Whoa there, Mr. Kraus," Julia said, putting up a hand to stop the damaging words. "You're just a visitor here." She raised her hand higher, stopping his objection. "I'm not saying you're not welcome, and I wouldn't presume to think your showing up was a fluke—I've stopped believing in coincidences since I've come here—but the fact remains that all of us have been assigned a mentor and have received special counseling, as it were. You have not. Therefore, I don't think it's appropriate for you to butt in where your opinions are not wanted."

"Well, I—"

Kathy put a hand on his knee. "I'll listen to your opinions after the meeting is over. But Julia's right. You're here, just like the children are here, but you are not a part of this."

"Maybe I should leave," he said, but he looked more hurt than angry.

"Don't go," Natalie said. "Chief brought you here. They want you to stay. We want you to stay."

"As long as I keep my mouth shut."

"To a certain extent, yes," Julia said. "No offense intended."

He shrugged, crossed his arms, and slumped in his chair.

Julia took a deep breath. "Now then. To the decision we're supposed to make. Any ideas?"

"Why don't we start with what we all have in common?" Kathy said.

"Stupidity?" Lenny mumbled.

She ignored him. "We were all invited—or welcomed—to Haven. John said there were other Havens, in other states and other countries. Perhaps we're supposed to make some decision to get together with those other people?"

Walter snickered. "I can see it now. A Haven reunion. We

344

can have matching T-shirts with Haven stamped on the front and a drawing of the bell tower on the back. We can OD on potato salad, baked beans, and trite conversation."

"What's wrong with that?" Kathy asked.

Natalie shook her head. "If they wanted us to meet, why didn't they have us go to one location in the first place? Gather in a football stadium somewhere? Or in a huge auditorium?"

"I don't think that's the decision," Julia said. "It's got to be more personal than that."

"Maybe the decision we have to make involves telling people about Haven," Walter said. "Maybe they want me to put it on the news, though I doubt the wire services would touch it."

"They'd distort the message even if they did," Julia said. "Again, I don't think we're supposed to advertise Haven. They could have done that with a good marketing firm. Full-color ads and infomercials. Jingles on the radio. Billboards."

"Excuse me?" Del said, his voice fraught with pain. They all looked at him, realizing it was the first time he had spoken.

"Can I get you something, Del?" Walter asked. "Water? Pain pills? Just tell me—"

"You can shut up," Del whispered. "All of you."

Lenny snickered.

"You think you know all the answers, Del?" Walter asked, his tone offended.

Del shook his head. "I don't. I know I don't. But I do know you've gotten on the wrong track. You didn't listen to John's words."

They all hesitated a moment, thinking.

"He said we need to make a decision," Walter said.

Del shook his head, wincing. "He said it's time we made *our* decisions. Plural. More than one."

"Like we each have a different decision to make?" Julia said.

"Exactly."

Walter stood. "I know what my decision is. I'm getting a second chance."

"To do what?" Lenny said. "Be obnoxious?"

Walter froze him with a look. "Fine. Make fun of me. At least I've made my decision."

"It doesn't sound like a decision to me," Natalie said. "*You* haven't done anything except announce you're willing to accept a fresh start. Big deal."

Walter sat down. "So what's your earth-shattering decision, girlie girl?"

"I'm not a girl. I'm eight—"

Walter twirled a finger in the air. "Just out of the nursery."

"That wasn't necessary, Walter," Julia said. "Natalie's age is no more an advantage or disadvantage than mine."

"Which is?" Walter asked.

"None of your business."

Natalie listened to this exchange, then made up her mind. She didn't want to do it, but she would. Quickly she stood up. "I don't know about the rest of you, but I've had an amazing thing happen here in Haven. A Bible that I was pretending was my bestselling novel showed up in two places at once—"

"That's nothing," Walter broke in. "The TV in my room flipped channels and blared." He looked at them. "Even *after* I'd unplugged it."

"I hardly think a television trick is as important as the Bible," Natalie said, frustrated. Why couldn't the man ever let her finish what she had to say?

"The school had my high school file containing original letters to Mrs. Robb, my counselor," Kathy inserted. "And there were letters *from* Mrs. Robb—"

"What'd she say?" Lenny asked. "Did she say anything about me?"

Kathy looked at her husband, startled. "I don't know, Lenny. I don't remem—"

"Hey, people," Julia said. "I'm the one who got kidnapped and had to spend the night in the school, a prisoner, alone and afraid."

"You said you *weren't* afraid," Kathy said. "You said you liked the boy who kidnapped you. You thought he was a good—"

"Well, he *is* a good kid. Basically. But that doesn't mean what I went through doesn't count for anything." She raised a finger, remembering the window. "Then there was the window that was broken, but then was fixed, locking us inside. The school wouldn't let us leave. That's why we had to stay there all night."

Walter gave her a look. "The school…wouldn't let you leave?"

She raised a hand. "Honest."

"I saw a sunrise," Del said quietly.

Natalie turned to him, wondering what that had to do with anything. "No offense, Del, but we've all seen a sunrise."

Del opened his mouth to answer, then shut it.

"I let Del save my life," Walter said. "I made him a hero."

There was a brief moment of stunned silence. Then chaos as everyone talked at once.

"*You* made him a hero?"

"Your ego is showing, Walter."

"The gall of some—"

The door to the meeting room opened, banging against the stone wall with enough force to make it swing back again. John caught it with a trembling hand. He took one step into the room. "Silence!"

Those who had been standing sat. Lisa and Ryan took refuge in their parents' laps. Natalie crossed her arms. Julia squirmed, Walter fidgeted, and Del placed a protective hand across his side as if reminding John he was injured.

John strode into the center of the circle, running a hand through his hair—an act of frustration, not grooming. He pointed a finger at them, spinning in a circle so everyone felt his wrath. "'For they loved praise from men more than praise from God.'"

"We were just—" Walter said.

"You were just holding up the miracles of God to be judged and assessed. 'Mine is better than yours.'"

"We were comparing experiences," Julia said. "We meant no disrespect."

"And none would have been felt if you had compared miracles with your eyes focused on the giver instead of the receiver. On *his* glory, not your own."

No one had an answer for him. John studied their chastised faces, then raised his eyes, as though seeking instructions. Natalie frowned. John seemed confused...then he gave a nod, looking for all the world as though a point had been silently clarified. He took a deep breath, calming himself.

"It takes courage to make a decision and act. Because of your petty egos, you failed to fulfill our request. Therefore..." He paused. A siren began its plaintive wail, capturing Natalie's raw nerve endings, stringing them taut.

"What's that?" she asked.

Kathy put a hand to her mouth. "It's...it's a tornado siren!"

Walter sprang from his chair, looking around the windowless room. "A tornado? We've got to get out of here."

"We've got to get to a basement," Lenny said, running toward the door, dragging Ryan with him.

John made a small motion toward the doors. The bolts echoed shut.

Lenny turned the knob. "It's locked! Unlock it! Let us out!"

John moved toward the only other door—the door leading to the bell tower. He opened it and stood to one side. "Enter here."

"You don't go *up* in a tornado," Lenny said. "You take cover below ground."

"'What he opens no one can shut, and what he shuts no one can open. I have placed before you an open door that no one can shut.'"

"Open, shut," Walter said, trying the other doors. "You're

speaking in riddles. We need to get out of here!" He put his hands over his ears. "That siren is driving me nuts. Turn it off! Turn it off!"

Julia moved to John. "Can't you let us go outside and see what's going on? Without windows all we have to go by is the sound of the siren."

"And the open door."

She looked at John's eyes, assessing him. "You want us to trust him. That's what all this is about, isn't it?"

"'I am the gate; whoever enters through me will be saved.'"

Natalie went to stand beside Julia, listening to John's words. "This is more than being saved from the tornado, isn't it?" she asked softly.

John swung his hand toward the door. "'Trust in the LORD with all your heart and lean not on your own understanding; in all your ways acknowledge him, and he will make your paths straight.'"

Julia nodded. She backtracked toward Walter and Del, waving an arm toward Kathy and her family. "Follow John, people. We can trust him."

Kathy moved toward the door, but Lenny pulled her back. Natalie paused, watching the drama unfold.

"You stay here with me," Lenny ordered. "Going up in a tower during a tornado doesn't make any sense. You're making yourself tornado bait."

"But John's telling us it's safe. He wouldn't lead us into danger."

Lenny threw his hands in the air. "Why not? He's mad at us. He just got done yelling at us. And now you're going to trust him with your life, with the lives of our children?"

Kathy swallowed, and Natalie felt her struggle as though it were her own. Could Lenny be right? Were they crazy to trust John?

Kathy's answer was firm and confident. "Yes, I'm going to trust him. I have to let go of my own logic and submit myself to God's."

349

"Even if it goes against everything the world has taught you?"

"Especially if it goes against everything the world has taught me."

Kathy held out her hand to Ryan and joined the others at the door. With a sigh of relief, Natalie turned and went into the tower. Walter was helping Del negotiate the spiral steps. Julia waited with John, herding the others in.

I sure hope John is right, Natalie thought as she started up the stairs.

Lenny watched in disbelief as Kathy headed for the tower. She paused and turned toward him. He was alone, standing near the exterior door.

"Come with us, Lenny," she said, and he heard in her voice how much she wanted him to follow. "Trust me. Trust him."

The sound of the wind roared outside. Rain slapped against the stones in sheets; lightning cracked. Something blew into the side of the building, scraping and knocking violently.

Lenny wanted to run. Not seeing, only hearing, was unbearable. But he wasn't going to show them he was scared. Not Kathy. Not any of them. She watched him for a moment, then turned sadly and led their children into the tower. Lenny could hear Lisa's whimpers echoing in the stairwell as Kathy carried her higher, higher.

"Now," John said. "It's the only way."

Lenny's eyes flit from John to Julia. He felt like a caged animal.

"Let go of your own will, Lenny," Julia said. "Submit to the Lord. Trust him."

John motioned for Julia to go into the tower. She shook her head. "I'm not going without him, we're in this together."

John turned to Lenny, and his tone was hard when he spoke. "Listen to the words of the Lord, little man. 'Wide is the gate and broad is the road that leads to destruction, and many enter through it. But small is the gate and narrow the road that leads to life, and only a few find it.' Jesus knows your name, Lenny. You've been invited. The invitation will not come again."

The door to the outside blew open. Debris swirled past, highlighted by flashes of lightning. Rain blew through the door like sharp fingers threatening to touch them, grab them, pull them into the destruction.

Lenny gave John and Julia one last look of desperation. They were crazy! They all were crazy. They were following a crazy man who was leading them to the one place they would all die.

Well, he wasn't going along with any of them. He would find his own way—without God, and without this Jesus. Before he could change his mind, he turned and bolted into the storm.

⁓

John locked the door to the bell tower. Julia stood on the steps, frozen. She wanted to weep.

"How can we…how can I tell Kathy?"

"It was his choice, Julia. 'In his pride the wicked does not seek him; in all his thoughts there is no room for God.'"

She leaned against the curving wood of the staircase, feeling tired and terribly sad. "Will he die out there?"

"'The mind of sinful man is death, but the mind controlled by the Spirit is life and peace.'"

Julia met John's eyes and held them. "God has tough standards."

"For which he offers wondrous, eternal rewards." He put a hand on Julia's arm. "Shall we go? We need to join the others."

"But what will—"

"It's time you led them."

"Me?"

"Who led them to the tower? Who stayed behind, appealing to the last of them?"

"For what good it did."

"It *was* good, Julia. You cannot blame yourself for another's choice. You can only lead them, not force them. Free will prevails."

She took a few steps up the staircase, then she stopped. "Is this the choice you wanted me to make? To be a leader?"

"You *are* a leader. Your choice is whether to use that gift. And how."

A scream ripped the air from above. Heavy footsteps ran down the steps toward them, and Natalie rounded the corner, nearly colliding with Julia.

"It's awful!" she cried, leaning a hand against the wall, catching her breath. "There are four of them!"

Dread filled Julia. "Four twisters?"

She nodded and looked to John. "Everyone wants out. They want to come down and try the other door."

Julia glanced at John, but he shook his head. "Go to them. I will follow."

Natalie glanced upward, uncertainty evident on her features. Julia couldn't blame her. She wasn't all that sure she wanted to join the chaos above. But there didn't seem to be much choice. She gave Natalie a slight prod, and the girl turned and headed up the stairs. Julia and John followed.

As they neared the top of the tower, the sound reached deafening levels. The shouts of the people came as staccato bursts, mere fragments amid the clamor around them.

Kathy was the first to see them. She ran to Julia, Lisa clinging to her neck. She looked past John, waiting, obviously expecting to see her husband mounting the last few steps.

"Lenny?" Her eyes widened as she grabbed onto Julia's arm. "Where's Lenny?"

Julia looked to John, hoping he would answer. John walked past them, silent. Julia led Kathy down a few steps, hoping the short distance would give them the quiet her explanation deserved. It was of little help.

Julia didn't know what to say, so she just shook her head. The roar of the storm added credence to her action.

"He stayed in the room?"

Julia shook her head again and pointed outward.

Kathy pushed Lisa's head against her shoulder as if shielding the little girl from the truth. "He went outside?"

Julia nodded.

Instinctively, Kathy took a step down. Then another. Then she stopped and looked back to Julia. "Why did you let him go?"

Julia's first impulse was to defend herself; to tell Kathy that she and John had stayed until the last minute, to tell her they had cajoled, pleaded, and threatened Lenny.

"It was his choice," she finally said.

Kathy's legs buckled. She sank onto a step, her shawl rippling into a heap behind her. Julia lunged for Lisa, rescuing her from her mother's weakened grip. Kathy stared at nothing, unaware the child was even gone.

"Mama!" Lisa yelled, holding her arms out for Kathy.

Julia looked up to see Natalie staring down at them and she motioned for the girl to take Lisa. Natalie's eyes asked questions, but Julia shook her head. *Not now.*

Free of Lisa, Julia descended to Kathy's step. Standing beside her, she put a hand of comfort on Kathy's head, holding it there, praying it would say what words could not.

Eventually, Kathy raised her head, her eyes moist but clear. "It's out of our hands, isn't it?"

Julia nodded and held out a hand. Kathy took it and stood. Together they walked to the top of the tower.

The circular stairs came out at a landing near the center. A five-foot aisle skirted the outer wall, a wall that was punctuated with glassless openings. The bells hung above them, concentrated among the intricate rafters. The inhabitants of the tower stood at the openings, their attention drawn outside.

Julia was lured to the scene unfolding before them. The fury of the storm was unbelievable.

Walter came to her side. "Quite a show, don't you think?" He leaned his back against the wall as if the view had become boring.

Julia pointed at the funnel cloud moving close from the eastern horizon. She turned full circle, spotting the other three. "I've never seen…how can there be four tornadoes coming at us from different directions?"

Walter rested an elbow on the ledge and looked at his manicure. "That was my second question. My first question was, why isn't the wind blowing in here? in the tower? There's no glass to keep it out. All logic says we should be wet and blown to bits."

Julia made another slow circle, taking it in. The noise of the storm was full and ominous, yet not a breeze breached the walls of the tower.

John joined them.

"I don't understand," she said to him.

"'No eye has seen, no ear has heard, no mind has conceived what God has prepared for those who love him.'"

Julia threw an arm into the air. "*This* is what he's prepared for us? Destruction?"

"His ways are not the ways of man," John said.

"Obviously."

John glanced beyond Julia at the funnel clouds looming closer, their swirling tails backlit by lightning.

"He will use whatever means are necessary to further his plans."

"And *this* is necessary?"

John's eyes were drawn upward as if hearing some instruction. "It is time."

"Time for—"

A gust of wind forced Julia backward into the wall, then

another wind pushed her forward to the place she'd been. The green chiffon of her skirt danced madly in the swirling air. She looked at John, beseeching him. He stood firm in the wind, his hair and caftan thrashing back and forth.

The screams of the people were swallowed up in the storm, their mouths open in anguish and fear as they clung to each other, cowering against the tempest. The bells clanged against each other overhead, their music harsh and dissonant.

The lone light in the tower extinguished itself, accentuating the oppressive darkness of the storm. A great crackling cut through the din.

"The stairs!" Kathy yelled, holding her shawl and her body like a shroud over her children.

Those who could not hear her words saw her pointing finger. Disbelief flashed on their faces as they watched the wooden stairs rip away from the stone walls and tumble into the depths of the tower. A rafter tore away from the roof and plunged across the hole.

The four funnels were close, their teeming tails hidden by the vastness of their upper clouds' greedy inventory of fractured houses, dismembered trees, and mangled cars.

Natalie buried her head in her knees and put a protective hand over the baby growing inside her. "I don't want to die!" she screamed. "I don't want to—"

"Look!" Walter yelled. "The tornadoes aren't going to get us. They're circling around us!"

One by one, heads lifted to see. Bodies unfolded. Tense arms relaxed. The people stood, their feet spread, braced against the wind. Their eyes darted between the whirling clouds spotted with debris. They watched them surge, their heads in constant motion as if they were the occupants of a carousel watching the rest of the world flash by.

"It's beautiful," Julia said, staring.

Walter tore his eyes away from the storm. "Beautiful? How can you say—"

"It's his power," she said. She turned to Walter. "He's showing us he's in control."

"A simple parlor trick would have sufficed," Walter said. "Isn't this a bit extreme?"

Julia shook her head. Five stubborn people had needed powerful proof. And this was it. She cocked her head, noticing a change in the sounds around them. "It's dying. The storm is dying."

The roar was replaced with a sucking sound. The funnels drew upward as if God were inhaling, siphoning them toward heaven.

Silence.

The suddenness of it was shocking. The people stood frozen, reveling in the stillness. "It's over" shone on every upturned face.

Julia was the first to see it. The words caught in her throat, her hand waving outward into the calm air.

Haven was gone.

Twenty-nine

Do not neglect your gift, which was given you through a prophetic message when the body of elders laid their hands on you.
1 TIMOTHY 4:14

HAVEN WAS FLATTENED. For as far as the eye could see, not a tree grew, not a building stood. Vivid testimony to the wrath of the tornadoes.

"*No!*" Kathy wailed as she stood with one child clutched against each hip.

"Where are the buildings, Mommy?" Ryan asked.

"They're gone."

"But what about our room? Our toys?"

What about your father?

"This is unbelievable," Walter said, moving around the perimeter of the tower. "Even the church is gone." He stuck his head over the ledge and looked down. "I can't see the meeting room at the base of the tower."

"We're the only thing standing," Natalie murmured.

Del leaned against the wall. "Where are the people?"

Good question, Kathy thought, watching as the others scanned the horizon. "Surely some of them took cover in basements. Surely some of them are safe."

Walter shook his head. "I don't see anyone."

"Fran is dead?" Natalie asked.

Walter looked stunned. He swallowed. "Gabe too."

"And Anne."

"Louise."

Del looked around the tower. "Where's John?"

They looked at each other, amazed they hadn't noticed his absence before.

"The last time I saw him," Julia said, "was right before the winds came through. Before the stairs fell, before the rafters broke off and—" She moved toward the hole that used to hold the stairs. She studied the rafters bisecting the space. "It's a cross," she said. "The rafters form a cross."

They each stepped forward to look. Two aged rafters lay across each other, one a bit above the center point of the other. A perfect cross.

Kathy stared at it, chills running up and down her spine. "It's a sign," she said, as sure of it as she'd ever been of anything in her life.

"A sign? Of what?" Walter asked.

She met his questioning gaze. "Of God. It's a sign he's here. With us."

Natalie nodded. "We *were* saved. We were the only ones saved."

Del sank to the floor, using the wall as a guide. "I don't feel so good," he said. Walter rushed to him and pried Del's hand away from his side.

"You're bleeding!"

Del looked down at his shirt. It was crimson with blood. He and Walter exchanged a look.

"He needs help," Walter told the others. He yanked off his suitcoat and wadded it into a pillow, then helped Del lie down.

Julia went to help. She loosened Del's tie and carefully opened his shirt. The bandage that had covered the wound was soaked with fresh blood.

How can a man lose that much blood and still be conscious? Kathy wondered.

"We need some cloth to press against it," Julia said, looking to the others.

"Here." Kathy removed her shawl, folding it quickly into a many-layered compress. She handed it to Julia, who pressed it against Del's wound. Del grimaced.

"Hold it tight," Julia told Walter. "We've got to stop the

bleeding." She looked around the tower. "If only John were here."

Del licked his lips, as though speaking were a chore. "Why were the people of Haven punished? We were the selfish ones."

Natalie took a step forward. "If only we'd made our decisions like John asked us to do. None of this would have happened."

Julia reached up to tug on Kathy's hand. Following Julia's direction, she knelt, taking Del's feet and placing them in her lap. Julia rose, leaving Del in Walter and Kathy's care. She stood, pushing a strand of hair away from her face. "Then let's do it. It's not too late. God let us live while he destroyed everything around us. There has to be a reason for that. *We* are the reason."

"You make us sound too important," Natalie said. "At the moment, I feel very unimportant."

"Which is as it should be," Julia said, her voice gaining strength. "Although the storm didn't destroy us, perhaps it did destroy our pride."

"Making us an empty vessel, ready to fill," Natalie said to herself.

"What?"

She looked at the others. "Fran said God wants each of us to be an empty vessel, ready to be filled with his will for us. We have to think of what we can do to help him. What have we learned here in Haven that we can use back in our lives?" Natalie thought a moment. "I guess my decision is—"

"You *guess*?" Julia fixed her with a hard stare. Kathy was glad she wasn't the recipient of that look. "Don't you think God had a more definite commitment in mind?"

Natalie didn't flinch. She straightened her shoulders and nodded. "Okay then, I dedicate my writing to God. I'll write about real people and real romance. People who experience the kind of love God had in mind." She looked to Kathy, and the expression in her eyes filled Kathy with gladness. "And I dedicate my baby to God. Whether Sam and I are together or apart, this child deserves to live, and I will do everything in my power to see that it gets the best life has to offer."

"Excellent," Julia said. She turned to Kathy. "What about you, Kathleen?"

Kathy still held Del's feet in her lap, and she looked down at them, biting her lip, filled with uncertainty. "I want to do what you say, but my talents don't seem to fit like Natalie's does."

"What about your paintings?" Julia said. "And your fire?"

She looked up, frowning. "My fire?"

"Your fire for children, for life."

Del opened his eyes and looked at Kathy. He nodded, urging her on.

"Okay. All right." She pushed her fear and feelings of unworthiness aside and cleared her throat. "I dedicate my paintings to God, and I promise to do everything in my power to promote the sanctity of children. Whatever he wants to do with me, I'll do."

"How can he ask for anything more?" Julia said, and her smile warmed Kathy's weary heart.

Next Julia looked to Walter. "Your turn, Mr. Prescott."

Walter looked away. "I was hoping you'd forget me. He'd forget me."

"Fat chance."

"Don't I know it." Walter adjusted the bandage on Del's wound, easing the pressure when Del winced. "Okay. What I've learned during our wonderful Haven adventure is that I have to take responsibility for doing the right thing. It's not enough to believe, I've got to act on those beliefs, even if it's hard, or awkward, or embarrassing—"

"Gee, Walter," Natalie said. "Cut with the pep talk, you're depressing me."

Walter shrugged. "I'm a newsman. I know TV. I dedicate my expertise to God. I have no idea how he wants to use it. I'll leave that up to him." He looked to Julia. "Is that good enough?"

"Perfect."

"You next, Julia," Walter said. "Take a spoonful of your own medicine and see if it comes out bitter or sweet."

Julia put a hand to her throat, thinking. "I didn't want to get back into politics. What I saw while I was governor was hardly encouraging, but now…" She took a deep breath, raising her chin. "I dedicate my leadership abilities to God. However, wherever…I'll do my best not to disappoint him."

Walter raised a hand in a mock toast. "All hail, Queen Julia, leader of planet Earth!"

Julia spread her skirt and curtsied.

Ryan tapped Kathy on the shoulder. "Mommy? What about me?"

Kathy drew him to her side, leaning her head on his chest. "Do you want to dedicate yourself to God, sweetie?"

He nodded. "I ded-cate to be good and eat my dinners without spilling and…" He looked to the ceiling, thinking hard. "I ded-cate to be a good brother to Lisa. I'll even let her play with my cars…once in a while…if she's careful." He looked to his mother for her approval. "Is that okay?"

Kathy couldn't speak. She only nodded.

Lisa moved next to her brother, her finger hooked in her mouth. "Lisa good too."

Kathy laughed and brushed a curl away from her daughter's eyes. "Lisa good too."

Julia put her hands on her hips. "Now, this is truly amazing. Surely, he is satisfied. We should have done this—"

Del raised a hand. "Don't forget about me."

Julia reddened and closed her eyes, obviously mortified at her omission. "Antonio. Of course. I'm so sorry."

He shook her apology away. "It's only natural. I don't have much to offer God or the world."

"Don't say—"

"It's true." He licked his dry lips. "It's been thrilling to see all of you come alive with your talents. God was wise in choosing you. As for me—" he closed his eyes—"all I can give God is myself. He gave me a gift I can never earn or repay. He gave his life so that my sins would be forgiven. And I *am* a sinner." He smiled ruefully. "Oh, what a sinner I am."

"You're being too hard on yourself," Kathy said, reaching to touch his arm.

He shook his head, his voice surprisingly strong. "I know what I am and I know what he is. Therefore, I dedicate my life to God. As I am right now. No more. No less. It's all I can do."

Kathy stared at Del, suddenly ashamed. She had struggled to find some scrap of worth…some prideful scrap. Del had simply offered the most valuable thing of all: himself. And he'd done it with true humility and sincerity.

Jesus, help me be more like—

Suddenly, Del flinched. His eyes grew wide. He drew his legs toward his body as if the pain had worsened and taken a chunk out of him.

"Del!" Walter cried. "Don't move like that. You'll make things worse. You'll—"

Inch by inch, Del straightened to a prone position. His body relaxed. His eyes lost their frenzy. He smiled.

"It's gone," he whispered.

"What's gone?" Walter asked.

"My wound." His voice was filled with wonder. "It's healed."

"Your—" Walter lifted the compress from Del's side. Kathy watched in amazement as Walter peeled the blood-soaked bandage away.

The skin beneath it was new. Perfect. Unmarred by the previous day's violence.

Walter's mouth hung open in disbelief.

"He's healed!" Kathy said in hushed awe. She looked down

at Del's smiling face and felt tears pricking at her eyes. "You're healed!"

Del's eyes shone with rapture as tears streamed down his face. "Thank God," he said.

The others fell to their knees and joined him in worship.

The bells rang in celebration.

~

"He is pleased."

Heads whipped toward the quiet voice.

"John!" Relief swept over Julia. "You're back!"

John nodded, walking to Del's side. He knelt beside him and put a hand on Del's forehead. "He *is* pleased, Antonio."

Del nodded, sprouting new tears.

John stood and surveyed the group. "Our Lord says, 'Whoever acknowledges me before men, the Son of Man will also acknowledge him before the angels of God.'"

"We could use a few angels," Walter quipped.

John laughed.

Julia stepped forward. He'd told her it was time for her to lead. Now she knew he was right. "We know our places, John. And healing Antonio like that…it's something we'll never forget. But what about Haven? Did God have to destroy all those good people just to make us act?"

"Your tower of decision was a haven in the storm," John said.

Julia nodded. "We understand and appreciate that. But what about the town? The people?"

"'But if it were I, I would appeal to God; I would lay my cause before him. He performs wonders that cannot be fathomed, miracles that cannot be counted. He bestows rain on the earth; he sends water upon the countryside. The lowly he sets on high, and those who mourn are lifted to safety.'"

"So if we pray…?" It made sense, but Julia watched John

carefully for some kind of confirmation that she'd understood correctly.

"Jesus said, 'Again, I tell you that if two of you on earth agree about anything you ask for, it will be done for you by my Father in heaven. For where two or three come together in my name, there am I with them.'"

Julia stood quiet a moment. Then she turned to the others. "Come close, everyone. We need to ask for a miracle."

They gathered in a tight circle, their hands clasped, their heads bowed. Together, they prayed for the people of Haven.

"Look!" Ryan yelled, pushing past his mother.

Julia and the others rushed to the wall. The trees were back, lining the streets. Green. Lush. The roofs of the buildings were just as before: gray-and-red dots amid the green. Birds soared above the town. Cars stopped at intersections.

"It's back!" Natalie yelped. "It's as if it was never gone." She shook her head with awe, then turned toward the others. "It *was* gone, wasn't it?"

"Wiped out," Walter confirmed, shaking his head. He grinned at Julia. "How would I ever report something like this? They'd put me in the loony bin."

Julia smiled, joyful laughter bubbling inside of her. "Well, you said it wouldn't be easy."

"Me and my big—"

"The stairs!" Natalie said. "They're back too. We can leave."

Julia saw she was right. "Come on, everyone. Let's go see God's handiwork."

⌒〜⌒

As the others hustled down the stairs, anxious to see the old Haven restored, Kathy held the children back until they were alone with John.

"It's time to go, Kathy," he said.

She leaned down to Ryan's ear. "Take your sister downstairs, sweetie. I'll follow in a minute." Ryan did as he was told, taking hold of Lisa's hand.

"You have questions." It was more a statement than a question.

Kathy looked down the stairs, making sure the children were out of sight. "Is my husband...is Lenny okay?"

"'God cannot be mocked. A man reaps what he sows.'"

"Which means?"

"Lenny was given the choice. He rejected it."

Kathy sucked in her breath, feeling as though she'd been struck, square between the eyes, by a two-by-four. "He's dead?"

"I assure you, God takes no pleasure in anyone's death."

"Then why did Lenny have to die? Maybe he didn't understand the choice."

"He understood. The Lord knows every thought, he knows what's in a man's heart. The Lord cannot be fooled."

"And Lenny didn't...Lenny wouldn't..."

"Because he rejected the word of the Lord, the Lord rejected him."

Kathy felt her knees give way. She was vaguely aware of John's supporting hand as she sank to floor. "No, it can't...I'm just as guilty as he is. It wasn't all his fault. I'm to blame as much as—"

"You chose God. He did not. That choice is between each man and his Maker."

Kathy moaned, fighting the despair that was threatening to swallow her. "I'm so alone."

John raised her to standing. He put a hand beneath her chin and lifted it. His eyes were gentle and full of compassion. "You are not alone, Kathy. Your Father is with you. Always."

"And my children?"

"He is with your children."

Jesus! her heart cried. *Help me. Help us.*

A sense of peace settled over her, like a blanket being thrown about her shoulders. She looked down the winding steps. "My children," she said.

She wiped her tears and descended the stairs.

Kathy was not prepared for what she saw when she rounded the last few steps of the tower. The meeting room was aglow with light. Everywhere, gold and crystal shimmered. In the center of the room were tables set to perfection with gold lamé tablecloths, gold-rimmed china, and gold flatware. On each table sat the same centerpiece: a filigree golden cross surrounded with sprays of gold stars and sparkling dust. A golden seat cushion had been tied to each wooden chair. Fran was filling goblets from a cut-glass pitcher.

"So what do you think?" Fran asked Kathy.

"It's like a fairyland," she said, waving at Chief across the room.

Fran put a hand on her hip and scanned the room. "Hmm. I was trying for a heaven theme."

Kathy smiled. "That too."

Ryan and Lisa came running, two golden balloons trailing behind them.

"Look, Mama!"

She gave them a kiss on the tops of their heads and they ran away, their heads turned to watch the dance of the balloons.

Kathy stood alone a moment, then turned her back on the crowd, not wanting them to see her tears. She felt an arm around her shoulders. It was Anne.

"God is with you, Kathy. Don't despair. He is with you, and so am I."

She nodded and took the handkerchief Anne offered.

"It's a time of celebration," Anne said. "Even in sorrow, we need to find the celebration."

Kathy turned around, taking a deep breath to calm her tears. "Yes," she said. "We have much to be thankful for." She took Anne's hand. "Will you pray with me, Anne? For us? For...for Lenny?"

Anne smiled approvingly and squeezed Kathy's hand. "Of course I will."

Together they bowed their heads, and Kathy felt a deep peace sweep over her as together they lifted her requests to God. "Amen," she whispered, wiping a tear away.

Anne put a comforting hand beneath her chin. "You're in his hands, Kathy. Always. And—" She motioned to the tables—"he will provide." She smiled, her eyes twinkling. "What do you say we go pig out on the decadent hors d'oeuvres Fran whipped up?"

"Decadent?" Kathy asked in a shaky breath. She returned Anne's smile. "Does God approve of decadent?"

Anne laughed. "Only in very small doses and only when garnished with pimientos."

Ryan stirred the last of his corn into his mashed potatoes. "Mommy, where's Daddy?"

Kathy closed her eyes. *Help me, Lord.* When she opened them, she saw Anne looking at her expectantly. Kathy put a hand on Ryan's. "We'll talk about this later, sweetie."

Ryan yanked his fork away from Kathy, catapulting a lump of potatoes across the table. It landed on Walter's suitcoat like an errant button.

"Ryan!"

"I didn't mean—"

Walter held up a hand, stopping their argument. Using his spoon, he scooped off the potatoes and ate them. "Not bad," he said, smacking his lips. "Though my middle usually prefers to forgo the middle man."

"Ryan, you tell Mr. Prescott you're sorry."

"There's no need, Kathy," Walter said. "I'm sure if the kid meant to throw potatoes at me, they would have come much closer to my mouth. Right, Ryan?"

"Uh-huh," Ryan said.

Lisa maneuvered some potatoes unto her spoon and held it

up. "Me, Mama. Me!"

Kathy cringed and applied a restraining hand. "No, sweet-cakes. We don't throw food."

Lisa pushed out her lip and slumped in the chair.

"Mommy," Ryan said again. "Where's Daddy?"

Del looked at Kathy with a sudden frown. "Where *is* Lenny?"

The mentors exchanged a look. Kathy leaned an elbow on the table and shielded her eyes with her hand.

"Your father went out in the storm," she heard John tell Ryan. "We tried very hard to get him to go into the tower with us, but he chose to go outside."

"He went out with the 'nadoes?" Ryan asked.

"Yes, he did."

Kathy opened her eyes to see her son's gaze flit back and forth as though he was back in the tower, seeing the devastation of Haven. He turned to his friend, Donnie, who was sitting beside him. "Donnie's here. He was outside, but he's here."

Kathy reached out to touch her son's cheek. "Donnie and his family were under cover. They were protected from the storm. God took care of them."

Ryan bit his lip. "Why didn't God take care of Daddy?"

John sat forward, clearing his throat. Kathy gladly relinquished the floor. "Ryan," John said, "has your mother or father ever wanted to hold you, and you didn't want them to? Have you ever wriggled away from their arms even though you knew it was a nice place to be?"

Ryan looked uncertain. He looked to his mother. Kathy nodded at him, urging him to think.

"Yeah, I guess so," he conceded.

John looked relieved. "During the storm, your daddy did the same thing. God wanted to hold him close and keep him safe, but your daddy wriggled away, even though he knew God's arms were a nice place to be."

"God could have kept him safe?"

"God kept you safe, didn't he?"

Ryan considered this. "Is Daddy dead?"

Kathy shoved her chair back and ran from the table. She stood near the wall, breathing heavily, her heart beating a frantic pace. *How do I tell them, Lord? How do I explain this?*

A soft touch on her arm turned her around, and she saw Ryan standing there, looking up a her, his eyes wide. She drew him in, and they held each other.

Neither one wriggled away.

~~~~~

"You don't have to help clear the dishes, Natalie," Fran said. "That's my job."

"I want to," Natalie said. "After all you've been through…"

Fran set two plates on a back table. "What do you mean?"

Natalie glanced at the others, not wanting them to hear. "You know…being wiped out during the tornado and then having God bring you back whole."

Fran blinked twice. "I don't know what you're talking about."

Natalie hesitated, studying her face. "The tornadoes? We were up in the tower and we saw their aftermath. Haven was destroyed. I was just wondering how he did it."

Fran's laugh was tight and unnatural. "I bet when you were a kid you asked the kind of questions that had no answers like, 'Why is there air?' Am I right?"

"Don't put me off, Fran. Not you."

Fran grew serious. "Don't try to fathom the unfathomable, Nat. Look at the results, not the technique."

"So you *do* admit it happened?"

Fran sighed. "'The LORD reigns. The world is firmly established, it cannot be moved; he will judge the peoples with equity.'"

"That's a Bible answer," Natalie said. "That's not a Fran answer."

Fran handed her two plates of strawberry cheesecake, nodding toward the tables. "Perhaps they are one and the same."

⟋⟍

John stood, tapping his spoon on a goblet. "May I have everyone's attention?"

People turned around in their chairs.

"It's time to say good-bye." There was a communal moan. He held up a hand. "I know how you feel. We feel the same way about you. What we've experienced together in Haven is a memory to be cherished and reviewed often."

Natalie raised a hand. "Why can't we stay here? After spending time in Haven, everything seems clearer. I don't want to lose that. I'm afraid when we leave, the rest of the world—our everyday lives—will take over and..."

"Make us forget," Julia finished for her.

John nodded, understanding. "It's easy to live *in* his glory at a time and place like this, but God wants you to do more than that. He wants you to live *through* his glory in every aspect of your lives. That's the hard part, but that is his will. You must carry his inspiration with you in every breath you take, with every meal you consume, to every person you meet."

"That's a tall order," Walter said.

"And such a victory will only happen through your faith in God, not by your own efforts."

"So we don't have to try?" Julia said. "That doesn't sound right."

John put a hand to his brow, as though struggling to find the right words. He smiled. "'If you have faith as small as a mustard seed, you shall say to this mountain, "Move from here to there" and it shall move; and nothing shall be impossible to you.'"

"The verse," Kathy whispered.

"It seems so simple," Del said, "and yet it's hard to understand."

"There is great power in even a small amount of faith," John said. "When God is with us, all things are possible as long as we trust in his abilities instead of depending on our own." John nodded to Fran. "We have a gift for each of you that will be a reminder of this simple, yet immeasurable lesson."

Fran came forward with a purple velvet box. She held it open and John removed one of the items and held it for all to see. It was a piece of jewelry, a pin. A hollow glass ball the size of a marble dangled from a gold bar. Inside the ball was a single mustard seed.

"This pin is a symbol. Wear it as you go about your daily lives as a testament to your faith. And when others ask you about it, tell them. Tell them the power of God's love for the world. Show them how the world can be changed by a single man doing God's work."

John turned to Del, who was sitting beside him. He gave him the pin. "Antonio Delatondo. You, who have nothing, have everything. 'The man who loves his life will lose it, while the man who hates his life in this world will keep it for eternal life.'" He put a hand on Del's shoulder.

John moved to Walter. Walter had trouble meeting his eyes until John touched his arm. "For you, Walter Prescott." He handed him a pin. "Be strong, Walter. Strong in him and strong through him. 'For the foolishness of God is wiser than man's wisdom, and the weakness of God is stronger than man's strength.'" Walter nodded, accepting the challenge.

Kathy had tears in her eyes as John walked toward her. He placed the palm of his hand against her cheek. "Kathleen Kraus, 'The eyes of the LORD are on the righteous and his ears are attentive to their cry.'" He brushed a tear from her cheek, then placed a pin in her hand. "'Tell it to your children, and let your children tell it to their children, and their children to the next generation.'" Kathy nodded and kissed the palm of his hand. Anne leaned over and gave her a hug.

John moved to Natalie, placing a hand on her head.

"Natalie Pasternak, he blesses your child even now." Natalie bit her lip, clutching the mustard seed in the palm of her hand. "'Do not conform any longer to the pattern of this world, but be transformed by the renewing of your mind. Then you will be able to test and approve what God's will is—his good, pleasing and perfect will.'"

"And lastly," John said. "Julia Carson. 'From everyone who has been given much, much will be demanded; and from the one who has been entrusted with much, much more will be asked.'" Julia clutched the mustard-seed pin, holding it against her heart. "'Hold firmly to the trustworthy message as it has been taught, so you can encourage others by sound doctrine and refute those who oppose it.'" Julia held out her hand, and John shook it, sealing the agreement.

John moved away from them, then turned, holding his arms wide. "It is not enough to change your mind, you must change your heart. 'For you are a people holy to the LORD your God. The LORD your God has chosen you out of all the peoples on the face of the earth to be his people, his treasured possession.'"

He raised his face toward heaven, then lowered it, content. "Sow the seeds of God's message. Our Lord said, 'Go: I will help you speak and will teach you what to say.'"

⌒

"Gabe?" Walter called out as the man passed by. He'd held back behind the others.

Gabe backtracked. "It was a nice dinner, wasn't it, Walter?"

"Yeah. Nice." His voice was flat.

Gabe gave him a look. "You have something on your mind?"

Walter took Gabe's arm and led him to the side of the meeting room. He couldn't let the others hear. It was too presumptuous. It was too selfish. It was too *Walter*.

Gabe clasped his hands in front of him, waiting. Walter fingered his mustard-seed pin as if it could give him courage.

"Just say it, Walter," Gabe finally said.

Boy, oh boy, do I need a cigarette.

Walter inhaled deeply and exhaled a series of coughs.

"This," Walter said, pointing to his mouth during the middle of a spasm. "This is what I wanted to ask you about."

"Your cough."

Walter sputtered. His body relaxed. "Actually, I'm talking about the cause of the cough."

"Your smoking."

"No," Walter said. "I mean whatever's growing inside me. The disease. The cancer. The…whatever it is."

"The consequence."

Walter opened and shut his mouth. He should have known Gabe wouldn't let him shirk the blame. "I admit it, I've smoked for over thirty years and now I'm paying for it. And I have to say, I'm pretty scared."

"The biopsy."

"Yeah. The biopsy. And I was wondering…I saw what God did for Del up there in the tower and I was thinking that maybe…"

"God would heal you too?"

"If I was good."

"You cannot buy God's gifts."

"I'm not trying to buy them, I'm hoping he'd give—"

"Give you a miracle?"

"Well, yeah. If he wasn't busy."

"What makes you think you deserve a miracle?"

Walter looked to the floor. "Maybe I don't deserve it, but since God did it once, I thought—"

"'Do not put the Lord your God to the test.'"

"But how am I supposed to do the work he wants me to do if I'm sick?"

"'It is God who works in *you* to will and to act according to his good purpose.'"

Walter thought a moment. "God is going to make me want what he wants?"

"Yes."

Walter shook his head. "I'm not used to this. I'm used to doing things my way."

"That's obvious," Gabe said with a wry grin. "And that's why you have to pray that his desires become yours."

"So no miracles?"

"Maybe. Maybe not. He knows what's best, for you and for his larger plan."

"But can I give my opinion?"

"Certainly. God hears *all* prayers."

"But answers some more than others," Walter said.

Gabe shook his head. "God answers *all* prayers. But sometimes God says no."

"Uh-oh."

Gabe put a hand on Walter's back and walked with him out of the meeting room. "He loves you, Walter. Let that be enough."

~

The edge of the curtains were bathed in moonlight. Ryan moaned in his sleep, turning over, pulling the covers with him. Lisa curled around her Bunny Bob, her feet drawn close to her body.

Kathy readjusted Ryan's sheet and blanket. His moans subsided, replaced by the soft breathing of a contented sleep. She put a hand on Lisa's back, willing her to feel safe and loved.

Kathy moved to the table by the window and sat, fingering an apple but not eating it. Unable to sit still, she stood and cracked the curtain, letting in the moonlight. She closed her eyes and willed Lenny to appear outside, his forehead tight with anger because she'd left the dinner without him. His mouth mumbling the words he'd say if she opened the door and let his argument in. She opened her eyes. He was not there.

"Oh, Lenny." The words were intruders in the still of the night.

She felt a fresh batch of tears but held them in. She was tired of crying. She wondered if she'd ever again take a breath or have a thought that wasn't linked to Lenny—to her life with him…and her new life without him.

What would she do? with the children, the house, the bills? with the responsibility God had given her?

Lenny's clothes were tossed on the bed, evidence of his quick change with Chief waiting outside. A few hours ago, he'd been alive. And now he was dead.

She was alone.

She was free.

Kathy shook this last thought away. It was disrespectful. It was selfish.

It was true.

Although Lenny had provided monetarily to the family, he had never been a part of it. He was like a neighbor who stopped by for a few hours now and then.

No, not even that.

A neighbor would have taken time to talk. To listen. To care. Lenny cared when his own cup needed filling but was oblivious to the empty cups around him. No matter how much Kathy or the children held out their cups—like beggars hoping for a scrap to sustain them—Lenny turned away, unless by a miracle, their need coincided with his own.

Kathy's days had been spent in joy with the children. Her nights—when Lenny was home—had been spent walking on eggshells, preventing arguments, surviving until the morning when he'd be gone again and they would be free to be happy.

Like now.

She picked up his shirt and held it to her face. It smelled salty. Like sun and wind and worry.

"I loved him," she said. "Once."

Was that true? When they'd dated in high school, she'd been attracted to him. His muscles. The dimple in his right cheek when he smiled. His way of looking at her like he knew secrets that maybe, just maybe, he'd share if she were lucky.

She'd loved the idea of him. The idea of being a couple. And then when she'd gotten pregnant, she'd loved the idea of having a family of her own. Away from her parents. A baby made her feel grown. Having the title of wife made her feel special. But what if...

She'd considered giving the baby up for adoption. Maybe she'd known she didn't love Lenny and he didn't love her. Maybe a part of her had seen ahead, down the road of their marriage. How different her life would have been if she'd chosen to give the baby up. Not a bad life, but different.

She looked across the room at her children. The title she cherished the most was the one they brought her. Mother.

Her children needed her. She needed her children. She needed...

There was a knock on the door.

Lenny!

Kathy sprang out of her chair and yanked it open. "Del!" She saw by his face that her disappointment showed. "I'm sorry. I was expecting—"

Del put a hand on her arm. "I know." He looked past her into the darkened room. "Were you asleep? I didn't wake you, did I?"

"No, no," Kathy said. "I can't sleep."

"Me neither." He cocked his head outside. "Do you want to sit out here and talk awhile?"

She looked back at the kids. They were quiet. She tied her robe around her waist and joined him outside, leaving the door slightly ajar.

Del wiped off a place on the curb and offered her a seat. She sat, tucking her robe around her legs. Del sat beside her. She glanced at his shirt, looking for blood. He'd changed it. There was no evidence he'd ever been wounded.

"That's quite a miracle," she said, pointing at his side.

He touched the spot gingerly. "It's the reason I couldn't

376

sleep. I don't understand why God did it."

"He healed you because you're a good man, Del. You deserve it."

Del shook his head. "No, no, that's not it." He hesitated, looking at her profile. "If that were true, then it would mean that your husband deserved to die."

Kathy sucked in her breath. Hadn't that been exactly what she'd been thinking? In spite of the August heat, she suddenly felt cold. She drew her legs to her chest, drawing herself in, protecting herself from the truth.

"Kathy?"

She felt the tears come and this time she let them fall. They were not tears for Lenny, but for herself. For her own ignorant, egotistical self. She felt Del's arm wrap around her shoulders. "I need to confess something," she said.

"You've come to the right place." Del cleared his throat. "I used to be a priest."

She pulled back to look at him. "You?"

He shrugged. "What's bothering you, Kathy? Besides Lenny's death."

She shook her head, finding it hard to say the words. "I'm hating him, Del. I'm sitting in my room thinking of all his faults, trying to rationalize why he deserved to die." She turned to face him. "And the scary thing is, I was doing a good job of it. I'd convinced myself that Lenny was a bad person, a bad husband, a bad father....I'd convinced myself that I'll be better off without him. That his death is a blessing. After all, he wasn't worth much any—"

Del shook his head. "No, Kathy. Don't."

She nodded. "You see? I know it's not right to think that way, but I'm doing it anyway. In fact, I'm enjoying it. It makes me feel..." She grappled for the right word.

"Superior?"

Oh God...She wanted to crawl away, to hide from him. From herself. *Yes. Superior. Forgive me*...She nodded.

"No one is worthless in God's eyes, Kathy." Del flicked pieces of gravel away from his feet. "Even though some of us feel that way."

Kathy wanted to die. She was no different than Walter. She'd been furious with the way he'd treated Del, and yet wasn't she, in her heart, treating Lenny just as badly? "Del. You proved yourself to Walter. You saved him. You proved your worth."

Kathy watched Del's jaw tighten. Oh dear, she'd said something wrong. She was so confused. Maybe she should just go back inside and shut the door. She was only making things worse.

Del bowed his head. *Please, please hear him. Answer his prayers,* Kathy pled silently. When Del turned to look at her, his eyes were kind.

"None of us is disposable, Kathy. We all matter to God. I may have been a stowaway, but I am not a throwaway. And neither was Lenny. We all do wrong; we all fall short of what we should be. That's where Christ comes in. He, in his perfection as all God and all man, showed us what we can be, if only we will accept his gift of salvation and love God. If only we will obey him." Del looked to the ground. "But we don't do that. We keep messing up. And it makes God sad." He sighed deeply, squinting up at the moon. "I can't imagine how frustrated God must be when we continue to go against him. He has every right to kill us all, to blot us out with the press of his thumb."

Kathy shivered. Del was right. She deserved to be blotted out.

Del smiled at her, his face radiant beyond the moonlight. "But he doesn't do that. God doesn't give us what we deserve. He gives us his love and his forgiveness. He gives us every possible chance to turn to him. He created each and every one of us to love him, and when we do—" Del filled his lungs with the thought—"he stirs in us a breath of life. He completes us."

Kathy put her hands to her mouth, stifling the sobs that came from deep inside her soul. "Oh, I am so sorry. I've sinned! I have sinned! How could I have ever—" She hid her head in her hands, feeling totally broken. "Lord, forgive me!"

She felt Del's arms circling her shoulder, offering comfort— but the inner peace that began to fill Kathy surpassed any physical touch. It came from the sure knowledge that she was held close in the comfort of God's forgiving arms.

When Kathy went back into her room, she expected to feel drained, but she didn't. There was a new kind of invigoration flowing through her. A hunger. A thirst for...what? Something more. She made a beeline for the Bible on the nightstand.

Why haven't I opened this before?

She switched on the bedside light and sat down, holding the Bible in her lap. A red ribbon marked a page. She nodded and slid her finger next to the ribbon. Her eyes were drawn to the left-hand page. "For it is by grace you have been saved, through faith—and this not from yourselves, it is the gift of God—not by works, so that no one can boast."

Kathy felt a smile light her face. She would be saved—her *family* would be saved—not by anything they did, but by their faith in Christ and by the grace of a God who loved them in spite of themselves.

She closed the book, filled with a new contentment. "Be with us, Lord. And be with Lenny."

She curled up on the bed and, cradling the Bible to her chest, closed her eyes and slept.

Thirty

Praise the LORD, you his angels, you mighty ones who do his bid-
ding, who obey his word. Praise the LORD, all his heavenly hosts,
you his servants who do his will. Praise the LORD, all his works,
everywhere in his dominion. Praise the LORD, O my soul.
PSALM 103:20–22

THE MENTORS GATHERED outside the motel rooms of their charges. In a moment they would knock on the doors and wake them so the disciples of Haven could begin their journeys home.

"I'm going to miss her," Fran said, pointing toward Natalie's room.

Gabe nodded. "It's not like we're never going to see them again."

"It won't be the same," Anne said, fingering her cross neck-lace.

John held up a finger. "It'll be better."

They shrugged, conceding the point.

Louise tried to corral the wisp of black hair that pointed left when it should have pointed right. "They've been through a lot."

"So have we," Gabe said. "It wasn't easy getting them to see the light."

John stifled a smile. "Some were harder than others."

Louise sighed. "We're going to miss this place, too."

"And each other," Fran said. "Our charges will be spread across the country."

"It won't be easy, seeing them struggle," Gabe said.

"Since when have you been one to shun work?" John asked.

"This *is* a big assignment."

"With the potential for big results."

"I pray you're right," Gabe said, glancing toward Walter's door.

"I think that's a perfect idea." John took Fran's hand. "Let's pray."

They joined hands and bowed their heads. John did the honors. "'The LORD bless you and keep you; the LORD make his face shine upon you and be gracious to you; the LORD turn his face toward you and give you peace.'"

~~~

Fran knocked on Natalie's door.

"Go away." The response was a whine.

"Come on, Nat, it's time to get up. We're setting up coffee and donuts in Kathy's room. All of you have a long drive ahead of you." She knocked again. "Open up, Sunshine."

There was silence, and then, "Chocolate donuts?" Natalie asked through the door.

Fran laughed. "Is there any other kind?"

Natalie opened the door, squinting at the sunlight. Fran walked in. "Not your most appealing look, squint-face."

Natalie walked to the sink. "I don't take criticism until I've been up at least twelve hours."

"You must go to bed very early."

"Ha ha. The only reason I got up now was because you called me Sunshine." She fixed Fran with a look. "My mom calls me that."

Fran didn't respond.

"But then, you knew that, didn't you?" Natalie said with a smile. When Fran only smiled in return, Natalie gave a bemused shake of her head, then turned back to the sink and splashed water on her face. As she patted it dry, Fran perched on the foot of the bed. "I do love this room," Fran said. "You and I have similar tastes."

Natalie studied the room a moment. "You certainly treated us well."

"We aim to please."

Natalie pulled a pair of jeans shorts under her nightshirt. "So what's next for you, Fran? Taking a little time off, or are you getting a new batch of guinea pigs to inspire?"

Fran thought a moment. "I'm going to be working out of town for a while."

Natalie buttoned her blouse. "What about the café?"

"It'll get along without me."

"What kind of work will you be doing?" Natalie asked, searching under the bed for her sandals.

"Consulting," Fran said slowly. She nodded, pleased with herself. "Yeah, consulting. That's what I'm going to do."

Natalie put her shoes on, then pinned the mustard seed to her shirt. She opened her arms, presenting herself. "So, what do you think?"

"I think you'll change the world."

"The world will have to fend for itself. But *I'm* changed. You changed me."

Fran shook her head. "I didn't do it, Nat. God did."

"Give credit where it's due, huh?"

"Never bite the hand that feeds you."

Natalie laughed. "Is that biblical?"

"More likely cynical."

Natalie sat next to her on the bed. "I'm going to miss you. I can write to you, can't I? Or call?"

Fran gave her hand a squeeze, willing Natalie to understand what she was about to say. "You can count on me any time of the day or night. I'll be there for you, Nat." She took a deep breath, wishing she could say more. But the choice wasn't hers. God knew best. "Now then. Let me help you pack and we'll go drown ourselves in chocolate."

$\backsim$

"Donnie. Ryan," Anne called from the table. "You boys let Lisa play with the cars. Otherwise, *I* get them all."

"But Mom—"

Anne extended a hand, palm up. Donnie hesitated, then gave his toy to Lisa, who immediately made motor sounds and drove it into her doll house.

"It's never too soon to learn the fine art of negotiation," Anne told Kathy, smiling.

Kathy sat at the table, mute, glassy-eyed. She fingered the box holding the donuts.

Ann watched her for a moment. "You don't look so good, Kath." She patted Kathy's hand. "Anything I can do?"

Kathy blinked, then raised her chin. "You can be here for me, Anne. Things aren't going to be easy. Going home, telling my parents, telling Lenny's mother. What do I say to them?"

"You tell them the truth." Anne knew it sounded simplistic, but that didn't make it any less right.

Kathy looked at Anne, uncertain. "That Lenny was killed in a tornado because he rejected God?"

"Maybe not that last part." Anne paused, reconsidering. Actually, now that she thought about it…"Then again—"

"No way." Kathy slashed her hands through the air. "It's not something they'd understand. I'm having trouble with it myself."

"They aren't people of faith?"

Kathy shrugged. "My parents go to church. But having a strong faith and going to church don't necessarily go together. I know. I've always believed in God and known about Christ. Until I came to Haven I even thought I was fairly close to the Lord, but now…"

"Now, what?"

"Now I realize how far I have to go. I've only skimmed the surface of my faith. I know there's more to this than just believing in God. I have to let Christ be the head of my life…I need to fix my heart and dreams on him, on following him."

Anne smiled. She understood Kathy's struggle. "It's an ongoing process, Kathy. When God thinks you're ready, he reveals more. Then more. And more."

"I can hardly wait." She sounded far from enthusiastic. "It's overwhelming. At the moment my whole life is overwhelming."

"It won't be," Anne said, trying to encourage her. "I'll help."

"From hundreds of miles away?" Kathy looked out the window, blinking back tears. "I need you close to me, Anne. You...you've come to be like a sister to me."

Anne scooted around the table and wrapped her arms around Kathy, feeling ties closer than she'd ever imagined possible. "No matter how far away I am, I'll be there for you. I promise."

⟡

Gabe looked around Walter's motel room. The bed was made. A suitcase stood by the door. "Early riser today, Walter?"

"I couldn't sleep. Got a lot on my mind."

"Sorry about the miracle."

"Or lack of one," Walter said. He waved a hand in the air. "Forget I said anything. I don't want to leave on a negative note."

"I'll agree to that."

Walter pulled some papers out of the side pocket of his suitcase. "In fact, I want you to have this."

Gabe took it and skimmed the pages. "Your article about the robbery."

Walter smoothed the bed though it didn't need smoothing. "I thought you'd like to see it. To show you I wasn't a total lost cause."

"I never thought—"

He shook his head, stopping Gabe's objection. "I gave you reason enough to believe it. I'm not the easiest person to get along with. My girlfriend will confirm that. I'm not good at letting people know they've touched me. Letting them know I've changed."

"So, have you?"

Walter nodded. "The old Walter is still holding on, but I'm determined to do my best and beat him down if I have to."

"Not everything about the old Walter was bad."

Walter snickered.

"There were some good traits," Gabe insisted.

Walter laughed.

"Hey, he liked my chili."

"Indeed he did. And does." Walter went to the door and opened it, taking a deep breath of the morning air. "You going to be around, Gabe?"

"Certainly. Just because you're leaving Haven doesn't mean our friendship is over."

Walter nodded. "Good. I have a feeling I'm going to need you."

"*And* someone else?"

"There's Bette."

"*And* someone else?"

Walter stuck his head out the door and looked skyward as if expecting God to be peeking over the rooftop. "You too," he shouted.

"You don't have to shout," Gabe said, laughing. "He hears the quietest whisper."

"Just wanted to make sure. I want to start my new life with things out in the open." He rubbed his hands together. "Let's go eat. I'm starved."

Gabe followed Walter from the room. As he pulled the door shut, he glanced heavenward. "I hope you know what you're doing," he muttered, shaking his head.

⌒

Del held the bloodstained shirt at arm's length, studying it.

"What are you going to do with it?" John asked.

Del brought it to his chest. "I feel like I should frame it. Proof of the miracle."

Will they ever understand, Lord? "You are the proof, Del."

Del touched his side. "I am, aren't I?"

"Are you riding back to St. Louis with Walter?"

"St. Louis is as good a place as any."

John tilted his head slightly. "To do what?"

Del studied the crucifix hanging over his bed. "I wish I knew."

"You'll be fine, Del," John said. "You, of all people, will be fine."

"Me of all—" He fixed John with a pondering look—"You act like I'm better than the rest."

"No, not better. Perhaps more focused. You don't have the distractions the others do."

Del laughed. "That's for sure." He spread an arm to the dresser where his new clothes were neatly stacked in a paper sack. "Behold the extent of my worldly goods."

John watched Del's face carefully. "Does that bother you?"

Del sat on the bed and stroked his mother's quilt. "I've never cared much for material things—I have simple tastes. Still, not having things is like not having an identity. I did it once willingly, but I'm not sure...I don't have a car, or a house, or even clothes to show the world who I am—or who I think I am." He looked directly at John. "Who am I, John?"

If you only knew... "That's something you'll have to find out."

Del snickered. "So I need to 'find myself' at age thirty? Most people have lives by now."

"You've *lived* a life. Now it's time to live another." He motioned Del off the bed, then leaned down to remove the quilt and fold it. He held it out. "This is yours, Del. Take it. Your mother would want you to have it."

Del looked at him, startled, then he reached out and took the quilt, hugging it to his chest. His expression was pure delight. "If only I had a bed to put it on."

John put a hand at the back of Del's neck, as he'd done as they watched the sunrise. "Everything will work out, Del. Anytime you need me—"

Del swung around. "*All* the time I need you."

John shook his head and moved his hand to Del's shoulder.

"All the time you need *him*."

Del nodded. Then he went to the crucifix and took it from the wall. Reverently, he placed it on top of the quilt. Only then did he look at John, asking for permission. "Is that all right? I want to have him with me."

Hesitantly, John nodded. "But you don't need any*thing* to have him with you."

Del stroked the head of Jesus, as if giving the suffering Savior comfort. "I know. I have him in my heart. He knows my heart is his."

"'Create in me a pure heart, O God, and renew a steadfast spirit within me,'" John said.

"Amen," Del whispered in a choked voice. "Amen to that."

⟡

Louise stood inside the door to Julia's room, shifting from foot to foot, folding her arms, unfolding them. Julia bustled about, getting ready to leave. The silence between them was awkward.

"I want to apologize, Julia," Louise finally said.

Julia stopped in midroom, a skirt in her hand. "What for?"

Louise looked out the window, hoping for help with the right words. "The other mentors had a chance to get to know their charges, but you and I...with the kidnapping and Arthur...I hope you don't feel I neglected you. I was with you...in spirit, you might say."

Julia tossed the skirt on the bed and motioned for Louise to sit down. They sat across from each other at the walnut table, a lace doily separating them.

"And I regret not getting to know you," Julia said. "But I also relish my experience with Arthur. I know that sounds ridiculous but—"

"It doesn't sound ridiculous. It sounds gracious."

Julia raised her eyebrows. "No one has ever accused me of being gracious. Gratuitous, gabby, and grating, maybe. Gracious, never."

Louise laughed. "I can hardly wait to see how far you'll climb."

"Climb?"

"As a leader. Your promise to God." If only Julia could know all God had in store for her.

"Word gets around, doesn't it?"

Louise shrugged.

Julia got up and packed the skirt, smoothing its wrinkles. "I'm not sure about this leadership business. It's easy to say it and quite another thing to do it."

"But you will do it."

Julia gave her a level stare. "Are you sure?"

"I'm sure."

"Absolutely sure?"

Louise tilted a hand left, then right. "Pretty sure."

Julia sighed. "Well, that's better. I never bet on a sure thing. Long shots are much more invigorating."

"Then maybe you should prepare yourself to be invigorated."

Julia hesitated. "Unfortunately, I understand. It's going to be tough, isn't it?"

"I'll be around to help, if you need it," Louise said. "It's only proper we become better acquainted, considering."

"Considering?"

Louise blushed at her slip. It was too soon to let Julia know what was coming. "Considering we're two friends who share a life in public service. We share a responsibility to the people, a goal to—"

Julia let the top of the suitcase fall shut and turned to face Louise. "You can stop with the public service announcement, *Mayor* Loy."

Louise looked away. "I don't know what you mean." *Oh, Lord, I'm sorry. Forgive me if I said too much.*

Julia returned to her seat across from Louise. She reached across the table and put a hand on Louise's arm. "It's only proper we become better acquainted considering...you're an angel.

My angel. Isn't that right?"

Louise fingered her unruly hair. *Lord, guide…*

Tell her.

Louise smiled. She looked directly into Julia's eyes. "Yes, I'm an angel."

Julia slapped the table. "I *knew* it!"

"I hope I wasn't *that* obvious. It's not our place to reveal ourselves to our charges. It's up to—"

"God?"

Louise nodded. "Christ is *your* Savior, but he is *our* King and Master. We were created to worship him and minister to you at his instruction." Louise saw Julia give her an intense once-over. "What?"

"You don't look like an angel."

"How do you know?"

Julia cocked her head. "Good point."

Louise lifted her chin, trying to look as dignified as possible under her limiting circumstances. "Actually, you're right. This is not my natural form. We were given these appearances for your comfort, not ours. We didn't want to overwhelm."

"We?" Julia's mouth dropped open. "Then all of you?"

"All of us."

Julia leaned back in her chair, obviously trying to take it all in. Her eyes cleared. "Do the others know?"

Louise opened her mind to any heavenly instruction. "No," she finally said. "They do not. They may suspect, but none of them have asked in such a direct manner as you have."

"Can I tell them?"

"No. Just as it wasn't up to me to tell you of my own volition, neither is it up to you to reveal such a thing. God will do so in his appointed time. When each of them are ready."

"Shucks." Julia grinned. "That's one piece of news I would have enjoyed passing along. But maybe it's best. What would Walter the newsman do with such a piece of knowledge?"

"That's not up to us to determine."

"I guess you're right." Julia looked out the window.

Louise followed her gaze and saw some of the others gathering. Their time togther had been so short.

"Oh, Louise…"

Louise put an understanding hand on Julia's arm.

Julia sighed. "When you said you'll be around to help me? That has new meaning now, knowing what I know. I find it particularly comforting."

"I'm glad," Louise said, truly meaning it.

Julia sighed and stood. "I'm not making any promises about all I can accomplish. I hope God knows that."

"God only insists on one promise."

"And what's that?"

"That you'll obey." Louise took Julia's hand and looked at her intently. *Help her understand.* "Remember, Julia, the work is secondary. Your relationship with God is the primary objective."

Julia nodded. There was honor in her eyes. "I'll give it my best shot."

Julia sighed.

~⌒~

Stomachs were full, rooms emptied, and trunks packed. The chosen people hugged each other, hugged their mentors, and got in their vehicles.

A few blocks away the bells began to ring.

As Julia put her car into reverse, she called out the window. "By the way, how exactly do the bells ring? When we were in the tower I noticed there weren't any ropes."

The mentors exchanged a look, then they burst out laughing.

It took Julia a moment to let the answer sink in. "Oh," she said with a grin, giving them a wave. "Dumb question."

The visitors pulled away, heading north, south, east, and west. Their promise to each other was to keep in touch.

If they only knew.

Thirty-one

Teach me, O LORD, to follow your decrees;
then I will keep them to the end.
PSALM 119:33

NATALIE LAY IN BED, her hands resting on her stomach. Subconsciously, she started small circular motions over the baby growing inside her.

There was a knock on her cabin door. "Sunshine?" her mother called. "I've got some breakfast for you."

She sat up in bed, scooting back against the pillows. "Come in."

Her mother entered carrying a bed tray loaded with oatmeal, milk, orange juice, and a blueberry muffin.

"You didn't have to—"

"I wanted to." Her mother positioned the tray and handed Natalie a napkin. "You've got to start eating healthier. No more junk food."

Natalie took a sip of milk, then set it down and looked at her mother. "You're unbelievable, you know it?"

Her mother blushed.

"I leave for days without telling you, then I come back and inform you I'm pregnant. I thought you'd—"

"Throw you out?"

Natalie shrugged. "I'm a mother's worst nightmare."

"Not exactly." Her mother pushed a strand of hair behind Natalie's ear. "Your *hair* is a mother's worst nightmare. You really should get it cut. How about a nice, controllable wedge?"

"Ma…"

She held up her hands in surrender. "I know. You're old enough to choose your own hairstyle."

"Exactly."

Her mother hesitated. "But are you old enough to have your own child?"

"Old enough. But hardly wise enough." Natalie took a spoonful of oatmeal. "I may not keep it."

"You didn't mention that last night."

"I figured you could only handle one crisis at a time."

"But adoption...my grandchild."

"That's the point. Right now it's only *your* grandchild. Dad doesn't want anything to do with it. Or me."

Natalie's mother put a hand on top of her daughter's. "He'll come around. You're his little girl. And you being pregnant—and unmarried—well, that's definitely his worst nightmare."

"Sam said he'd marry me."

Her mother smoothed the bedspread. "Sam's a nice boy."

"But?"

She met Natalie's eyes. "Do you love him?"

"Of course I do," Natalie said too quickly. She sighed. "But what do I know about love?"

"Marriage is forever, Sunshine. Don't hurry into it."

"Marriage is *supposed* to be forever. It doesn't always work that way."

Her mother's chin grew hard. She raised a single finger to Natalie's face. "I will not allow you to go into a marriage thinking there's an easy way out."

"Divorce is hardly the end of the world, Ma." Even as she spoke the words, she felt the tug inside, as though her heart were disagreeing with her.

And so, apparently, was her mother, who was shaking her head adamantly. "If we don't do something to stop the habit of divorce it *will* be. Families are falling apart left and right, Natalie. Divorce isn't a solution. It's a problem in itself." She fixed Natalie with a stern look. "You can't go into a marriage thinking there's an out if you don't like it. You have to go in committed to making it work. Even when it gets hard."

Natalie looked at her mother with new eyes. "I didn't know

you felt so strongly about it."

Her mother looked embarrassed. "I'm sorry, Sunshine, I didn't mean to—"

"No, Ma, it's okay. I...I think you're right." And she did. In fact, she was sure of it. She glanced at the mustard-seed pin on the dresser. "Get me that pin, will you, Ma?"

Her mother picked it up and turned it over in her hand. "Did those people at the retreat give you this?"

Natalie opened her mouth, then stopped. *Can I tell her?*

"It's a mustard seed, isn't it?" her mother said. "Like the verse in the Bible."

"You know the verse?" Natalie looked at her mother, surprised.

"I knew it. It's been years and years since I've read the Bible. But as a little girl...we used to go to church every Sunday."

Do it.

"Ma," Natalie said, pushing the breakfast tray away. "I have something to tell you. It all started with an invitation...."

"Natalie?" her mother called from the kitchen. "You got a package in the mail."

Natalie ran in from the living room where she was weather-stripping the windows. With one look, she knew what was in the package. Her manuscript. Rejected by an agent. Back in her hands again to be revised or—

"Aren't you going to open it?" her mother asked.

Natalie held the package in her lap. "I know what it is."

Her mother did too. "Remember what your mentor told you about your writing. Fran? Was that her name? Maybe you just need to do a bit of editing."

Natalie laughed. "A bit." She took a deep breath and positioned her hand to rip open the package. "Here goes." A letter sat on top of the manuscript. She picked it up and scanned the first line for the usual, "We are sorry." It was there—but there was more.

"Ma, listen to this," Natalie said in wonder. "'The writer shows a talent for imagination and visual description. However, the characters are superficial and cardboard, lacking in depth and dimension. Write about real people. Make them whole: physical, psychological, emotional, intellectual, *and* spiritual. Don't write what everyone else is writing. Write what you know from your own experience. A pyramid gets smaller as it reaches the top.'" Natalie stopped, staring at the paper.

"What's wrong? A personalized rejection is special. At least they gave you some encouragem—"

"The initials." Natalie pointed to the closing salutation.

Her mother took the letter. "F.P.," she read. "How strange they didn't write out their full name. And this is odd—" She pointed to the passage Natalie had just quoted—"This part you read aloud is handwritten. The rest of the letter is typed."

Natalie nodded. She began to laugh.

Her mother stared at her. "Now that's an odd reaction to a rejection."

"Oh, Ma! This letter makes me happier than any letter I've ever received."

Her mother's eyebrows raised. "Am I missing something?"

She went to her mother's side and pointed. "The initials. F.P. They stand for Fran Pendleton. My mentor from Haven. *She* wrote the encouraging words."

"How did she get hold of the letter?"

"Oh, they have their ways, Ma." Natalie took the manuscript and ceremoniously dumped it in the wastebasket.

"But I never got to read it," her mother said. "Don't throw it—"

"It's exactly where it belongs," Natalie said, refolding the rejection letter and holding it to her heart. She walked away.

"Where are you going?"

Natalie turned toward her mother, filled with hope and determination. "I'm going to write. The top of the pyramid is waiting."

Thirty-two

Give me understanding,
and I will keep your law and obey it with all my heart.
PSALM 119:34

THE LIGHTS OF ST. LOUIS enveloped Del and Walter, bathing the van with an unnatural glow. Walter reached over and nudged Del.

"Wake up," he said. "We're home."

Del sighed and opened his eyes. "I wasn't asleep."

He saw Walter sneak a glance at him. "What's with you? You haven't slept a minute since we left. I'm beat. Count to two and I'm gone."

"I should've driven more," Del said, his voice flat.

"No way. As it was we nearly ended up in Springfield. If I hadn't been awake when you drove through Kansas City, we'd be winding our way through the Ozarks by now."

Del shrugged. "I have a lot on my mind."

"So I figured." Walter sat up straighter in the driver's seat, resting his arms on the steering wheel. "I've been doing my own thinking. You can stay with me if you want. I've got an extra bedroom and I'm not home half the time. Especially now. Work will be piled chin high. I'm not the greatest housekeeper, but most of the cobwebs are above eye level."

"No thanks."

"What?" Walter looked at him as though he wasn't sure he'd heard right.

Del forced himself to show some life. He turned toward Walter. "I appreciate the offer, but I don't need a place to stay."

Walter was clearly confused. "You don't? Since when?"

"Since Haven."

"Did John arrange an apartment for you here? A job maybe?"

Del laughed. "In a way."

"In what way?"

Del shook his head. "I don't want to say anything until I see what happens. But I'll let you know."

"Look, I may not have been the most friendly guy in the world, but I do like you, Del. I owe you. And I care what happens to you."

"That's encouraging."

Walter laughed. "It is, isn't it? Who'd have—"

Del bolted upright. "Exit here!"

"Wha—?"

"Now!"

Walter jerked the wheel, swerving into the exit lane. At the bottom of the ramp, he hit the brakes and shoved the gearshift into park. Turning, he fixed Del with a glare. "What's going on?"

Del peered out the window at the dark night. He pointed up ahead. "Let me off at the bus stop. I'll take it from there."

Walter checked his watch. "Do the buses run this late?"

"I'll be fine."

They pulled in front of the bus shelter. It was deserted. "Do you have any money?"

Del thought of the few coins in his pocket—coins stolen from this very van. "You could help me there, Walt. I don't need much, just a few dol—"

Walter pulled out his billfold. He flipped through a few bills, paused, then handed Del the entire wad. "Here."

Startled, Del looked at him. "I can't take this much."

Walter laughed. "It's mostly ones."

Del hesitated, then he smiled. "Thanks, Walter. I owe you." He opened his door.

Walter put out a hand to stop him. "Take care of yourself."

Del saluted and watched Walter drive away, the van taillights blinking a good-bye.

He adjusted the quilt under one arm and held the sack containing his clothes and the crucifix in the other hand. He had no idea where he was going. He closed his eyes. "I'm here, Lord. Now what?"

He looked up and down the street. He saw cars parked at the curb. A discarded Coke can. Cigarette butts. Street lights spotlighted summer moths and the occasional dog. Apartments lined one side of the street. A sprinkling of windows were lit and alive, the rest were dark.

Del held the bundled quilt in front of him like a buffer against the unknown. He walked slowly down the street, studying each building, wondering if this one was it. Or this one.

He moved past a barber shop, a used book store, an insurance agent. There was an alley that was way too dark for Del's tastes. He kicked a rock on the sidewalk.

A dab of orange on the pavement caught his eye. He leaned down, picked it up, and stared. A marigold. He heard his mother's voice as clearly as though she were standing beside him. "Marigolds...named by the Holy Mother herself." A shiver coursed through him. He took a deep breath, closed his eyes, and straightened. He turned toward the building on his left and faced it fully before allowing his eyes to open. There was a door. Nondescript. Brown paint peeling. The brass handle was worn from many comings and goings. He took a step back to get a fuller view. The building was a squat two stories, as though time had sat long and hard on the roof and shortened it by its weight. The brick was chipped, yet it added a solid element to the tumble-down surroundings.

Behind the building was a larger structure. Del made his way into the deserted street so he could get a better view of it. When he made a first guess at its purpose, his heart jumped. And when he saw the dark silhouette of a cross crowning the tower, he sank to his knees, oblivious to street or sidewalk, day or night.

The door opened, and a young man ran outside, stooping to steady Del's arm.

"Are you all right?" he asked.

Del's head was bowed. He didn't dare look up.

"Come on, man. Look at me. Are you all right?"

Del raised his face and looked at the man.

"It's you!" the man said. He helped Del to standing. "We've been waiting for you, Father Delatondo. We are so honored."

Del looked down at the marigold as if it were precious metal instead of a flower. "Honored?" he whispered.

"Of course, Father," the young priest said. "We received word that a very important priest would be joining us." He gave Del a once-over. "Although I must admit you're not what I expected. You're young. Too young to have the reputation—"

"Reputation?" Del cringed at the word.

"I'd like to talk to you later, if I might, Father. There is so much I can learn from you." He started to lead Del inside.

Del stood his ground. "I don't understand. I—I sinned. I left the priesthood. My reputation is tarnished. I can't teach you anything."

The young priest patted Del's arm. "You can teach us humility, sacrifice, and honor."

Del shook his head adamantly. "I am not honorable. I have sinned."

"We all have sinned."

Silence sat between them. Then Del looked into the eyes of the priest. "Would you hear my confession, Father? I feel the need for communion."

The priest smiled. "Come inside, my son."

Del let himself be led inside. As he passed the door he saw a brass plaque, scratched with the years and obscured by climbing ivy: The Brothers of Safe Haven.

Del was home.

⌒

Walter sat in the dark. It had been over an hour since he'd entered his apartment, set his suitcase aside, and fell onto the

couch. He hadn't even turned on a light. It was as though seeing this testament to his old life had erased all possibilities of
his new one. He took a drag on a cigarette.

The phone rang. Walter's heart dropped to his toes, then
bounced back to its proper place. He reached to answer it,
knocking the ashtray onto the carpet.

"Hello?" he said, his energy gone.

"Walter? Honey? Is that you?"

Walter righted the ashtray, snuffed out his cigarette, and set
the phone in his lap. He slumped on the couch until the back
cushions supported his head. "Bette."

"A stunning greeting. Can't you do better than that?"

"I love you."

She cleared her throat. "That's definitely better."

Even as he wished she were sitting beside him in the dark,
he wished she'd leave him alone. The clash of old and new—
before and after—felt so risky.

"How long have you been home?" she asked.

"Not long."

"Any more televisions go bonkers on you?"

"No."

"Did you have a good time in Haven?"

"Yes."

"Anything exciting happen?"

"Yes."

There was an extended pause. "Help me, Walter, I'm dying
here. What's wrong?"

Walter rubbed a hand against his eyes. He wasn't...no he
couldn't be. He was! He was crying.

Bette must have heard his sobs. "I'm coming over," she said.

Walter didn't have the strength to say no.

A different Walter answered the door.

"Walt—"

He pulled her in, yanked her back in a low dip, and kissed her.

She righted herself, out of breath. "Is this going to become a habit?"

"Why not?" he said, pulling her into the living room. "Isn't that the way a husband should greet a wife?"

Her sudden stop caused him to whiplash into her. "Wife?"

"Sure," he said with uncharacteristic happiness. "Husband. Wife. Me. You. Do ya wanna?"

She slapped his hand away. "'Do ya wanna?' What kind of a proposal is that?"

He held up a hand, conceding. He drew her to the couch and offered her a seat. Then he got on one knee and took her hand between his. "Bette, I love you. Will you marry me?"

"Are you sure ya wanna?"

"I do."

"Then I do too." She flung her arms around his neck and kissed him. Then she pushed him back. "What brought this on? What'd you do in Haven that made you feel guilty enough to get married?"

"I was a very good boy."

"Uh-huh."

He crossed his chest. "So help me God."

"It appears he did just that."

"You'd never believe…I hope you believe it because it's true." He sat next to her and told her about Haven. She listened in silence, taking it all in.

"So?" he finally asked. "What do you think?"

"If it weren't you, Walter Prescott, newsman, talking, I'd think you'd been nipping dandelion wine and perhaps a few other sundry beverages. But since it *is* you…" She considered a moment. "I'm impressed. And a little scared. It's a huge responsibility they've given you, Walter. And as your wife, I'll be a part of it."

"I was counting on that."

"So what are you going to do at work tomorrow? You can't change the world in a day."

"No, not one day. But one day at a time," Walter said. "That's how I'll do it."

She took his hand, her face clouding. "And what about the biopsy? It's scheduled for the day after tomorrow."

"I have to go in tomorrow afternoon for a final X-ray. Then…it's out of my control." He stood, pacing. "Do you know how hard it is for me to say that?"

Bette nodded. "And I'm proud of you, because you're right. God is in control of everything. All of it."

"There's nothing we can do."

"You're wrong, Walter," she said. "With God's help there's nothing we *can't* do."

Walter sank beside her, taking her hand. "I don't deserve you, Bette."

She snuggled into his shoulder. "I wouldn't have it any other way."

Dave Hanlin stood at the table of the conference room, extending his hands palms down, quieting the news staff.

"Hold up, everyone. We're never going to get anything done unless you at least pretend I'm in charge."

A ripple of snickers.

"That's better." Dave turned toward Walter, who was sitting beside him. "We'd like to welcome Walter back to the fold after his short vacation. I'm sure we're all anxious to hear about his exploits in the Cornhusker state."

More snickers.

Walter reddened and hated himself for it. He caught what Dave wasn't saying, loud and clear: Walter had some explaining to do about his "vacation."

Dave cleared his throat and took a sip of water. "I called this meeting to go over the newest ratings for the six and ten news." He shook his head, holding a paper in front of him. "Down two points at six, three at ten. Not good, people. Not good at all."

Miranda, one of the ten o'clock news anchors, raised a neatly manicured finger. "We should have pounced on the story about the school board scandal. Juicy stuff. The other stations beat us to it. We're never going to be number one if we aren't willing to tackle the big ones."

Walter raised a hand. "Did I miss something?"

Miranda shrugged her shoulders, balancing the ever-present chip. She looked in the air as if a list of the school board's transgressions were written there. "One member declared bankruptcy ten years ago, one is going through a nasty divorce, and a citizen came forward saying that one board member sold him a house that had a defective furnace—"

"Any substantiation?" Walter asked.

Miranda shrugged. "Enough."

"What does that mean?"

A bit of the woman's polished veneer flaked off. She looked to Steven, the other anchor, for support.

"We've got it covered, Walter. Don't worry—"

Walter leaned forward, resting his elbows on the table. "I do worry. People's reputations are at stake. Their careers. What right do we have to report anything unless it's confirmed by—"

"The other stations went with it."

The jump-off-a-roof analogy flashed through Walter's mind, but he dismissed it. "What right do we have to butt into the private lives of the school board? Their personal finances, a divorce, the sale of a house? If it doesn't affect their work as an elected official, it should be off-limits."

"Walter," Dave said. "That's not always feasible. The public has a right to—"

"No," Walter said. "N-O, not K-N-O-W."

Miranda rolled her eyes. "Any public figure has to realize people are interested—"

"Are they?" Walter asked. "Do you really think the public wants to hear about the personal problems of—"

"Yes," Steven said, chewing on the end of a pencil. "They eat it up."

"Just because dogs eat their own vomit doesn't mean you should feed it to them."

Miranda made a face. "How crude."

"Yes," Walter said. "That is a perfect description of our news programs. Of other programs too, but that's another—" He stopped in midsentence as a rain of images and thoughts drenched his mind. He blinked twice. *You can't be serious, Lord.* But he knew the answer…and he knew what he had to do. He turned to Steven. "Should the world know you have a lover named Marty and he is HIV-positive and you're going in for tests on Friday to see if you—"

Steven nearly bit off the end of the pencil. "How—?"

Walter turned to Miranda. "Should we broadcast that your father is being investigated by the IRS for tax evasion for the years 1985, '87, and '90?"

"He's…he's taking care of that," she stammered. "It's all a big mistake."

Walter looked around the table at the people who put the news together behind the scene or in front of the screen. "I could go on. Nina? Reg? Or maybe you, Vicky?"

Dave stood. "Walter, that's enough. I don't know how you found out these things, but you have no right—"

"To pry into people's personal lives?"

"Yes."

"But, Dave, we do it all the time and call it news. What's the difference?"

Miranda took a chewed index finger out of her mouth. "My business is nobody's but my own."

"But you're a public figure."

"I don't hold office."

Walter nodded as if he were digesting some gem of information. "So we only butt into the personal lives of people who hold public office."

Miranda began to nod, but stopped, suspecting a trick.

"How wise of you to think before you said yes," Walter said.

"What about the lives of movie stars? They don't hold public office. They are not elected."

Vicky from the six o'clock news held up a hand. "But they're in the public eye. They're famous."

"So there's a new criteria," Walter said. "We can butt in if a person holds public office or is famous."

Vicky thought a moment before answering. "Yes."

"Define famous."

"Known by lots of people," Reg said.

"You anchors are known by lots of people," Walter said. "You are celebrities in St. Louis. According to your own criteria that makes your personal lives fair—"

"I don't like this conversation," Miranda snapped. "We've gotten off the subject."

"No, we haven't," Walter said. "We were discussing ratings and you made a suggestion how to get higher ones. By poking into, and reporting about, the personal lives of our school board."

Steven tapped the pencil on the table. "My personal life has no bearing on my work or how I do it or—"

"Exactly," Walter said. "You are 100 percent right." He put a hand to his chest. "I wouldn't want my past transgressions flashed over the airwaves. None of us are perfect. All of us have sinned."

"Sinned?" Dave said, raising an eyebrow. "What's sin got to do with it?"

A verse popped into Walter's head. "'The Judge is standing at the door.'"

"What?"

Walter sat a moment, trying to digest his thoughts. He took a deep breath, shaking his head. "Come on, everyone. Isn't it time we take responsibility for our own actions? Our words can help the world or hurt it. We need to stop bending to what we misguidedly call popular opinion. God's opinion is the only opinion that really matters."

"God's—" Dave stared at Walter. "What happened to brash, determined Walter who was merciless in his quest for the news?"

Walter stood to leave. "He found mercy is a two-way street."

Belinda's voice came over the intercom. "George from the photo lab is here to see you, Mr. Prescott."

Walter didn't look up from the mountain of papers on his desk. "Just have him leave the pictures with you. I don't need to talk to—"

"He says he needs to talk to you, Mr. Prescott."

Walter looked at the intercom. "Send him in."

George came in the office, an envelope of photos in his hands. He took two chews of his gum, then stuck the wad in his cheek. "Afternoon, Mr. Prescott."

"What's up, George? You could have left the pictures with Belinda, you didn't need to hand deliver—"

"It's about the pictures," he said, turning the envelope over in his hand. "There's something strange…I'm afraid I ruined them."

"Ruined?" Walter held out his hand. Reluctantly George gave him the photos. Walter flipped through them, slowly at first, then faster.

"I'll say you ruined them. Something's big-time wrong." He held out a photo. It was the one taken outside the school while they were waiting for Julia and Lisa to be released. Kathy and Lenny stared at the front door of the school, hope and fear mixed on their faces. Walter remembered that he'd snapped this while Gabe and Fran were consoling the frightened parents, yet only Kathy's and Lenny's images were clear. The others were hazy at best.

"And this?" he asked George. "And this, and this?" He pulled out the other photos, none of which had turned out.

George switched his gum to the other cheek. "They look like ghosts or something. I don't know what went wrong, Mr.

Prescott," George said. "That's why I wanted to give you the pictures in person, to let you know I tried everything to get them to come out plain—I printed them three times. This is as good as they'll get."

Walter continued to flip through the photos, shaking his head. *I don't have a single good picture of the mentors, not a single—*

He stopped flipping. He swallowed. He had a sudden need to be alone. "Thanks, George," he said, moving behind his desk.

"I suppose I could try it one more time, Mr. Prescott," George said. "Maybe if I opened a box of fresh paper? It could be the paper. Maybe it's old—"

"No, George. Thanks. You can go."

As the door clicked shut, Walter sank into his chair. He rubbed his eyes as laughter threatened. "It's not the paper that's old, Georgie boy. Something else—some*one*, actually—in Haven is old. Eternally old."

Bette and Walter sat in the waiting room at the doctor's office. Bette squeezed his hand. They exchanged looks but no words. Words weren't necessary.

"Walter Prescott."

The nurse stood at the door leading to the examination rooms, a file in her hands. Walter stood and held up two crossed fingers toward Bette. She reached for him and uncurled the fingers. She held his hand a moment. "You won't be alone, Walter."

He nodded and followed the nurse. She led him into a generic room, with pale-on-pale wallpaper, that smelled of antiseptic and fear. Charts on the wall detailed the milestones in a person's life: when one was supposed to get immunized, poked, and prodded. Walter looked at the space reserved for a forty-six year old male. At least he wasn't due for any shots.

"How are we doing today, Mr. Prescott?" the nurse asked.

"*We* need a cigarette."

She looked over the top of her glasses and pursed her lips. "There's nothing to be frightened of, Mr.—"

"Only death, destruction, and a wayward scalpel."

"Dr. Barry is an excellent doctor, I can assure you—"

"That I don't have cancer?"

She gave him a gown. "A positive attitude heals, Mr. Prescott. Take off your shirt and follow me. Doctor wants one more X-ray before—"

"He slices into me."

"You do have a way with words, Mr. Prescott."

"You should hear the ones I'm saying under my breath." *Please, God. Be here with me.*

Walter had the X-rays taken and returned to the examination room to wait. He flipped through an ancient issue of *Good Housekeeping* and found himself studying an article about closet organization. He was just getting to the part where they found a place for necklaces and scarves when Dr. Barry tapped on the door and came in. He carried a file and an oversized envelope of X-rays.

"Afternoon, Mr. Prescott," he said, extending a hand. "How are you feeling?"

"Peachy keen."

"Glad to hear it." He switched on a light board and stuck the X-rays under the clip. Walter's insides glowed to life. The doctor pointed to the one on the left, pinpointing a dark shadow. "See this?"

"It looks like Florida during hurricane season."

"That's your left lung a month ago."

Walter's eyes flitted to the X-ray on the right. The hurricane was gone except for the southernmost tip of the peninsula. "And that one is...?"

"Today's X-ray."

"It's different."

"Indeed, it is," Dr. Barry said. "Have you stopped smoking?"

"Yes...well, kind of. Sort of. Pretty much."

"Kind of sort of pretty much seems to be working."

Walter stared at the X-rays. "I don't have cancer?"

"We never knew if it was cancer, Mr. Prescott. That's what we were going to find out with the biopsy."

"Were?" Walter gripped the side of the examining table. "I don't have to have the biopsy?"

Doctor Barry studied the X-rays again, tracing a finger along the lung where the shadow should have been.

"Dr. Barry? The biopsy?"

The doctor blinked, as though finally hearing the question. "Um. Biopsy? Uh, no. We don't need to do the biopsy. There's still a small area that will need to be watched, but..." He removed the films and placed them in the envelope. "I'm curious, Mr. Prescott. Are you a religious man?"

"Why do you ask that?"

He cleared his throat, a bit uncomfortable. "It's just that I've found if a person believes, if they pray...I know it's totally unscientific, but—"

"They seem to get better faster?" Walter suggested.

"Exactly."

"I believe," Walter said, fingering his mustard-seed pin. Dr. Barry noticed.

"What's that?" he asked.

Walter glanced down at his lapel, unaware of what he'd been doing. "It's proof I believe."

"A mustard seed," the doctor said.

"You know about it?"

Dr. Barry made a notation in Walter's file. "I haven't thought about it for years, but when I was a boy I had to memorize that verse for Sunday school." He looked to the ceiling. "'If you have faith as small as a mustard seed, you will say to this mountain, "Move from here to there" and it will move. Nothing will be impossible for you.'" He shook his head. "I'm amazed I still remember it."

"I'm not," Walter said to the room as the doctor left. "I'm not."

Walter dressed quickly and burst into the waiting room. Bette popped out of her seat.

"What?" she asked. Fear streaked her face.

He took her hand and pulled her toward the door. "I'm hungry."

"Hungry?" she asked. "Walter, what happened?"

He stopped her in the hall and faced her. "It's gone, Bette. He healed me!"

"Doctor Barry?"

He laughed. Had he ever felt this good? "No, silly. God."

Her face flipped from disbelief, to awe, to joy in a matter of seconds. She bowed her head. "Thank you," she whispered.

Walter said a thank-you of his own. Then he grabbed her hand and raced down the hall. "We need to celebrate. With dinner."

"What do you feel like eating?" she asked as they burst onto the street.

Walter stopped to take a deep breath of fresh air. He did not cough. Instead he laughed with pure joy. "You know what I want?"

"What?"

"Chili. Chili with oyster crackers. It'll be my treat."

Thirty-three

Direct me in the path of your commands, for there I find delight.
PSALM 119:35

JULIA STOOD BACK from the painting, cocking her head. "Tilt it up a hair on the right," she told Edward.

"You just told me to tilt it up on the left."

"You did it too much."

"You *are* too much."

"So I've been told." She nodded when he got it right. The painting of Lisa looked perfect in its new home above the couch in the den. Here, she could look at it, be inspired by it, when she worked at the desk. She could remember Haven through it.

Edward sank onto the couch and patted the space beside him. "Break time. Julia's quest to organize the world will have to be put on hold as her head slave is on the verge of rebellion."

"It hasn't been that bad," she said, sitting down beside him. "Has it?"

Edward put an arm around her shoulders. "Haven may have inspired you, but its aftermath tires me. Perspires me. Conspires against me. Makes me want to retire. Has me considering—"

She put a hand across his mouth. "I get the idea, you whiner."

"I don't whine," Edward said. "I complain creatively. Especially when my wife—who thinks a messy house is a sign of an unorganized thinker—decides to unclutter the Carson Castle of Chaos. And has the audacity to make me help."

Julia tucked her legs beneath her and rested her head on his chest. "Isn't it nice to have everything organized? The entire house is clean. You can see the top of my desk. My piles are filed."

Edward knocked on her head. "You're not pregnant, are you?"

"Why would you say that?"

"The last time the cleaning instinct surfaced, you were about to give birth to Bonnie. Remember your absurd burst of energy?"

She grinned. "Our refrigerator was never cleaner."

"It was as if you sensed you soon would be busy and you wanted to be prepared."

"I went into labor that evening."

"So..." he waved his arms to indicate her newest project.

"I promise you, babies will not complicate our golden years."

"Thank heav—"

"But, I have a feeling..."

"Uh-oh."

She sat up to face him. "Remember the promise I told you about? The one I made in the tower?"

"Why do I have the sudden urge to clean the garage?"

"Well, I've been thinking about how best to implement that promise and I—"

The phone rang. Julia reached for it.

"Saved by the bell," Edward mumbled.

"Oh, hello, Benjamin," Julia said. Edward rolled his eyes and got up, collecting the hammer and picture wire. "They've what?"

Edward sat back down. "Who's what?" he whispered.

She batted his question away, intent on the conversation. She listened to Benjamin, her eyes flitting about the room, matching the speed of his words. "Slow down, Benjamin. If you'd take a breath while you're trying to convince me, I could understand—"

Edward crossed his arms, the hammer still clutched in one hand. He gave her his "What are you up to?" stare.

She put a hand over the receiver and whispered to him.

411

"You know Benjamin has been after me to run for Congress."
Edward raised his left eyebrow. "You said you approved before."
His left eyebrow lowered, his right one raised. "But there's
something more I wanted to talk with you—"

She turned back to the receiver. "Benjamin, hold on just a
minute, will you?"

Julia carefully pried the hammer from Edward's hand and
set it safely on the floor. His arms remained crossed. She took a
deep breath and made sure the receiver was completely covered
so Benjamin wouldn't hear her words. "I made a promise to
God, Edward. I promised to dedicate my leadership abilities to
him." She paused, waiting for some reaction.

Finally he said, "And...?"

"I want to run for president."

He sighed deeply, studying her face. He cocked his head. "I
refuse to be called First Lady."

She smiled at him, loving him more than ever before. "How
about First Man?"

He considered this. "How about Number One Man?"

"You are that, you know."

He nodded. She raised the receiver, still covered with her
hand. "So may I? May I tell Benjamin the news?"

"He'll faint."

"It wouldn't be the first time."

"Or the last." Edward shrugged. "Go for it, Madam
President."

Julia leaned over and kissed his lips, his nose, and his forehead. Then she stood and paced as her energy flowed.
"Benjamin, I will agree to get back into politics with a few conditions." She paused as his yelps of victory rang out. "Number
one, I will speak my mind. My mind, Benjamin. Not yours, not
that of the other advisers you bring into this. Not that of any
political party. I will speak my mind, true and plain. I'm going
to take a stand and keep standing." She closed her eyes as he
made his objections. "There is no compromise on this,

Benjamin. Do you understand?" He conceded half-heartedly. "Before I mention my final condition, I'd like you to sit down...don't argue with me, boy, just do it."

She held her hand toward Edward. He took it and brought it to his lips. The action firmed her resolve. She could do this with his help. And God's. She closed her eyes and said a prayer.

"Sitting yet, Benjamin?" she asked. "Good. My final condition is that instead of running for Congress, I want to run for president." She laughed at his reaction, the joy of making the decision, voicing the decision, changing her from a half-empty glass to one brimming over.

She held the receiver away from her ear, letting Benjamin's exuberance explode onto the unsuspecting air. Edward patted his lap. She claimed her place, wrapping her arms around his neck. Edward took the phone from her and hung it up, silencing Benjamin.

They celebrated in their nice clean house.

Julia and Edward were heading out the door to go to the cabin when the phone rang.

"Don't answer it," Edward said. "Ever since your decision, you've talked to *it* more than to me."

"But *it* doesn't have big brown eyes or a dimple in its chin."

"My eyes are hazel."

"Who said I was talking about—" She ducked his playful swing and picked up the phone. "Hello?"

"Gov?"

She hesitated. "Arthur? Is that you? Where are you? *How* are you?"

Edward set the suitcase down and moved closer to listen. Julia had told him all about Arthur.

"I'm in Kearney. I'm out of the hospital but I'm in county jail."

"Oh, Arthur, I'm so sorry."

"My fault, Gov. It's not so bad, really. Anyway, I had this

413

urge to call. I don't know why exactly, but when I got my turn to use the phone…well, here I am."

"How did you get my number?" Julia asked, wondering at the possibilities. *Did it mysteriously appear on the wall of his cell block? Did the number come to him in a dream? Did lightning strike, marking the—*

"I called information," Arthur said.

Julia laughed at her newly honed sense of theatrics. Of all people, Arthur *would* bring her down to earth.

"My lawyer says with your help I may be able to get a shorter sentence."

"I'll do everything I can, Arthur. You know that."

"I know," he said, his voice catching. "That's why I called. You make me feel…like I'm worth something, I guess."

"You are worth something."

"I'm not wasting my time in here, either, Gov. I'm reading. The Bible's all they'll give me right now."

"That's enough, don't you think?"

"Yeah. It is."

Her voice softened. "Take care of yourself, Arthur. And call me anytime."

"Night or day?"

"Preferably day, but I suppose—"

"Thanks, Julia."

"God bless you, Arthur."

~～⌐

On the way back to his cell after the phone call, a guard intercepted Art. "Here's a package for you, Graham."

Art took the package gratefully. There was no return address and no postmark.

"Who's it from?"

The guard shrugged. "Some officer brought it by. Chief something-or-other. He said it was yours. Only reason we didn't rip it open ourselves was 'cuz he was a police officer."

Art tore off the brown paper.

"What is it?" the guard asked.

"A book." Clutching it to his chest, Art hurried back to his cell. More than anything he wanted to read—or, rather, finish reading—*A Tale of Two Cities*.

～

Kathy sat in the kitchen and looked at the wrinkled note. "Dear Lenny, I have gone to Haven with the kids. Will be back in a few days. Please don't worry. Love, Kathy."

She'd found it on the floor by the refrigerator. Crumpled. Apparently heaved across the room by Lenny when he came home to an empty house, most likely accompanied by a few choice epithets.

No wonder he'd come after them. If she'd been a compliant wife and stayed behind, Lenny would still be alive. She would still have a husband. Her children would still have a father. All because she made the decision to go.

She wadded the note into a tiny ball and took it to the wastebasket. She needed to be rid of it, rid of the evidence of her rebellion. She gazed down at it, sitting among the bread wrappers and banana peels. The note was the beginning of the end of their life together.

What would her life have been like if she hadn't gone to Haven? The experience had changed her. Tested her. Enriched her.

"Mommy?" Ryan said. She hadn't noticed him coming up beside her. "The washer's buzzing like it does when it gets too heavy."

She perked her ears. The washer was wailing from the basement. She hadn't even heard it.

"Thanks, sweetie. You and Lisa wash your hands for supper."

Kathy went downstairs, the washer's complaint echoing off the unfinished space. She rearranged the clothes and started it up again, pausing to make sure it was satisfied. On the way upstairs, she detoured to her studio area. She hadn't been in it since returning from Haven. She had no urge to paint, even though she knew it would soon become her primary means of support.

She flipped on the light—and gasped.

Her paintings lay scattered about the room, the watercolors torn, the oil canvases slashed. Her brushes were broken. Tubes of paint were squeezed dry, the colors smeared on every surface.

She knelt beside the painting she'd been working on the day she'd received the invitation to Haven. A toddler's head was cut from his body as he played in a sandbox.

"Oh, Lenny."

She got to her feet and turned out the light. She went upstairs. When she got to the kitchen she retrieved the crumpled note from the wastebasket. She unfolded it and smoothed it against the counter. It wasn't the beginning of the end at all.

It marked the beginning of her new life.

She put it in a place of honor on the refrigerator, a smiley-face magnet marking its place among the other treasures of her life: Lisa's painting of a three-eared doggy; a torn page from a coloring book completed by Ryan; a photo of Lenny and the kids holding Easter baskets. She looked at the gallery. Something was missing.

Kathy went to her Bible on the shelf in the living room. She pulled out the invitation to Haven and placed it on the refrigerator, making a place for it front and center. She stepped back to admire the collage.

Amen.

Kathy nodded as the people filed by at Lenny's memorial service.

"So sorry."

"My condolences."

"If you ever need anything…"

She wanted it to be over. How could she and the children start to heal until it was over?

She let her eyes focus on Lisa and Ryan sitting across the room with their three grandparents. She pitied Lenny's mother. Her son gone. His body never recovered. Her questions would remain unanswered because the answers were unfathomable.

"Kathy?"

She turned toward the voice, ready to force a smile. The woman in front of her waited until Kathy's eyes focused, really seeing who she was.

Kathy blinked. "Mrs. Robb?"

Kathy's high school counselor nodded. "I've been thinking about you so much lately," she said. "It's strange. Not that you weren't an important student in my life, but it has been five years and I—"

"I've been thinking about you, too," Kathy said. She thought of her high school file in Haven with the encouraging note from Mrs. Robb. "In fact, I planned to call you to tell you how much your encouragement meant to me."

"My encouragement?"

"Back in high school, when I was pregnant with Ryan. That note you wrote that said I needed confidence to use my many gifts."

"Note?" Mrs. Robb asked.

The note in my file. The note I was never meant to see.

Kathy shook her head. "I'm glad to see you."

They paused to let another mourner say a word to Kathy and pass on by.

"What are you going to do now, Kathy? Do you still paint?"

"Yes, but I don't know if that will be enough to live on. I need a real job."

Mrs. Robb nodded. Then her eyes brightened. "I might even know of one." She put a hand on Kathy's arm. "Maybe this is why I've been thinking of you. During the summer I volunteer with the crisis pregnancy center, but they are growing so strong, they need to hire someone full time to go around and speak to high school kids, do a little preventative counseling along with pregnancy counseling. It doesn't pay much—"

"I'll do it."

"You'll—"

Kathy tenderly touched the mustard-seed pin. "It's a long story, and if you're interested, sometime I'll tell you the entire thing. Let's just say that you and your job are a gift from God."

"That's mighty high billing."

"The very highest."

⁓

"Fran, would you sit down?" Gabe said. "You're making me crazy."

"I'm just excited." She paced around the room. "Everything is working out so well. I intercepted Natalie's rejection letter, she's having the baby." She clapped her hands. "It's wonderful!"

Louise ran a hand through her unruly hair. "I'll be glad to get rid of this hairdo, that's for sure. Why did I have to be the one to have the eternal bad-hair day?"

"It was important that our appearance made our charges comfortable," Gabe said. He looked down at himself. "Actually, I rather like this sweater vest."

John dusted off his Rockies baseball hat, gazing at it fondly. "We should all give thanks. Julia is running for president, Walter is making a stand in the television industry, Kathy is going to be working with the pro-life forces."

"And Art," Louise said. "Don't forget about Arthur."

"He's a bonus," Gabe said. "A blessed bonus."

"Amen," Anne said. "We lost one but gained one." She sighed deeply. "I do hope Kathy will be all right."

"She'll be fine," John said. "Especially with you to watch over her."

"I do like that part," Anne said, her mood brightening. "It's rewarding."

"How is Del doing?" Gabe asked John.

"He's been called back."

"But has he answered?" Louise asked.

"Indeed he has." John spun a marigold between his fingers.

"Then our work here really *is* done, isn't it?" Fran asked with a sigh.

"Not done," John said. "Not entirely. This was just the invitation. Now the real work begins for our charges."

"Our friends," Fran added.

John nodded and went on. "Now it's time for them to begin their quest to understand the call God has given each of them."

"It won't be easy." Louise leaned back in her chair. "They'll have to make major adjustments in their lives to join God's work."

"But in the working—in the quest for learning—they will find their true goal, and God will be glorified." He held out his arms. The others moved to join hands and together they all raised their faces to the heavens.

"Take us home, Lord," they said together.

~~~~~

Kathy hung up and dialed the number again, carefully placing each finger.

"The number you have dialed has been removed or is not assigned."

"It can't be. This is the number of Anne's house. She gave it to me herself."

Kathy picked up the receiver and dialed information for Nebraska.

"What city please?"

"Haven."

"Just a moment…I'm sorry, but we don't list a Haven in Nebraska."

"Haven," repeated Kathy. "H-A-V-E-N."

"That's how I was spelling it, ma'am. But I'm sorry, there's no such city."

The receiver remained in Kathy's hand until the busy signal woke her out of her daze. She rushed to the garage to her car. She opened the glove compartment and pulled out the map.

"Haven, Haven," she chanted. "Be there. Be there."

She flipped to the map of Nebraska and let her finger trace the route she had just traveled. There was Interstate 80. There was the Platte River. But there wasn't any Haven. She carried the map into the house with her and sat at the kitchen table. She pored over it, inch by inch.

But no amount of searching would change the facts.

Haven was gone.

⟡

The sunset on the Nebraska plains was especially vivid that night. The sun lingered at the horizon until all the colors of the sky were impeccably aligned; the essence of perfection. The essence of God.

The wind blew across the cornfields, unimpeded by homes, motels, schools, and bell towers. The birds skimmed the ground before rising toward heaven.

God and his angels were pleased.

⟡

Therefore, as God's chosen people, holy and dearly loved, clothe yourselves with compassion, kindness, humility, gentleness and patience. Bear with each other and forgive whatever grievances you may have against one another. Forgive as the Lord forgave you. And over all these virtues put on love, which binds them all together in perfect unity.
COLOSSIANS 3:12–14

Dear Reader:

At first I thought I was crazy. I'd never written anything like this before. I had no grand plan, no meticulous outline. All I had was an idea: what if some ordinary people got an invitation from God?

I approached the writing of *The Invitation* exactly as the characters approached their trip to Haven, with a good dose of skepticism, fear, and excitement. And just like them, I took a deep breath, accepted God's invitation, and moved forward. By faith.

As my characters learned about God, so did I. Their failures and doubts were mine—as was their wonder. Even now when I reread certain passages, I find myself asking, "Who wrote this?" Though my fingers did the walking, my heart did the talking, with God as my head.

Through it all, my family and friends didn't laugh or tell me no. They gave me encouragement and the kind of blind trust that pushed me forward. How could I turn back with them standing behind me? As for God? I am forever grateful he doesn't give up on us.

That's the reason I wrote this book: I hope each of you has come away with the knowledge that you too have been invited by our Lord to join him in his work. Forget about your flaws and the fact that you are just an ordinary person.

God uses ordinary people in extraordinary ways…*if* we let him.

So let him.

A word about two extraordinary ladies: My sister, Crys Mach, heard every idea, read every word (at least once), and was blessedly honest. This is your book too, Crystie.

And much gratitude to Karen Ball, my editor—what a joy! Every question made me dig deeper, every suggestion made the book better. Your faith in me—and in our Lord—was an inspiration.

Finally, "Whatever your hand finds to do, do it with all your might" (Ecclesiastes 9:10).

Go on. Accept the invitation.

Nancy Moser

Write to Nancy Moser
Alabaster Books
c/o Multnomah Publishers
P.O. Box 1720
Sisters, Oregon 97759

* Verse paraphrased

Watch for *The Quest*,
the exciting sequel to *The Invitation*,
coming in the spring of 1999!

ALABASTER BOOKS

Look for these releases at your local bookstore. If the title you seek is not in stock, the store may order you a copy using the ISBN listed.

Homeward, Melody Carlson
ISBN 1-57673-029-8

Meg Lancaster returns to the hometown she left in anger twenty years before, but what she finds there is far from the peace she'd hoped for. Instead, Meg uncovers secrets that have been hidden for decades—secrets that force her to confront the family she ran away from and to reevaluate the beliefs she's held her entire life.

Redeeming Love, Francine Rivers
ISBN 1-57673-186-3

California's gold country. 1850. A time when men sold their souls for a bag of gold, and women sold their bodies for a place to sleep. A time when two people are brought together by an all-knowing, all-loving God—and neither will ever be the same. A powerful retelling of the book of Hosea; a life-changing story of God's unconditional, redemptive, all-consuming love.

Enough! Gayle Roper
ISBN 1-57673-185-5

Molly has had enough of her children's lack of respect. And so she stages a walkout: no cooking, no laundry, no cleaning, no chauffeuring. No *nothing* until her kids learn to treat her with the honor God commands children to show a parent. But how much time—and pandemonium—will it take before the kids cry "uncle"?

Tangled Vines, Diane Noble
(who also writes as Amanda MacLean)
ISBN 1-57673-219-3
When K.C. Keegan's aunt, well-known but eccentric mystery writer Theodora Whimple, disappears, K.C. risks everything to find her—even joining forces with her ex-fiancé, Sheriff Elliot Gavin. Following Theodora's trail, they come to an elegant winery in the sun-drenched Napa Valley, where something is going on...something far more sinister—and dangerous—than either K.C. or Gav can imagine.

The Invitation, Nancy Moser
ISBN 1-57673-115-4
Four ordinary people receive anonymous invitations to a small Midwest town they've never heard of. Each dismisses the invitations as a prank—until strange, even miraculous, things start happening. Soon all four embark on a journey that will test their mettle—and their faith—to the breaking point.

The Prayer Tree, Annie Jones (May 1998)
ISBN 1-57673-239-8
Naomi, Gayle, Rose, and Mary Lucille are southern, born and bred. So when New Bethany's fine tradition of praying for others is threatened with extinction, they step forward as a group to plant the town's last prayer tree. Characters all, each woman has a secret reason for taking part in the prayer circle. But what none of them realize is that God, not their agendas, has called them together—and what he has in store for them is beyond their wildest imaginings.

Of Apples and Angels, Annie Jones (September 1998)
ISBN 1-57673-330-0
Though Naomi, Gayle, Rose, and Mary Lucille are as close as

sisters in their hearts, the bond they share has grown fragile. Can a loony old lady bring them together again? And just who—as the women appoint themselves guardian angels over the old dear—is really helping whom?

Arabian Winds, Linda Chaikin
ISBN 1-57673-105-7
British field nurse Allison Wescott finds herself face-to-face with—and at the mercy of—the enemy, handsome and cynical Major Bret Holden. But there's something odd about this German soldier, something that makes Allison think the major isn't what he'd like her to think he is. An exciting tale of espionage and romance in World War I.

Lions of the Desert, Linda Chaikin
ISBN 1-57673-114-6
Allison and Bret are caught up in a sinister plot that pulls them into an unexplainable murder, a search for treasure, and frightening encounters that make Allison wonder if she can trust anyone—even Bret. The thrilling sequel to *Arabian Winds.*

Valiant Hearts, Linda Chaikin (June 1998)
ISBN 1-57673-240-1
The story of Allison Wescott and Bret Holden concludes as the Great War breaks across Palestine. As a field nurse, Allison must follow the Australian Lighthorse Cavalry to capture Beersheba—and then on to take Jerusalem from the Turks! But love flares to life again when Allison unexpectedly finds Bret wounded—and they end up trapped together behind enemy lines.

Where Yesterday Lives, Karen Kingsbury (July 1998)
ISBN 1-57673-285-1
At thirty-one Ellen Barrett has already won a Pulitzer Prize, but her skill as a reporter far surpasses her ability to sort out a troubled past. When her father dies, she returns home, where she must reopen old wounds before true healing can begin—and where a long-lost love unexpected reappears, drawing Ellen to make peace with her past—and put Christ in her future. A stirring novel that is the basis for an upcoming 1998 Hallmark Hall of Fame Movie.